THE TAPESTRY OF THE LAW

Law and Philosophy Library

VOLUME 26

The titles published in this series are listed at the end of this volume.

ELSPETH ATTWOOLL
University of Glasgow, Scotland, U.K.

THE TAPESTRY OF THE LAW

Scotland, Legal Culture and Legal Theory

Springer-Science+Business Media, B.V.

A C.I.P. Catalogue record for this book is available from the Library of Congress

---

Printed on acid-free paper

ISBN 978-90-481-4767-0 ISBN 978-94-015-8800-3 (eBook)
DOI 10.1007/978-94-015-8800-3

Originally published by Kluwer Academic Publishers in 1997.
Softcover reprint of the hardcover 1st edition 1997

For Hugh Robert Rhind Attwooll

ACKNOWLEDGEMENTS

There is a sense in which this book has been more than thirty years in the making. In consequence, it is impossible to make individual mention of everyone who has contributed to its development. I owe a considerable debt to discussions over the years with colleagues in law and philosophy in the University of Glasgow and other Scottish Universities, to my students, to various members of the United Kingdom Association for Social and Legal Philosophy and, more recently, to a number of people involved with the IVR and the Erasmus ICP in Law and Philosophy. Although some of them are acknowledged in it - either directly or through the medium of their writings - others are omitted only because the text does not aspire to cover the whole of jurisprudence.

I am, however, particularly grateful to Beverley Brown, Sean Coyle, Andy Devlin, Hilary Hiram, Mervyn Lewis, Neil MacCormick, Claire McDiarmid, John Tasioulas and Joe Thomson, all of whom read various drafts of the text and made valuable comments on them. Thanks are especially due to the last two of these, as also to Tom Mullen, for updating me in their own areas of expertise. I am similarly grateful to various individuals in the Scottish Courts Administration, the Crown Office, the Central Office of Industrial Tribunals (Scotland), the SFA and in the offices of the political parties for help with particular points. To none of the above are any of the errors due.

I would also wish to make special mention of Neil Cooper, who guided my first footsteps in the philosophy of law; of David Goldberg and Esin Örücü, for many happy years of working together; of Damian Henry, for the illustration; and of Don Henry, for taking on the proofreading as well an excessive share of more obviously domestic duties.

EMMA
Glasgow, July 1996.

CONTENTS

POST MODERN
restaurant
Damian Hardy

INTRODUCTION

Although its concern is jurisprudence, *The Tapestry of the Law* is intended to offer neither an original theory of or about law nor an account of other people's theories in textbook form. It is, rather, an attempt to approach the subject without following either of these conventions. The reasons are as follows.

Those engaged in legal theory are prone to assert that one cannot properly understand the law unless one takes a jurisprudential approach - preferably their own - to it. Equally, those engaged in exposition of the law may counter that legal theory fails to pay adequate attention to actual law. There is at least some truth in these claims. Analyses, courses and textbooks on both sides do often seem to be produced without reference to the other. Yet such isolation is probably more apparent than real. Most, if not all, so-called "black letter" lawyers do operate on the basis of certain jurisprudential understandings, even if these are not articulated ones. In the frequently quoted words of F C S Northrop:

> There are lawyers, judges and even law professors who tell us they have no legal philosophy. In Law, as in other things, we shall find that the only difference between a person 'without a philosophy' and someone with a philosophy is that the latter knows what his philosophy is, and is, therefore, more able to make clear and justify the premises that are implicit in his statement of the facts of his experience and his judgment about those facts.[1]

Equally, many, though not all, legal theorists are trained in the law and their theorising is likely to be coloured accordingly. In addition, a considerable amount of commentary on the law nowadays makes explicit use of legal theory,[2] whilst legal theory, too, appears to be looking increasingly to actual examples to inform itself. In both cases, though, the concern is effectively confined to specific areas of the

---

[1] F C S Northrop, *The Complexity of Legal and Ethical Experience* (Boston: Little, Brown & Co,1959) p 6.

[2] International law is particularly striking in this respect.

law.[3] What follows is an attempt to engage in both kinds of enterprise at a more general level and to do so in a way that highlights the extent to which they are interdependent.

In consequence, a relatively broad account of a particular body of law and certain approaches to legal theory are set up against one another with the object of identifying at least some of the things that may be learnt about both in the process. The body of law chosen for the purpose is the law of Scotland. The reasons for this are twofold. First, it is the law most accessible and most familiar to the writer. This is not just a matter of convenience. Certain authors would argue that one can only fully understand concepts as they are formed within one's own culture.[4] Taken to extreme, this approach would seem to rule out all comparative social studies, including comparative law.[5] It need not be taken to extreme, however, since it is clearly possible to arrive at a reasonable understanding of the concepts to be found in similar cultures.[6]

Indeed, the second reason for choosing Scots law is that it is generally regarded as a hybrid, sharing features of both the continental civilian tradition and the English common law approach. As a result, it has the potential, at least, to be more informative than some "purer"

---

3 Not surprisingly, for example, feminists tend to concentrate on rape, on the law of provocation and on domestic violence.

4 E.g. Peter Winch, *The Idea of a Social Science and its Relation to Philosophy* 2nd edn (London: Routledge and Kegan Paul, 1990).

5 See e.g. Alasdair MacIntyre, 'The Idea of a Social Science' and 'Is a Science of Comparative Politics Possible?' in *Against the Self Image of the Age* (London: Duckworth, 1971) reproduced in Alan Ryan ed, *The Philosophy of Social Explanation* (London: Oxford University Press, 1973).

6 Winch himself seems to concede as much, at least by implication, see *The Idea of a Social Science* (cit. n. 4) at pp 89-90.

form.[7] At the same time, and to the same end, the discussion is not entirely confined to Scotland. Reference is made to other jurisdictions, England fairly prominent amongst them, for various illustrative purposes.

The first three chapters provide a lead-in to the main discussion. Chapter I highlights some of the puzzles that are thought to exist about the world in which law is situated and law's situation within it. Their nature is argued both to explain the variety of views that are taken about its form, its function and its content and to justify beginning with something of which reasonably certain knowledge can be had - a particular body of law operating in a particular social context. Readers experienced in philosophy and those without any philosophical background may both find the chapter disconcerting. For the former this will be because the treatment is necessarily a simplistic one, amounting, perhaps, at times to little less than caricature. For the latter it will be because both the chapter and the book as a whole do not provide solutions to the puzzles concerned. By the end, though, the reader new to philosophy may well have reached his or her own view as to what some, at least, of these should be.

Chapter II covers a number of the problems that arise even when it is simply a particular body of law operating in a particular social context that is under consideration. These include identifying both the law and the society concerned and finding ways of viewing both that allows an assessment of the influence they exert on one another. The idea of a shared culture, of which the law forms part, is seen as helpful here and Chapter III develops this approach by looking at the relationship in Scotland between aspects of its constitutional law and the recurrence in its wider culture of certain ideas about the proper location and use of political power.

---

[7] It may, for example, allow something of the 'fusion of horizons' to which Gadamer refers (*Truth and Method* trans W Glen-Doepel, ed G Barden and J Cumming (London: Sheed and Ward, 1971) p 269ff, esp p 273 or use of what Charles Taylor calls 'the language of perspicuous contrast'. See *Philosophy and the Human Sciences* (Cambridge: Cambridge University Press, 1989) ch 4 esp pp 125-6.

Chapters IV, V and VI offer a more more general view of the law of Scotland using the criterion, developed by Konrad Zweigert and Hein Kötz,[8] of the "style" of a legal system. This has five components: history and development; characteristic mode of thinking; distinctive institutions; the sources acknowledged and the way in which these are handled; and ideology. In the course of these chapters a number of questions about how law and the legal system are to be identified and understood are raised and certain jurisprudential approaches to them touched on. Chapter VII then looks particularly at some of the problems involved in the interpretation of legal texts, with the suggestion that disagreements here are really just part of the wider debate about the proper basis for treating something as law.

Chapter VIII raises the issue of whether this basis is best established by finding grounds for identifying something as a legal system, the components of which may be regarded as laws, or by finding grounds for identifying matters as laws and then adopting a notion of legal system that will allow appropriate laws to be classified as part of one. The chapter then discusses how far, if the second approach is adopted, such identification can successfully be made by reference to the behaviour of officials. Chapter IX reviews a number of possible bases, variously appropriate to the two approaches, for treating something as a legal system. In particular it considers the claims made by autopoietic theory as opposed to more traditional understandings.

As in the latter part of Chapter IX, in Chapters X to XIII what are mainly contemporary approaches to legal theory are introduced and commented on. These include various different assessments of law both as a system of communication and/or from the point of view of its rationality, including semiotics, feminism and postmodernism, the hermeneutic approach, economic analysis, natural law thinking, communicative rationality and rational reconstruction. Chapter XIII - the final one - ends with some tentative conclusions, drawn in the light of the body of law surveyed, both about such approaches to legal theory and the nature of legal theory itself.

---

[8] See Konrad Zweigert and Hein Kötz, *Introduction to Comparative Law*, 2nd edition (Oxford: Oxford University Press, 1989) Vol I pp 64ff esp p 71f.

I

SOME PUZZLES ABOUT THE NATURE OF LAW

There are times in most of our lives when we become aware that we do not know what the law on this or that particular matter is. The very fact that we can have this kind of awareness, though, shows that we must already have some understanding, however undeveloped, of what law is and where it fits into our world. Yet, as soon as we try to express that understanding, the task proves much more difficult than expected. And, if we ask why this is so, we find that the idea of law has almost always been a contested one.

In our own age at least - by contrast with earlier times - it is generally accepted that the word "law" has two different senses. The first is the descriptive or scientific sense, where we use the word in relation to regularities of behaviour we find in the physical world - for example, Ohm's law, to the effect that a potential difference of one volt produces a current of one ampere. The second is the prescriptive or normative sense, where we use the word in relation to standards of conduct that are there for us to follow. An example here is that all societies apparently forbid their members to commit incest, even though what amounts to incest differs considerably from one society to another.

The second of the two senses is the one with which this book is primarily concerned. It will become clear, though, that one of the most difficult problems for jurisprudence is the extent, if any, to which there is an overlap between them. For, when we come to consider law as a set of standards of conduct that are there for us to follow, all sorts of questions begin to arise.

Where, for example, do such standards come from? Are they all produced by human activity or can other sources for them be found? For example, is there, as St Thomas Aquinas thought, an eternal law created by God, which includes standards for human conduct that we can discover by using our reason? Or, as Grotius argued, can we, by looking into our own natures, formulate a set of standards that we cannot deny without doing violence to ourselves? In other words, does there exist some kind of natural law by which human beings ought to govern their lives, even if in practice they fail to recognise it or abide by it?

If we do answer yes to this last question, what then do we make of human "laws" that do not match up to the natural law? Do we deny that they are laws at all; or argue that they are somehow an inferior kind of law; or accept them as law but deny that we are morally bound to obey them; or both accept them as law and insist that we are bound to obey them? Does it make any difference just how corrupt or evil they are by comparison with natural law?[1]

Whether or not there is a natural law, do human beings have to produce their own laws or could they manage to live together without them? If they could not, why not? Is there something about human nature that makes law a necessary feature of human society? If, on the other hand, human beings could live together without producing their own laws, what is it about the way they actually do so that makes us find such laws almost wherever we look?

Further, so far as laws can be, or - for those who reject any kind of natural law approach - simply are, produced by human beings, does this have to be in any particular way? Must, for instance, there be some deliberate act or can laws just emerge over time? If laws are created, whether wholly or partly, by deliberate acts, just whose acts count for the purpose? Also, whichever view we take, why is it that we regard such things as laws rather than anything else?

One way to tackle such questions is by defining their terms. Take, for instance, the issue of whether it is possible for human societies to exist without law. It is thought that, once we have clarified, first, what we mean by "human societies" and, second, what we mean by "law", we shall be in a position to resolve the matter. For, if we find that we

---

[1] The traditional view of the natural law position has been that it treats corrupt or evil human "laws" as not being law at all. This is disputed by John Finnis, who argues that, even for Aquinas, they are simply not laws "in the focal sense" and that the main line in natural law thinking is that, in appropriate circumstances, such laws do not have the power to bind in conscience. See *Natural Law and Natural Rights* (Oxford: Oxford University Press, 1980) pp 359-62. The focal meaning of law is defined at p 276. There are, however, passages in Aquinas which suggest a stronger line, as identified later in this chapter.

are able to explain what we mean by a human society without bringing in what we understand by law, then the answer is yes, societies can exist without law. If, on the other hand, we find that we cannot offer an explanation of the former unless we mention the latter, then the answer is: no, societies cannot exist without law.

The trouble with this kind of approach is that it does not work very well. The explanations given are likely to turn out to be either circular or culture bound. How they might be circular can be illustrated - unfairly in this case - by using the following quotation from Hans Kelsen:

> Society . . . is a normative order of the mutual behavior of men. These belong to a society so far as their behavior is . . . commanded, authorised or positively permitted by the order . . . society consists in nothing but this order and . . . if society is designated as a community then essentially that which these men have "in common" is nothing else but the order regulating their mutual behavior.[2]

Were someone to take the same kind of view but insist, unlike Kelsen himself, that the kind of normative order involved must be a legal one, then society and law would become defined in terms of one another. And, if human beings are only to be regarded as belonging to a society when their behaviour is governed by a legal order, then the conclusion that it is impossible to have a society without law beomes an inevitable one.

A man who did argue in this kind of way was the seventeenth century philosopher Thomas Hobbes. He contrasted two sorts of conditions under which people can live. First, there is the state of nature, which is a 'Warre, of every man, against every man', where life is 'solitary, poore, nasty, brutish and short' and there are 'no Arts; no Letters; no Society'.[3] Second, there is the Commonwealth or civil society, where an all powerful sovereign, whether one man or an assembly of men, prescribes the 'Civill Laws' which are maintained by the 'publique Sword'.[4]

---

2 Hans Kelsen, *The Pure Theory of Law,* trans Max Knight (Berkeley: University of California Press,1967) p 86.

3 Thomas Hobbes, *The Leviathan,* intro A D Lindsay (London: J M Dent, 1914) ch XIII.

4 Ibid, ch XVIII.

At one stage Hobbes does seem to allow that there are certain Laws of Nature that apply to people when they live in a state of nature.[5] Commentators differ on their status. To some, since they have their basis in reason, they are to be seen as obligatory. To others they are to be taken as simply counsels of prudence, to be heeded to the extent that self-interest dictates. Law, however, is usually thought of as imposing itself on people much more strongly than that.

It would appear that Hobbes took this view too, at least of what he considered to be law in any real sense of the term, even if obligations under it could ultimately be defeated by the demands of self-preservation. For he said of the Laws of Nature that they were 'but Conclusions or Theoremes concerning what conduceth to. . . conservation and defence . . .whereas Law, properly is the word of him, that by right hath command over others'.[6] Similarly, he claimed 'Where there is no common Power, there is no Law: where no law, no Injustice'.[7]

His argument, then, appears to run as follows: Society is a condition where peace is maintained between men. Peace cannot be maintained unless men's behaviour is controlled by the unfettered use of power. Law is the medium by which men's behaviour is so controlled. Granted all these premises, logic compels us to conclude: therefore, society cannot exist without law.

The question, though, is whether we do want to grant all these premises. We may want to dispute any or all of Hobbes' views about the nature of society; about what is required to maintain peace; about the character of law; and about the relationship that holds between them. One particular ground on which we may wish to argue with Hobbes is his pessimism about human nature. Rather than as competitive, insecure and power seeking, we might see people as cooperative, confident and unambitious. Or we might think that neither picture is an accurate one. We may even take the view that there is no such thing as a fundamental human nature, maintaining instead that human natures are shaped by the types of society in which they are

---

[5] Ibid, chs XIV and XV.

[6] *Leviathan,* ch XV.

[7] Ibid, ch XIII. On this kind of account the Laws of Nature are real laws only to the extent that there is a power willing to enforce them.

found. Or we may go further still, arguing that we cannot possibly know whether human nature is either constant or socially conditioned (or even a mixture of the two), simply because we cannot get access to the kind of evidence that would allow us to decide.

This disagreement about the nature of human nature is, though, only one of many that underlie attempts to resolve the question of whether societies can exist without law by defining the terms "society" and "law". Indeed, such disagreements affect all jurisprudential issues, no matter the line of approach. They concern both the very character of reality itself and the whole quality of our understanding of it.

For example, there is a so far unresolved debate as to whether there is such a thing as mind or whether there is only matter. Those who accept that there is such a thing as mind may still be divided as to whether there is some Universal Mind or Spirit or whether there are only individual finite minds, like yours and mine. Again, they may diverge about the role Mind or mind has in directing matter. For example, some may wish to endorse and some to challenge the claim that 'God is working his purpose out, as year succeeds to year'.[8]

Others may be more concerned with the question, of major importance for law, of whether our bodies are actually controlled by our minds, so that our physical movements are, normally at least, the result of thoughts and decisions and acts of will. For, if this is so, it becomes necessary to explain just how the mental does act upon the physical. As Richard Taylor asks us:

> Conceive, then, if possible how an *idea* . . . can render more permeable the membranes of certain brain cells, or how an idea can enter into a chemical reaction whose effect is the diffusion of sodium ions at a certain place, how an idea can move the particles of the cortical cells or otherwise aid or inhibit chemical reactions occurring therein. Try, I say, to form a conception of this, and then confess that, as soon as the smallest attempt at a description is made, the description becomes unintelligible and the conception an impossible one.[9]

The lack of what they regard as any satisfactory explanation of how mind and matter interact is one factor in leading some to maintain that

---

[8] Hymn 303, *The Church Hymnary* (Oxford: Oxford University Press, 1973) line 1.

[9] Richard Taylor, *Metaphysics,* 2nd edn (New Jersey: Prentice-Hall, 1974) p 25.

we are mistaken in our belief that we have minds. We are really just sets of physiological processes, operating in response to various stimuli. If this is so, then we need to ask why is it that we think of ourselves as being, all but occasionally, in control of the movements we make and as directing them in terms of some intention or purpose. We need to ask, too, what incredible injustices have we done to our fellows according to the criminal law, if we have executed or imprisoned them on the basis that they have acted with *mens rea*. For, if there is no such thing as mind, how can anybody have a guilty one? Yet, perhaps this should not trouble us overmuch, since, if we are just sets of physiological processes, notions like justice and injustice seem to lose most of their relevance anyway.

It remains to be seen how far the fact that scientists now explain matter itself in terms of energy will assist in the resolution of such debates, as also of other debates about the nature of reality that are of significance to legal theory. For instance, the law may well be shaped differently in a reality that has some kind of in-built structure and/or follows inevitable patterns of development and in one that has no set form, with change occurring as a matter of accident and taking no set path. It matters here, too, given that reality does indeed have some kind of in-built structure or follow inevitable patterns of development, whether these structures and patterns are the same throughout - in particular, it matters whether the social world behaves like the physical one.

Just, however, as there are disagreements about the nature of reality, so, too, are there disagreements about our capacity for knowledge of it. One issue is as to whether or not we can know what reality is actually like and, if so, how we come to do so. Some believe that the process is one of discovery. All sorts of questions arise about the character of this process. On one understanding, there are certain self-evident principles of reason from which knowledge can be deduced, without any need for experience. On another understanding, knowledge is arrived at by the application of such principles of reason, either self-evident or in-born, to our sense experiences. In either case we may ask whether the existence and/or employment of these principles allows us some kind of privileged insight, so that the knowledge we gain is of reality as such or whether we can only arrive at reality as it is for us as human beings. And, in the latter case, we may ask whether we are bound, given the nature of the principles of reason involved, to interpret our sense experiences in the way we do, so that our version of reality has to take the kind of shape it does.[10]

Others would contend that reality is just something we construct for ourselves. All sorts of questions arise about the character of this process too. On one understanding, we simply have certain sense experiences and order and interpret them in ways that seem convenient at the time. If so, we need to ask whether we can we accept everything that appears to follow from this - for example: that our reality is the only reality there is; that there is nothing fixed about the form this reality takes, since we make it up as we go along; and that our knowledge of reality consists in whatever, at any given time, we have accumulated by way of sense experience together with whatever account of that experience we find that we can agree upon. This seems to commit us to saying that we once knew that the sun revolved around the earth but that we now know that the opposite holds. Similarly, it seems to commit us to saying that we once knew that the individual human temperament was constituted by the balance of the humours or body fluids - blood, phlegm, choler (yellow bile) and melancholy (black bile) - but that we now know this analysis to be defective, although scientists continue to seek a similar but more convincing one, in terms of genetic make up and chemical balances.

On other understandings of the constructive approach, however, matters are rather less fluid than suggested above. First, it may be claimed that, however "ad hoc" our constructions of reality may once have been, we are now conditioned by them - so that the ways in which we are capable of understanding the world today are limited by the ways that we have done so in the past. Second, it may be argued that the manner in which we have constructed reality has, from the beginning, been more than just a matter of convenience - driven, perhaps, by certain interests and purposes common to us all. Or, indeed, both views may be held together.

In identifying what law is for the purpose of deciding whether societies can exist without it, we, consciously or unconsciously, answer various questions of a similar kind for ourselves. Is law already

[10] A materialist might also take the line that we are bound to interpret our sense experiences in the way that we do, not in terms of principles of reason but, rather, in terms of the ways in which our brains are structured.

there in the world, waiting for us to discover it and build our own human arrangements in its likeness? If it is already there in the world, can we get to know it as it really is or only as it is for us? If we can know it as it really is, how do we come to know it? Is law itself amongst the various self evident principles of reason or is it just that we can find it by making use of such principles? If, on the other hand, we can only know law as it is for us as human beings, does this mean that we can know it as it is for all humankind or only as it is for different peoples? Alternatively, is law something purely of our own making? If so, can we find any general basis for identifying it or must we accept that what counts as law can vary from one society to the next?

Such problems bedevil all attempts to offer a satisfactory account of law and largely explain the many different emphases we find within them. Some examples are:

> An ordinance of reason for the common good, made by him who has care of the community and promulgated.[11]
>
> A command of the sovereign backed by threat of sanction.[12]
>
> What . . . officials do about disputes.[13]
>
> A set of conditions for the legitimate use of force.[14]
>
> The customs, generated by the spirit of a people, living and working in common in all individuals.[15]
>
> A treaty to which members of the same community have agreed.[16]

---

[11] St Thomas Aquinas, *Summa Theologiae,* trans and ed Thomas Gilby et al (London: Blackfriars, 1964) Q91 A1.

[12] John Austin, *The Province of Jurisprudence Determined,* 2nd edn (London: John Murray, 1861) p 5.

[13] Karl Llewellyn, *The Bramble Bush,* revised 2nd edn (New York: Oceana, 1960) p 12.

[14] The thrust of Hans Kelsen's position, though not actually a definition offered by him.

[15] F K von Savigny, *System of Modern Roman Law,* trans W Holloway (Madras: J Higginbotham, 1867); see also *Of the Vocation of our Age for Legislation and Jurisprudence* trans A Haywood (London: Littlewood & Co, 1831).

[16] Adam Ferguson, *An Essay on the History of Civil Society 1767* (Edinburgh: Edinburgh University Press, 1978) p 155.

An instrument of force and ideology used by the ruling class to maintain its dominant position.[17]

A way of solving a community's coordination problems. . .[18]

The enterprise of subjecting human conduct to the governance of rules.[19]

The contest really begins, however, when some thinker, either expressly or impliedly, treats her or his understanding of law as definitive - as holding good on a universal basis and/or as adequate to the purpose of answering any question that might be asked.

For instance, those who maintain that law is already there in the world and that we can get to know it as it really is still manage to disagree amongst themselves about both its nature and its content. We gain very different pictures of the law from the Torah and the Koran and the New Testament, even though all three are believed to reveal the Word of the Almighty.[20] Within these faiths, too, there are fundamental disputes about how the Word is to be interpreted. Since each thinker holds his or her own picture to be the true one, each tends to dismiss those painted by others as reflecting mere and erroneous beliefs. Such beliefs, it is argued, have been arrived at because of some flaw in the operation of the process by which knowledge is acquired, such as a failure in vision or a defective use of reason.[21]

Similar disputes may arise between those thinkers who argue that law is already there in the world and that we can get to know it but

---

[17] Karl Marx, *Preface to a Contribution to a Critique of Political Economy*; Karl Marx and Friedrich Engels, *The German Ideology*, as discussed in Hugh Collins, *Marxism and the Law* (Oxford: Clarendon Press, 1982) esp ch 2.

[18] John Finnis, *Natural Law and Natural Rights* (cit. n.1) at p 276. This, however, leaves out the positivistic element in his account and also the reference to the common good. (For more on Finnis, see later in this chapter and ch XII).

[19] Lon L Fuller, *The Morality of Law* (New Haven & London: Yale University Press, 1964) p 91. See also the revised edn, 1969.

[20] There are also secular versions of this kind of thinking. For a discussion of them, see chapter XII on the ideas of Grotius and of John Finnis.

[21] For a very early exposition of this type of approach, see Plato, *The Republic,* ed F M Cornford (Oxford: Clarendon Press, 1941), in particular the metaphors of the sun (Book VI 502c - 509c, line (Book VI 509d-end) and cave (Book VII 514a - 521b).

only as it is for us as human beings. If they maintain, as most of them do, that there are principles of reason common to all humankind and that knowledge is acquired by applying those principles to our sense experiences, how is it that there seem to be so many different understandings of what law is? In common with the first group, such thinkers might respond that other people have just not done a good enough job with the principles concerned. Alternatively, they could suggest that an insufficient amount of experience has been brought into the reckoning.

Others, however, might adopt a different form of defence, involving an attack on the idea that common principles of reason must lead us to a single understanding of law. Planet Earth is a very diverse place, so that people on it just will have different experiences. Whatever they arrive at by applying principles of reason to those experiences does represent reality as it is for them at that time and in that place. The insight may be a partial one but it is valid for all that.[22] Thinkers taking this line, though, sometimes go on to argue that, despite their apparent dissimilarity, all the different appreciations of reality are actually the same at root. The task of the philosopher then becomes that of digging down to and exposing it, just as for some linguists their role is that of trying to lay bare the same deep structures underlying the different grammars to be found in human languages.[23]

For those who believe that reality is just what we construct out of our experience, in ways that seem to suit our convenience, such endeavours are fruitless ones. Law is nothing more nor less than what we happen to agree to make it. One obvious problem is, of course, just who are the "we" involved? The "we" chosen is rarely that of the whole of humankind but rather that of some identified group. Even then, is it the whole membership of the group, or those having power within it or some specialist élite? In attempting to resolve this problem, some of the thinkers tend to lose sight of their original position and slip into arguing that the "we" they have chosen is the

---

[22] This is, very very approximately, the kind of approach adopted by Hegel. see e.g. G W F Hegel, *The Philosophy of Right,* trans T M Knox (Oxford: Oxford University Press, 1967) Introduction at p 15.

[23] Based on the work of Noam Chomsky. See e.g. his *Syntactic Structures* (The Hague: Mouton, 1957). (For further discussion of linguistic approaches, see ch X.)

only "we" by whom law for that group can be constituted. Similarly, where they have identified to their satisfaction what law is for the group to which they belong, they are prone to assume that that is what law is for everyone and to deny others the right to call their own arrangements law.

The dangers in this construction of reality approach become even greater once it is argued that what we agree to be law is not just a matter of current consensus but heavily conditioned by our pasts. For we then appear to be in a trap of our own devising. We have no obvious means of breaking free and making law into something different from our previous experience of it. Nor, indeed, is it easy to see where, short of reference to some reality beyond what we have constructed, we might find these means. Yet the possibility of referring to any such further reality is one that the approach sets out to deny.[24]

Alternatively, if human beings come to create law because of certain shared interests and purposes, how do we set about identifying the interests and purposes concerned? Is it possible to find ones belonging to all humankind, particularly if the only way we can do this is by uncovering what is common to the realities constructed by numerous different social groups? For, since we cannot take any line that involves going outside the constructions - such as asserting that these interests and purposes are somehow inherent in human nature - it is difficult to see how we might set about this exercise, given the diversity of languages and practices that exist. If, even so, we can actually identify such interests and purposes, should we agree that it is appropriate to call anything law if it serves them, no matter how different the form it takes between one society and the next? Or should we regard law as one special way of serving such interests and purposes and distinguish it from other ways of doing so?

If we make the first choice, we risk foisting onto a society a concept that it does not actually have or, at least, does not make use of in some particular context. If we make the second one, then how do we distinguish law from other ways of doing things? We seem to be forced back upon our own culturally conditioned understandings of what law is. Take, for example, the much quoted words of Justice Oliver Wendell Holmes: 'The prophecies of what the courts will do in

---

[24] See later, however, in ch XI and (mainly) ch XII, the ideas of Jürgen Habermas.

fact, and nothing more pretentious, are what I mean by the law'.[25] Holmes himself was clearly not trying to give any kind of exhaustive definition of law. Rather, his object seems to have been that of drawing attention to the central role played by the courts in forming the law of the United States. Read on their own, though, the words 'prophecies of what the courts will do' might be taken to imply that a society does not have law unless it also has such institutions or that we cannot call standards legal ones if disputes falling under them are resolved by mediation or conciliation.

It may or may not be possible for us to develop some special kind of insight into a reality not purely of our own making and discover what law properly is, irrespective of what we actually call laws. Alternatively, it may or may not be possible for us to move beyond different constructions of reality and achieve some genuinely cross-cultural understanding of what counts as law. The fact is, however, that, when discussing law, we do somehow tend to assume that it must have the features found in developed - and usually western - legal systems. Much of the disagreement as to whether international law is really law arises because it does not fit cosily into this kind of model.[26] Yet to treat law in this way begs all kinds of questions about its nature. For just what features something must have to count as law or legal system is actually a matter of considerable controversy.

The debate is a wide ranging one. It covers issues about the form law takes, the function it has and the kind of content it can include. Where form is concerned, the argument goes well beyond the question of whether law needs institutions such as courts and legislatures. Does law have to be general in its application? Must it be coercive, either in every case or, at least, ultimately so? Can something fail to be a law simply because people disregard it? And so on. These kinds of questions preoccupy those engaged in analytical jurisprudence. But the answers they give to them often turn, consciously or unconsciously, on the understandings they have of the function of law. Such understandings themselves turn on the answers to various questions of

[25] O W Holmes, 'The Path of the Law' (1897) 10 *Harvard Law Review* p 457 at p 460-1.

[26] For example, there is no legislature as such, submission of disputes for judicial resolution is largely voluntary and there is no properly organised system of sanctions.

a different kind. Is, for instance, law somehow tied to certain aspects of human nature? To the requirements of social living generally? Or to particular types of human society? If so, will it be different depending on the type of society to which it is tied? Can it be used to achieve any kind of social purpose? If so, should it be used to achieve any such purpose? Alternatively, does law have certain in-built purposes of its own or ones that arise out of particular social arrangements?

Karl Marx affords a very clear example of someone whose answer to the question of whether law must be coercive in form is conditioned by his views on such functional matters. He regards law as arising out of the existing modes of production and as legitimising and sustaining the relations of production that stem from them. In a capitalist society it is thus a means through which, by force and ideology, the bourgeoisie maintains itself in power over and oppresses the working class. Given a change to social ownership of the means of production, however, state and law will become superfluous. As Engels put it 'The government of persons is replaced by the administration of things and by the direction of the processes of production. The state is not "abolished", it withers away'.[27] Since, for Marx, the function of law is to sustain the power of the ruling class, the system as a whole and many, if not all, of the individual laws it contains will be coercive in form. The kind of regulation employed in the truly communist society, on the other hand, will be there to enable and not to coerce and so is not to be accounted as law.

Again, for Hans Kelsen, the function of law is to regulate the mutual behaviour of men by prescribing the only conditions under which they may be deprived of life, freedom, economic and other values.[28] It follows that, for him, it is not just some laws that are coercive. Not only must the legal order as a whole have a monopoly over the means of coercion but so also must every norm forming part of it specify the conditions under which the imposition of sanctions is authorised. On

---

[27] Friedrich Engels, 'Anti Dühring' quoted in M. Oakeshott, *Social and Political Doctrines of Contemporary Europe* (Cambridge: Cambridge University Press, 1939) pp 130-1.

[28] Hans Kelsen, *The Pure Theory of Law* (cit. n. 2) esp pp 30-37.

this kind of approach, the function of law is seen as conditioning its very structure.

Further, views about the function of law do not just affect claims concerning its form. They also prompt different attitudes to its content. We have already seen how Hobbes, from a view that human nature is essentially quarrelsome, regards the very purpose of the law as coercive. He also, however, defines injustice as being in breach of what one has agreed to under the law. It follows that the all powerful sovereign, being outside the law, can never be unjust. Since law is made by the sovereign it, too, can never be unjust. Of course, the sovereign and the law may be iniquitous - run contrary to natural law - but that is a different matter. And there is no barrier to the sovereign committing whatever degree of iniquity is compatible with his role of preserving the peace.

By contrast, theorists such as Aquinas, who see the function of law as promoting the common good, question the status of what is done by those in power where this involves corruption or evil. Whether this means that they fail to issue laws at all or that they only manage to make ones that their subjects have no moral obligation to obey is a matter of dispute. For Aquinas himself it appears to be a matter of degree. For he writes:

> To the extent that it falls away from right reason it is called a wicked law: as such it has the quality of an abuse of law, rather than of law. Nevertheless, even a wicked law keeps some trace of legality, since it is backed by the established order which is supported by the Eternal law;[29]
>
> As already stated, every law is ordained for the common well being and to that extent it gets the force and quality of law, insofar as it falls short it has no binding force;[30]
>
> Another regime is tyranny, which is so thoroughly corrupt that it affords no law.[31]

Issues concerning the form, the function and the content of law are, then, so clearly inter-related that a coherent view of its nature as a whole depends on a consistent approach to them all. Further, those concerning function and content, at least, can only be resolved in terms of answers to a whole range of non-legal questions. These range across

---

[29] *Summa Theologiae* (cit. n.11) Q93 A3.

[30] Ibid Q96 A6.

[31] Ibid Q95 A4.

various fields of enquiry, particularly those of the biological sciences, of philosophy and sociology. In consequence, even identifying the questions poses a problem, let alone coming up with compatible answers.

Where, then, should we begin? One way would be to take a common knowledge approach. There are two problems with this, though. First, common knowledge can be very misleading. As mentioned earlier, we once "knew" that the sun revolved around the earth. Consider, too, the following statements: 'Life begins at conception';[32] 'I've flipped tails five times in a row - by the law of averages, it **must** come up heads next!';[33] 'When something gets cheaper, people buy more of it'.[34] Upon investigation, however, it becomes clear that all these assertions provide inadequate guidance for those considering terminating a pregnancy, continuing to gamble or cutting prices. Second, as with law, what we regard as common knowledge will in large measure be culture bound. For example, we organise our lives around a twenty four hour day. So, when Benjamin Whorf writes of the traditional understanding of the Hopi Indians, he remarks:

> What surprises most is to find that various grand generalisations of the Western world, such as time, velocity and matter, are not essential to the construction of a consistent picture of the universe. The psychic experiences that we class under these headings are, of course, not destroyed; rather categories derived from other kinds of experiences take over the rulership of the cosmology and seem to function just as well.[35]

In consequence, we do not find means in the Hopi language of expressing past, present and future but only of the degree of objectivity or subjectivity of what is being expressed.

Given all this, common knowledge seems not to offer a very secure basis, whether for arriving at conclusions in general or at ones about the nature of law in particular. An alternative approach might be to tackle all the non-legal questions by becoming experts in the relevant

---

[32] It does not. Conception is a re-formation, not an initiation of life.

[33] In fact the chances of flipping heads or tails remain constant at 50-50.

[34] Frequently, perhaps, but not necessarily. If it is something that already takes up a large part of people's incomes they may actually buy less of it (e.g. potatoes) and more of something else (e.g. bread).

[35] Benjamin Whorf, 'Science and Linguistics' *Language, Thought and Reality* (Cambridge, Mass: MIT Press, 1956) para 18.

fields of enquiry. Even if this were humanly possible, there would still be a major snag. It is by no means clear that all the experts are offering the same types of explanation of the world. So we would still need to produce an over-arching theory that would include and reconcile them all. In short, we would need to produce the key to 'Life, the universe and everything'.[36]

Should we then abandon jurisprudence as an impossible enterprise? The temptation may be great, but it has to be admitted that there is another possible approach. Our ordinary, everyday experience gives us a degree of certainty that there are things we call laws, that these arise out of human activity and that they are found by looking at societies. Something may, then, perhaps be learnt from looking at what is called law in a selected society, provided that earlier caveats are borne in mind. What is being investigated is highly partial. First, it is human law in a social context. Second, it is particular human law in a particular social context. The conclusions that can be drawn will necessarily be limited. Nonetheless they may be sufficient to demonstrate that certain views about the nature of law are inadequate or misleading as far as that particular law is concerned.

[36] Taken from the title of volume three of the Douglas Adams series, beginning with the *Hitch-Hiker's Guide to the Galaxy* (London & Sydney: Pan Books, 1979).

II

CONNECTING LAW AND SOCIETY

Examining the law of Scotland in the context of Scottish society meets with two immediate problems. First, how does one identify the law of Scotland? Second, just what counts as a society in general and as Scottish society in particular? Some of the problems of identifying law have been mentioned in the previous chapter. Those involved in determining what a society is are as great, if not greater. They are complicated, too, by the fact that some writers regard the ideas of "society" and "community" as interchangeable, whilst others believe that the two can be distinguished. About the only real point of agreement is that, when we are talking about a society, we are dealing with something that involves more than one member - that it is some kind of whole comprising various parts.

Where the disagreement comes in is as to what kind of whole it is and the relationship it has with the parts. There are at least three different views in this respect. For example, Jeremy Bentham writes:

> The interest of the community is one of the most general expressions that can occur in the phraseology of morals: no wonder its meaning is often lost. When it has a meaning, it is this. The community is a fictitious body, composed of the individual persons who are considered as constituting, as it were, its members. The interest of the community, then, is what? - the sum of the interests of the several members who compose it.[1]

At the opposite pole, various writers, in varying degrees, regard the whole as some kind of fusion of the parts. The ideas involved are forcefully expressed in the writings of Otto von Gierke.[2] He argues that we have only to consider things like the organisation of power, or the law, or the social code or the economy or the language of a community to realise that these cannot be explained as the sum of

---

1 Jeremy Bentham, *An Introduction to the Principles of Morals and Legislation*, 1798, ed W Harrison, published jointly with the *Fragment on Government* (Oxford: Blackwell, 1967) ch 1, para 4.

2 E.g. in *Natural Law and the Theory of Society*, ed E Barker (Cambridge: Cambridge University Press, 1934).

separate activities of separate human beings. They have a character of their own. For Gierke:

> . . . it follows that the community which produces them must also be something different from the sum of the individuals who constitute it. It must be a Whole, with a life-unity which is itself super-individual.[3]

Ernest Barker explains Gierke's approach as saying that 'When 100 persons unite to form a group which wills and acts as one, we must say that there is a new real person present - the hundred and first person, the super-person - in which these 100 individuals live and have their being, at the same time that they also continue to live and have their being as so many separate persons'.[4] This hundred and first person can then be seen as having a real will and a real mind of its own.

In between come those writers who see the group neither as something reducible to the human beings who comprise it nor as something that exists over and above them. Rather, the group, the whole, has to be seen as a matter of relationships amongst its members. Emile Durkheim explains the approach as follows:

> . . . society is not the mere sum of individuals, but the system formed by their association represents a specific reality which has its own characteristics. Undoubtedly no collective entity can be produced if there are no individual consciousnesses: this is a necessary but not a sufficient condition. In addition these consciousnesses must be associated and combined, but combined in a certain way. It is from this combination that social life arises and consequently it is this combination that explains it.[5]

The first approach, then, sees the notion of the whole as something fictitious. Although we may sometimes talk as if such wholes - for example, society or the community - actually exist, what we are doing in these cases is using a kind of shorthand to describe the only things that can genuinely be found: the parts or individuals which, for some purpose or another, we are treating "en bloc". The second two approaches, on the other hand, agree that wholes have a reality to them

---

3 Ibid at p lxviii.

4 Ibid at p lxvi. It is interesting that this kind of approach is reflected in the European Community, in that Community treaties are signed both by all member states and the Community as such.

5 Emile Durkheim, *The Rules of Sociological Method,* trans W D Hall, ed S Lukes (London: Macmillan, 1982) at p 129.

but differ about what this reality amounts to. For Gierke a whole has a reality of its own, separable from that of its various parts. With Durkheim, the whole is, instead, defined in terms of all the relationships there are between its component parts, together with various features that are peculiar to them. The reality of the whole arises simply because, whenever things are associated together, the relationships between them (and the features peculiar to these) become actual aspects of our world. They have to be explained as such.[6]

Which of these approaches we adopt has considerable implications for our identification of Scottish society. If societies just consist of various individuals, then we can draw the boundary around any group of them we please. Or, at least, we can do so "within reason". For, at its most basic, our understanding of the nature of a whole is that its parts have something in common. We have, therefore, to come up with some plausible principle by reference to which we can justify bracketing those individuals together. The need for such a principle becomes clearer if we consider the effect of ignoring it. I would, for example, be thought a little bizarre if I tried to assert that a tree on the other side of the city was part of the park I can see from my sitting room window.

If, on the other hand, a society is seen as existing "over and above" its individual members, then its boundaries are already drawn for us. It would appear, too, that these individual members must be ordered together according to some principle or principles belonging to the society as a whole. We are limited, then, to trying to discover where the boundaries are to be found and what the governing principles are. The situation within the Durkheimian model is, however, rather less clear cut. It is plain that, in the social world, things like custom, law and conventional morality may both determine the composition of a group and be, in part at least, constitutive of the relationships between its members. Custom, law and conventional morality are thus undoubtedly real in the sense that they affect our thoughts and behaviour. What is considerably less clear is whether their existence is purely dependent on that thought and behaviour or whether they have some kind of life of their own. More moot still is the extent to

[6] This remains true even though, for Durkheim, 'individuals are the only actors in social life'.

which such factors are constitutive not just of the relationship between the parts but also of the very nature of the parts themselves.

Setting such complications aside, however, it does seem clear that the kind of approach offered by Durkheim is likely to be the most useful one in an attempt to determine the ambit of Scottish society. Unlike that of Bentham, it directs our attention to certain specific aspects of the way in which we live our lives. Unlike that of Gierke, it does not saddle us with a super-person, for whom we have to account at every stage. Even if we do follow Durkheim, though, there are still difficulties in choosing the aspects of our lives that are relevant for the constitution of particular societies and in deciding which, if any, of these aspects is the most significant. One possibility is the law. We might argue that what makes an otherwise motley collection of human beings into members of Scottish society is the fact that they are all subject to the law of Scotland. This means that we can return immediately to our first problem, that of identifying this law. When we have done so, we shall be able to tell at once who the members of Scottish society are.

A critic of this way of going about things might wish to ask why priority should be given to law and not to some other factor, such as geographical location. Surely, it can be argued, what the human beings concerned actually have in common is the fact of living in Scotland. To which the response might be that this is a misunderstanding of the situation. The physical point of the universe at which someone is located is a matter of natural or brute fact. The name given to that particular point, though, is a matter of artificial or social fact - as, indeed, is the meaning we give to any word in our language.[7] What, then, actually gives all these human beings something in common is the use of the name Scotland for the area in which they live. Since this is a matter decided by the law, the priority given to it was clearly correct.

---

[7] On an allied distinction, see D N MacCormick, 'Law as Institutional Fact' in (1974) 90 *Law Quarterly Review* 102, at p 104: 'To say that a contract exists between parties as the result of certain acts is to develop one particular frame of reference in terms of which these acts can be considered, namely that of the law, or that specifically of an inter-related set of legal rules'; and the developed ideas in Neil MacCormick and Ota Weinberger, *An Institutional Theory of Law* (Dordrecht: D Reidel, 1986).

Unfortunately, upon investigation, this response proves not to be quite so convincing as it might first appear. The reason, again, has to do with our use of language. As jurists, we view the world, as it were, through bi-focals. We seek to know what the law is. In doing so, we use methods and concepts peculiar to us as lawyers. In cases of uncertainty, however, there is a point at which the lawyer in us retires and the ordinary citizen takes over. Admittedly the attitudes we have as ordinary citizens will be affected by the fact that we are lawyers. Yet wider aspects of our education and experience will go to shape them too. As jurists, also, we may seek to criticise the law. Here, too, there is a similar duality of approach - though with, perhaps, the ordinary citizen in us coming more readily to the fore.

This duality is not confined to the way we view the world. It comes out in the way we talk and write about it as well. This is so for most of the population, not just for lawyers. Even setting aside major cases of bilingualism - such as Gaelic/English in the Highlands and Islands of Scotland; Welsh/English in Wales; and French/English in Quebec - we still do not all speak quite the same language. Dialect is an obvious example. More important for our purposes, though, are the kinds of discourse engaged in by specialist groups such as medics, sociologists and lawyers.[8] Such groups may diverge considerably in the way they use words. "Automatism", for instance, is used for markedly different sets of circumstances in medicine and in law.[9]

Parallelling the divergences between specialists are those between the specialist and the ordinary citizen. Often this involves the two using different terms for the same thing. In some cases there is an exact equivalence of meaning between them: as in infectious mononucleosis and glandular fever; sodium hydroxide and caustic soda; sequoia and redwood tree. Unfortunately, where the law is concerned, it is likely that the kind of divergence between the lawyer and the lay person will resemble that between different groups of specialists. The same word will be used but not in quite the same sets of circumstances. Usually, in the case of the law, the circumstances will be much more precise ones. The lawyer, too, is likely to employ various "terms of art" that have little or no meaning to the lay person.

---

8 Known technically as "special registers".

9 See e.g. *Stevenson* v *Beatson* 1965 SLT (Sh Ct) 65.

It is probably only the most pedantic of lawyers who, in the family circle at least, would talk of a creditor acceptilating the obligation of the other party, rather than just releasing him from it, or of irritating, rather than just terminating, the lease of an unsatisfactory tenant. Properly, though, these are not quite the same things. Acceptilation is a unilateral renouncing by a creditor of his rights under a contract, which may require a different form - dependent on how the contract was entered into - this having the **effect** of releasing the other party. Similarly, irritancy is a narrower concept than that of termination, since it only applies where a lease is brought to an end by a specific procedure because its terms have been breached, whilst termination can take place by various means.[10]

When looked at more closely, legal language can be seen to fall into a number of different categories. First, there are words and phrases that have no meaning outside the legal context. The sense of these can only be conveyed to a lay person by means of a detailed explanation. Thus, a vitious intromitter[11] is someone who may be held liable for all the debts of a deceased person, in consequence of having meddled with the deceased's moveable estate without having been confirmed as his or her executor. Even this explanation is incomplete, though, since what amounts to moveable property, to confirmation and to an executor still needs to be spelt out.

Second, there are those words that, although they come from the same root, have a substantially different significance for lay-person and lawyer. To the former a conveyance is a form of transport, to the latter a transfer of title to property. To the former a curator has to do with museums, to the latter with looking after the affairs of those deemed legally incapable of doing so for themselves. Third, there are those words which have ordinary and legal meanings of the same type. Typical examples are 'possession' and 'murder'. As already noted, the legal term is used in much more precisely specified sets of circumstances than the ordinary one. These may even vary from one branch of the law to the next. Finally, there are those words which

---

[10] As, for example, by giving appropriate notice.

[11] D M Walker suggests this example in *The Scottish Legal System* 6th edn (Edinburgh: W Green & Son/Sweet & Maxwell, 1981) at p 179.

have no specialised legal meaning and which are used by Parliament, the courts and lawyers in general in their ordinary everyday senses.

The third is, however, the most interesting of the categories. For here the ordinary and legal meanings exert a considerable influence on each other. The legal meaning cannot be made to depart too far from the ordinary one without objections being made. For example, in the English case of *D.P.P.* v. *Smith*[12] it was held that an accused person should be deemed to intend the natural and probable consequences of his action. This was sufficiently distant from the ordinary conception of what it is for someone to intend something for Parliament to intervene in the matter.[13] Equally, the ordinary meaning may be heavily conditioned by the legal one. In this case the former is often a rather blurred version of the latter.

Here the relevance to the question of identifying Scottish society becomes apparent. In determining the proper scope or extent of a geographical name we look to matters of custom and to official or legal recognition. Sometimes these will not coincide - as where the inhabitants of a village persist in referring to one of its dwellings as 'Yew Tree Cottage', despite its appearance on the valuation rolls as 'Dunroamin'. In the majority of cases, however, it is from the law that we take our cue. This attitude is not confined to place names and their geographical limits. It extends to the names we use for people, too, whether as individuals or groups. It is to the law that we turn to identify individuals, associations, companies and nations. This also holds for links between people and places, both in terms of what people are said to belong to a particular place and of what places are said to belong to particular people. It is to the law that we turn to establish domicile, residence and nationality and to determine title, whether of a person to a particular piece of land or of a whole people to exclusive dominion over a particular territory.

In a settled situation, at least, we tend to accept what the law says in such matters. This does not mean, however, that we cannot think beyond it. First, what the law says may not be particularly clear. Where this kind of doubt exists, or a dispute arises, we may refer the matter for decision to an appropriate official or body. We usually do

[12] [1961] A.C. 290 at 327.

[13] Criminal Justice Act 1967 s. 8.

so, though, with a ready made view as to what the outcome should be. Further, even after the decision, we can hold an opinion of our own as to what it should have been. Second, we may be concerned with far more than the clarity of the law. We may wish to contest its determining matters in the way it does. Examples of this kind include the basis on which citizenship is granted under the British Nationality Act 1981 and the divergence of opinion between the governments of the U.K. and the Argentine as to the proper status of the Falkland Islands/the Malvinas. Third, while not questioning either the clarity or the rationale of the law, we may on occasion, and for our own purposes, operate according to criteria of our own devising. The area of "contract" is a particularly fruitful one, with vast numbers of business agreements, betting and gaming transactions and collective bargains not meeting with the criteria for legal recognition and/or enforceability.

How, then, does this affect the use of the term "Scottish"? It seems clear that, a few eccentrics apart, the legal criteria are the accepted ones for defining the physical area that is to count as Scotland.[14] The statement 'Berwick upon Tweed is in Scotland' is mistaken to lawyer and lay person alike.[15] This does not mean, though, that the legal criteria are accorded anything like complete control over what sorts of things are generally counted as Scottish or over the circumstances in which they are so. For example, actual location within the boundaries of Scotland may not be required. Origin or some similar connection can be enough. Scotch whisky is Scotch whisky no matter where in the world it is found, even if it is Scotch whisky only because it was produced in Scotland.[16] Scottish country dancing is as competent an activity in Hamilton, Ontario, as in Hamilton, Lanarkshire. The

[14] Although a question may arise as to which set of legal criteria, as, for example, when a state extends its fishing limits in a way not recognised by international law. Another such issue might be just what should be counted as Scotland's oil in the event of Scottish independence.

[15] Even if it is the case that Berwick Rangers play in the Scottish League.

[16] See e.g. *John Walker and Sons Ltd* v *Henry Ost Ltd* [1970] 2 All ER 106.

London Scottish was traditionally regarded as a Scottish regiment despite the place of its Headquarters.[17]

The case of Scotch whisky apart, the law, normally, is only relevant to defining the geographical area with which the connection is made: it does not determine the nature of the connection. More markedly, some usage is without legal warrant. The law knows no such thing as Scottish nationality. To most Scots, however, anyone born in Scotland has it. For some purposes, the link may be looser still. Apart from the necessary skill, the most one needs to play football for Scotland is a native grandparent.[18] Equally, the legal status of Scotland is not always evident to foreigners. Post from abroad is commonly addressed to Scotland, England. Indeed the Turkish word for Britain is Ingiltere. At the extreme, the notions "Scotland" and "Scottish" become hazy ones.

Two main conclusions seem to follow from all this. First, if we can find something we can call society that can be located by reference to the (legally defined) boundaries of Scotland, we are safe in calling that society "Scottish". Second, this may or may not include everything we are prepared, by ordinary usage at least, to count as Scottish society. Can, however, the law take us any further? Can it help us to determine not just when it is appropriate to call something a Scottish society but when it is appropriate to call it a society at all? Is a society constituted by the fact that a number of human beings are subject to the same law? This immediately raises two further questions. First, is their being subject to the same law a good reason for calling them members of the same society? And if so, second, is it the only reason for calling them members of the same society?

On the first question what, in any event, is meant by "being subject to the same law"? If we take the notion of British society, we find that its members are only in part subject to the same law. Even if one restricts the use of the term "British" to mainland Britain, the extent to which people located in England and Wales, on the one hand, and Scotland, on the other, can be said to be subject to the same law is

---

[17] At present, however, its status is rather that of being a Company in the London Regiment.

[18] By agreement between the Home Nations, i.e. England, Wales, Scotland and Northern Ireland.

strictly limited.[19] One could not then sensibly talk of British society if the criterion were being subject to identical laws, that is to the same law in respect of every aspect of life. The most that could be claimed is that people located in Scotland, England and Wales are members of the same society only because and to the extent that they have some shared law.

The question still remains, though, whether the sharing of law is a good reason for regarding people as members of the same society. Does the fact that Turkey imported the Swiss civil code make Switzerland and Turkey the same society?[20] Our intuitions, surely, suggest not. This may just be, though, because our notion of "sharing the same law" means more than people operating according to identical or nearly identical rules. It involves them conducting relationships with one another according to these rules. This the citizens of Switzerland and Turkey do not do on any consistent basis, except, perhaps, in the case of trade. Since, in fact, Turkey imported the German commercial code, the idea that Turkey and Switzerland are the same society appears even less plausible. Even with trade between Germany and Turkey, though, doubts may be expressed as to whether what the inhabitants are doing is "sharing the same law". For, identical or nearly identical though the rules may be in content, they are distinct as to source. The power and/or authority by which they are sustained is differently located.

It would seem, then, that any notion of people "sharing the same law" can only safely extend to cases where they are conducting relationships with one another according to identical (or nearly identical) rules and where these rules themselves have some kind of common foundation. It would seem too, though, that, where this is happening, we do have good reason for regarding the people concerned as members of the same society. For social action is explained by Max Weber as action which is '. . . oriented to the past,

[19] For example, Article XIX of the constituent Treaty and Acts of Union provided for separate courts 'in all time coming' and Article XVII gave protected status to laws concerning private right in Scotland.

[20] The same may be asked, for example, in respect of Japanese importation from Germany.

present or expected future behaviour of others'. [21] A society then may be understood as a grouping of people orienting their behaviour toward one another in terms of shared understandings and expectations. It will amount to what Talcott Parsons refers to as 'a stable system of interaction'.[22] Since law provides a medium by which people orient their behaviour toward one another in these ways, it does constitute them as a society.

The second question remains, however: namely, whether their being subject to the same law is the only reason for regarding human beings as members of the same society. The life of the ordinary citizen is probably more intimately governed by law than he or she realises - few think of themselves as entering a contract when buying a cabbage or hopping on a bus, for example.[23] Yet, equally, law - narrowly conceived, anyway - is probably less dominant a feature of the world than would appear to the person whose student or professional life is devoted to it. Only some of the shared understandings and expectations by which we orient our behaviour to others will be conditioned by the law.

Certain of these understandings will be purely habitual. A number, and certainly the most important, will have a normative dimension. That is to say, they will involve judgments about what ought or ought not to be done. Indeed, for Parsons, it is this normative dimension that lends stability to the system. Law clearly has this kind of dimension but it is not the only part of our social system that does so. Conventional morality and language also provide stable bases for interaction. Both, too, are of major significance in our lives. Indeed it might be argued that, where members of British society are concerned, more is held in common by way of language than of law.

Their being subject to the same law, then, does not appear to be the only possible reason for regarding people as members of the same

---

[21] Max Weber, *The Theory of Social and Economic Organisation,* trans A R Henderson and Talcott Parsons (London: William Hodge & Co, 1947) p 102.

[22] See, e.g., 'Outline of the Social System ' in Talcott Parsons, Edmund Shils and others eds, *Theories of Society* vol 1 (New York: Free Press of Glencoe, 1961).

[23] On this see William Galbraith Miller, *The Data of Jurisprudence* (Edinburgh: W Green and Sons, 1903) pp 18-26.

society. This is made more apparent by the fact that we readily regard people as belonging to different societies even where they are subject to the same law. For example, we distinguish Highland society from island societies and both from "industrial belt" and Borders societies. We distinguish Glasgow society from Edinburgh society. We even, within these cities, treat Easterhouse society as distinct from Hyndland society and Morningside society as distinct from Craigmillar society. Yet all the members of all these societies would appear to be subject to the same law - the law of Scotland.[24]

We justify such distinctions on a variety of grounds. Some of them are practical, such as the nature of the housing stock, distribution of employment (or unemployment), population density, ethnic or religious mix and so on. Some are to do with preferences as, for example, for certain types of food and forms of entertainment. Some are more directly psychological, to do with the members' own sense of themselves as a group. Such features do not themselves constitute the society but rather give rise to the set of understandings and expectations by which it is characterised. As already indicated, these may be merely habitual. Equally, they may amount to customary practices. Or they may reach the status of conventional morality, whether as an agreed set of values or as recognised rules for conduct.

Such distinctions may also owe something to the law. First, the name we give to the society usually derives from that of the area in which it is located. As suggested earlier in the chapter, this name is likely to have some kind of legal standing. At the same time, though, we do talk of societies in much looser geographical and historical senses - as with industrial society and agricultural society, medieval society and modern society. Second, however, and of far more relevance, is the fact that the law may engender societies. Used as an instrument of social change it can, of course, help create different types of society in a general sense - the affluent society; the open society; the permissive society. More interesting for present purposes, however, are the ways in which it may bring about the formation of societies within society.

This can happen indirectly, as a by-product of social policies that reinforce the practical, preferential and psychological differences

[24] At least as far as the formally established rules are concerned and subject to some variation in their application.

between the inhabitants of different areas. Or it can be of direct effect and a consequence of the fact that the law provides various procedures by which labels are attached to individuals and to groups. In some cases this is by desire of the persons involved - as with partnerships and companies. In such cases the interaction of the members is primarily governed by legal rules. Things do not, however, always operate on this voluntary basis.

One of the main thrusts of criminology in recent years has been to the effect that labelling people as deviant actually creates a deviant society.[25] It does this in more than a mere formal sense. It affects the deviants' view of themselves, as well as others' views of them, and may result in their associating together for mutual support. This, as well as other practical consequences of their being labelled deviant, can lead to the rejection of wider social standards. In consequence, rules of law and conventional morality having little connection with the original deviant act become set aside and relationships, both within and outside the group, are conducted according to the deviants' own shared understandings and expectations.[26]

Labelling may also operate in less obviously dramatic ways. In 1973, Rutherglen, though traditionally a separate Burgh, was made part of Glasgow where future parliamentary and local government elections were concerned.[27] Not all its inhabitants approved the idea of being turned into Glaswegians nor did they come to regard themselves as such, despite the direct practical effects the legislation had on their lives. The 1993 proposals for the reform of local government recommended the transfer of Rutherglen into a new 'South Lanarkshire', along with Clydesdale, Hamilton and East Kilbride, and this transfer was effected in the following year.[28] More controversial was the plan for various wards that had traditionally formed part of the city of Glasgow to be placed there too, with the Glasgow based

---

[25] See, e.g., Geoffrey Pearson, *The Deviant Imagination* (London: Macmillan, 1975) esp ch 3.

[26] This knock-on effect provides one of the most forceful arguments for those campaigning for the legalisation of drugs.

[27] The Local Government (Scotland) Act 1973 s. 1(5).

[28] The Local Government etc (Scotland) Act 1994. See especially Schedule 1.

Evening Times leading a successful campaign to keep them within the new Glasgow unitary authority. Of course, technical groupings can lead to genuine assimilation over time - but they need not do so.

Yet whilst the inhabitants of Rutherglen may question whether they have ever really been part of Glasgow society or whether they now wish to be treated as part of a South Lanarkshire one, they would have few doubts about their membership of Scottish society. The same could be said for the inhabitants of Glasgow or Edinburgh or the Highlands or the Borders or the lands in between. On the other hand, despite also being subject to the same law,[29] some residents, at least, of Orkney and Shetland appear to take a different view.[30] In a similar manner, the Basque people in Spain, although subject to various aspects of Spanish law, do not altogether see themselves as part of Spanish society but, rather, as belonging to Euskadi.

In sum, then, being subject to or sharing the same law does seem to be a good reason for regarding people as members of the same society. They are so in that and to the extent that the law provides a set of understandings and expectations by which they orient their behaviour to one another. As indicated earlier, however, law is not the only possible vehicle for shared understandings and expectations. They can also be encountered in the form of habits,[31] customary practices and conventional morality.[32] Taken together, all such understandings and expectations may be characterised as the culture of the society concerned.[33] Indeed, one basis for comparing and contrasting societies

[29] The complication of Udal law apart.

[30] Judging by the results of the 1979 Devolution Referendum, although recently a more favourable attitude seems to have developed.

[31] This covers both conscious habits and unconscious ones that give rise to expectations.

[32] Amongst which, for present purposes, are taken to be those understandings and expectations associated with religion, economic activity and so on.

[33] For this and competing notions of culture, see David Goldberg and Elspeth Attwooll, 'Legal Orders, Systemic Relationships and Cultural Characteristics: Towards Spectral Jurisprudence' in Örücü, Attwooll and Coyle eds, *Studies in Legal Systems: Mixed and Mixing* (London: Kluwer Law International, 1996) esp pp 320-7 and the references contained therein.

is in terms of the relative dominance of these different aspects of their cultures and of the extent, if any, to which each of these aspects influence one another.

Looking at its culture, so understood, however, will not give a complete picture of any society. Many understandings and expectations arise out of the need to adapt to existing conditions of social life, whether natural or human-made, welcome or unwelcome, intended or unintended, within or outwith the control of those concerned. Action according to the understandings and expectations so produced may, in turn, have practical effects of their own, thus creating new conditions to be contended with.[34] A culture, then, needs to be understood in the context of the conditions of social life of which it is both a cause and a consequence.

For Scotland today, such conditions might be listed as including: a particular religious mix, with Presbyterianism the biggest input but a considerable Catholic one too;[35] teaching across a broad range of subjects in schools, but with the emphasis (traditionally at least) on the imparting of information; a more or less even division between the public and private sectors in housing;[36] an economy in transition, with the decline of traditional heavy industry; a very uneven distribution of population, giving rise to particular problems in the provision of services; and so on.[37]

With the exception of the decline in heavy industry, where Scotland has much in common with the north of England, these factors serve to differentiate her from the rest of Britain. Indeed differences can even be found on the industrial front because of the particular oil-related, technological and financial directions in which the Scottish economy has moved. The distinct character of Scotland is reinforced at what may be called the institutional level. Scotland has, by name if not

---

[34] The invention of the birth control pill and the patterns and effects of its use provide a useful example in this context.

[35] Including the establishment of separate Catholic schools under the Education (Scotland) Act 1918.

[36] The effects of the Housing (Scotland) Act 1988 should be noted here.

[37] These features are identified and discussed, along with others, in James G Kellas, *The Scottish Political System* 4th edn (Cambridge: Cambridge University Press, 1989).

always by ownership and control, her own banks (with their own bank notes) and newspapers; her own television and radio channels, although this feature is shared with the regions of England; and her own sports teams.[38] A considerable number of voluntary and charitable organisations have either a purely Scottish base or a differently constituted Scottish arm.[39]

Scotland also has her own political and administrative bodies. For example, the local government structure is distinctive. Following a single tier structure, for just over twenty years - apart from three all-purpose Island authorities[40] - functions were divided between 53 District and 9 Regional Councils.[41] The Local Government etc (Scotland) Act 1994 abolished both of types of council, replacing them with twenty five new unitary local authorities. One scheme surviving the reform, however, is that introduced by the 1973 Act for very locally based Community Councils.[42] The latter are constitutionally non party political. There is a tradition, too, outside the urban areas, of independent membership and often control of local authorities, although nowadays councillors with party labels attached are clearly on the increase. The political parties themselves are also identifiably

[38] Interestingly, in athletics Scotland is treated as a unit for the Commonwealth games but as part of the United Kingdom for the Olympics.

[39] For example, the Scottish Society for the Prevention of Cruelty to Animals (the SSPCA), founded in 1839, is not connected with the RSPCA.

[40] Orkney, Shetland and the Western Isles.

[41] Local Government (Scotland) Act 1973, following the Report of the Wheatley Commission. The distribution of the population between the regions was very uneven, with Strathclyde accounting for nearly 40% of the whole.

[42] Their development has been patchy, they have little actual power and their influence is dependent on their individual effectiveness as pressure groups.

Scottish although - the SNP, naturally, apart - their status in relation to the British parties is varied.[43]

One of the major inputs of the political parties is, of course, through representation at Westminster. Even there, though, Scottish MPs can be separately identified and special arrangements exist for dealing with matters affecting Scotland alone. Scotland is also recognised at ministerial level, with a place in the Cabinet since 1892[44] and four junior ministers at the Scottish Office.

The Scottish Office itself is of major significance, providing a civil service concerned directly with administering Scottish affairs. This is effected through five departments - Agriculture and Fisheries, Development, Education, Home and Health; Industry - and a considerable number of linked agencies - for example, respectively: the Crofters' Commission, Scottish Homes, the Scottish Sports Council, the Mental Welfare Commission for Scotland, Scottish Enterprise. Alongside these come other Scottish departments involved with the administration of central services - among them the Scottish Information Unit - and of the law - the Scottish Courts Administration, the Lord Advocate's Department, the Crown Office.

Admittedly not all areas of Scottish life are subject to directly Scottish administration. Until recently the universities, for instance, came under the U.K.- wide Universities Funding Council,[45] although now, with the abolition of the binary divide, higher education as a whole comes under the Scottish Higher Education Funding Council.[46] Of immediate significance to a much larger proportion of the population, the welfare system is still operated through the Department

[43] The Scottish Labour Party exists within the United Kingdom one, but enjoys considerable devolved policy making powers; the Scottish Conservative and Unionist Party is a separate Party, cooperating with other parts of the UK through the National Union; the Scottish Liberal Democrats are a separate "State" Party within a federal structure.

[44] A Secretary for Scotland existed between 1707 and 1746, when the functions were transferred to the Lord Advocate. The post was reinstated in 1885 and the name was changed to that of Secretary of State for Scotland in 1926.

[45] Previously the University Grants Committee.

[46] The Further and Higher Education (Scotland) Act 1992 s. 31(1).

of Social Security and the income tax system by the Board of Inland Revenue - both British departments. Even in such cases, though, the Scottish dimension takes on some importance, especially in matters where consultation needs to take place with Edinburgh and not Whitehall.[47]

Whether all these features mean that Scotland has her own political system or just operates as a sub-system of the British one is a matter of debate.[48] For present purposes, however, it is enough to note that such features produce or reinforce distinct ways of seeing things and of doing things. Among many possible examples, the following one serves to illustrate the point. Industrial tribunals resolve the same employment-related disputes throughout Britain. The rules of procedure by which they are governed leave a great deal about the way the hearing is conducted to the discretion of the chairman.[49] By report, industrial tribunals in Scotland have come to operate on a rather less formal and rather less adversarial basis than their counterparts in England.

In sum, then, there appears to be little doubt that people in Scotland have shared understandings and expectations that are all their own.[50] Some are the product of contemporary society, many are the outcome of a shared history and inherited traditions - some of which have been passed down through many generations and some of which, like the current form of Highland dress, are of relatively recent adoption. Some traditions are widespread throughout Scottish society, others are particular to groups within it. Yet others play little more part in social life than is conditioned by the demands of the tourists trade.

---

[47] Consider, too, although it was not a matter of the kind referred to in the text, the significance attached to the then Secretary of State for Scotland's attitude to the proposal in the Riley Report, which recommended the closure of the Veterinary School at Glasgow University.

[48] Kellas, *The Scottish Political System* (cit. n. 37) ch 14.

[49] The Scottish rules are very similar to those in England and Wales. Compare the Industrial Tribunals (Constitution and Rules of Procedure) (Scotland) Regulations 1993 (1993/2688) with the Industrial Tribunals (Constitution and Rules of Procedure) Regulations 1993 (1993/2687).

[50] Even where these have much in common with those found in the rest of Britain, it is arguably a matter of similarity rather than 'sameness'.

However such understandings and expectations have arisen, they include and are both sustained by and criticised in the light of a strong national consciousness. This makes itself apparent in many areas of social life, sport being a prime example.[51] On the political front there is a continuing and widespread desire, going well beyond the bounds of any one political party, for Scotland to have greater control over her own destiny.[52] Where found amongst lawyers, the consciousness takes the form of pride in the distinctive character of Scots law and Scottish legal institutions and a fear of these becoming eroded.

What is clear, however, is that law is only one aspect of the shared understandings and expectations that are the mark of Scottish society - only a part and not the whole of what may be termed Scottish culture. It may of course turn out to be a very important part, exerting a great deal of influence on the rest of the culture - but that is a different issue. It follows that an approach to Scottish society which treats it as involving only those shared understandings and expectations that derive from the law of Scotland is unsound. So, if these are not the same thing, is there anything to be gained by examining them together? The answer would seem to be that there is and in two main respects.

The first respect has to do with the identification of society. As argued earlier, we can use the law as a means of establishing what amounts to Scotland for the purpose of locating Scottish, as opposed to any other, society and of determining, in some sense at least, the group of people who belong to it. The approach is, anyway, an unsound one only so far as it pretends to give an exhaustive account of the form Scottish society takes. There is, on the other hand, an important way in which it offers us a degree of certainty. Scotland is not entirely populated with native Scots unfamiliar with any other culture. Apart from those who have returned from foreign lands,

[51] It is sometimes argued, not altogether in jest, that if Scotland had been more successful in the 1978 Football World Cup, the outcome of the 1979 Devolution referendum would have been very different.

[52] This has been shown consistently in opinion polls. For instance six looked at, taken at intervals between November 1981 and May 1996, show the lowest percentage in favour of change at 69% and the highest at 81%, with those choosing the independence option varying between 22% and 34%.

England sometimes included amongst them, there is a considerable proportion of incomers. These both affect and are affected by the culture in varying degrees. What is more, in these days of mass communication, even the "pure" Scot is liable to be subject to other influences.

Further, as has already been indicated, Scottish society is actually composed of a considerable number of societies, each with its own culture or "sub-culture". It may, then, be difficult to establish just what overall set of shared understandings and expectations an Orkney fisherman and a former Ravenscraig steel worker, an Aberdeen lawyer and a Borders farmer, an Edinburgh shop assistant and a Glasgow social worker, an unemployed teenager in Ayr and a retired army officer in Dunoon have in common. What is significant about the law is that it provides a set of understandings and expectations in which they are expected to share, even if in practice they do not.[53] This suggests that the idea that people are constituted as a society by being subject to the same law is in need of qualification. They are substantially so only to the extent that they do actually share in the understandings and expectations it generates, rather than having these imposed upon them, whether by occupation or by other means.

The second respect in which there may be something to be gained by examining law and society together is a sociological one. Certain theorists have argued that law varies in form with other aspects of social life - with what is being understood here as the wider set of understandings and expectations entertained by the members of the group and the conditions of social life which provide the context of these understandings and expectations. Thus Durkheim contrasts a society characterised by mechanical solidarity (consensus arising from shared experience) with one characterised by organic solidarity (an awareness of interdependence arising from the division of labour). In the former, he suggests there is repressive law. In the latter the law is

[53] Hence the latin maxim *ignorantia iuris neminem excusat* or 'ignorance of the law excuses noone'. That, in practice, the Scots do not altogether share in the understandings and expectations required of them by law is testified to, for example, by the fact that Glasgow Sheriff Court is one of the busiest in Europe.

primarily restitutive, although, since elements of mechanical solidarity remain, there are repressive laws as well.[54]

More recently Unger has equated three different forms of law with three different forms of social life. These are customary or interactional law and tribal society; bureaucratic law (accompanied by priestly or sacred law) and aristocratic society; the legal order and liberal, that is group pluralist, society. This thesis continues that the legal order (otherwise the rule of law) is in the process of disintegrating in the face of the welfare statist and corporatist tendencies of modern or post-liberal society.[55]

Whether or not such theorists are correct in the correlations they find, it does seem that interesting questions can be asked about the relationship between law and other aspects of social life. First, though not necessarily most important, what sort of understandings and expectations in relation to the law are shared by those whose business it is and how do these understandings and expectations - sometimes called the "insiders" legal culture[56] - affect the shape of the law? Second, what sort of understandings and expectations in relation to the law are shared by the wider membership of society - is it, for example, used or ignored, respected or challenged - and what effect do such attitudes have on the law? Similarly, where both groups are concerned, what sort of attitudes to the law are produced by the law itself? Third, how do other kinds of understandings and expectations - be they economic, political, religious, moral or whatever - influence the law and, again, where both groups are concerned, how are such understandings and expectations influenced by the law? The following chapters begin to explore some of these issues in relation to Scotland, starting with understandings about the proper location and proper use of political power.

---

[54] Emile Durkheim, *The Division of Labour in Society* 1893 (New York: Free Press of Glencoe/ London: Collier Macmillan, 1964).

[55] Roberto Mangabeira Unger, *Law in Modern Society* (New York: Free Press of Glencoe/London: Collier Macmillan, 1976).

[56] Lawrence M Friedman, *American Law* (New York/London: W W Norton & Co, 1984) p 7.

III

A CONSTITUTIONAL CULTURE

In 1320, in the Declaration of Arbroath, various Scottish nobles and clergy addressed Pope John XXII, seeking his support in the War of Independence against the English. Of Robert the Bruce they wrote as follows:

> He it is that by the providence of God we have made our Prince and King, not only by right of succession according to our laws and customs, which we are resolved to maintain unto the death, but also with the due consent and assent of us all. Unto him, by whom salvation has been wrought unto our people, we are bound for the preservation of our liberties, both by force of law and by gratitude for all he has done, and unto him we are determined to adhere. But were he to abandon the task to which he has set his hand or to show any disposition to subject us or our realm to the King of England or the English, we would instantly expel him as our enemy and the betrayer of his own rights and ours, and we would choose another King to rule over us who would be equal to our defence.[1]

In those words may be found a very early expression of the view that political power rests upon consent and that it is to be used to effect some communal purpose. It would appear to reflect an even earlier tradition, found in the Celtic law, where rulers were chosen from amongst the membership of a kinship group, and it recurs throughout Scottish history. It comes through in the writings of the churchman and historian, John Mair (or Major), for instance in his descriptions of the attitudes of the Scottish peasantry toward the nobles.[2] Mair's pupil, George Buchanan, in his *De Jure Regni apud Scotos*,[3] justifying the deposition of Mary Stuart, regards the king as owing his position to the people and as dependent on his obedience to the civil laws. The law,

---

[1] Translation taken from Lord Cooper of Culross, *Selected Papers* (Edinburgh: Oliver and Boyd, 1957) p 337.

[2] See P Hume Brown ed, *Scotland before 1700 from Contemporary Documents* (Edinburgh: Douglas, 1893) pp 58-9. Mair's philosophical ideas are discussed in Alexander Broadie, *The Tradition of Scottish Philosophy* (Edinburgh: Polygon, 1990).

[3] Or *The Art and Science of Government amongst the Scots,* 1579, trans and comm D H MacNeill (MacLellan, 1964).

he argues, does not derive its force from the king. Rather, the king derives his force from the law. Similarly, the National Covenant of 1638, directed against the activities of Charles I, bound its signatories in a threefold manner - to the king 'in the defence and preservation of the . . . true religion, liberties and laws of the kingdom', to one another 'in the same cause' and to God, to conduct themselves 'as beseemeth Christians'. Samuel Rutherford's *Lex Rex* of 1644 expresses similar views to those of Buchanan.[4]

The Claim of Right of 1689 insisted that James VII had 'forefaulted the right to the Crown', itemising the grounds on which he had done so and summarising these as follows:

> Therefore the Estates of the Kingdom of Scotland, Find and Declare that King James the Seventh being a professed Papist, did assume the Royal power, and acted as King, without ever taking the oath required by law, and hath by the advice of evil and wicked counsellors, invaded the fundamental constitution of the Kingdom, and altered it from a legal limited Monarchy, to an arbitrary despotick Power, and hath executed the same, to the subversion of the Protestant religion, and the violation of the laws and liberties of the Kingdom, inverting all the ends of Government . . .[5]

Then there are the views of Andrew Fletcher of Saltoun, a vigorous opponent of the Treaty and Acts of Union, and, if not a republican, at least in favour of restricting the power of the Crown, for, in his view 'princes were made for the good government of nations, not the government of nations framed for the private advantage of princes'.[6] Thus, as Wight wrote in 1773:

---

4 1644 (Virginia: Sprinkle, 1982).

5 APS ix 37. See also the Articles of Grievance, APS ix 45 and the Coronation Oath of William and Mary, Nat Mss Scotland, ii, no cvii.

6 Andrew Fletcher of Saltoun, *Selected Political Writings and Speeches* ed D Daiches (Edinburgh: Scottish Academic Press, 1979) p 116. See also W C Mackenzie, *Andrew Fletcher of Saltoun* (Edinburgh: Porpoise Press, 1935) ; P H Scott, *Andrew Fletcher and the Treaty of Union*, (Edinburgh: John Donald, c 1992).

> As back as we can go with any certainty, we discover a limited monarchy, and find that all matters of consequence or public concern were transacted not by the king alone but by the king and his Great Council.[7]

Since the Union, however, the focus has shifted from the role of the monarchy to that of the "Crown in Parliament". There have been two further Claims of Right. The first of these, in 1842, was drawn up by the General Assembly of the Church of Scotland. It argued that the Treaty and Acts of Union had created a federal legislature and that all matters covered by the Act for the Security of the Protestant Religion and Presbyterian Church Government were outwith its 'cognisance and power'.

The trouble had begun as early as 1711, when the Westminster Parliament invaded the right of congregations to call[8] their own ministers by passing the Patronage Act. This placed the power of appointment in the hands of the aristocracy, the gentry and the Crown. The significance of the Act lay with the pervasive influence of the Church. Calvinist doctrine demanded that the Word of God was given priority. All behaviour should be in obedience to it. All power should be exercised in conformity with it. People should be educated in their faith and the responsibilities that they had according to it. Accordingly ministers, together with Kirk Sessions, exercised a high level of control over the daily lives of their parishioners.

Besides having responsibility for such matters as poor relief, they determined matters of doctrine and discipline. They had a statutory power to punish offences against morality not covered by the criminal law.[9] On the one hand it was pressure from the Kirk that brought legislation providing for locally funded schools in every parish as early as 1696. On the other, it was not until the mid nineteenth century that its grip over education, through imposing doctrinal tests on those who

---

[7] Alexander Wight, *A Treatise on the Laws concerning the Election of the Different Representatives sent from Scotland to the Parliament of Great Britain* (Edinburgh: Balfour and Smellie, 1773) Title II, Section I.

[8] i.e. appoint.

[9] General Assembly Act 1592 c.116. Confession of Faith Ratification Act c 3.

taught in schools and universities, began to be relaxed.[10] One notable result of the test was the refusal of Edinburgh University to appoint the philosopher David Hume because of his supposed atheism.

The patronage issue has, therefore, to be seen as part of a much wider struggle. First, was the dominant influence on people's lives to be that of Church or State? Second, within the Church, were evangelicals or moderates to have control? Third, should government be imposed or elective? Fourth, should it be directed from within or outwith Scotland? Some of the uses to which the Kirk put its authority, particularly in the seventeenth century, would not recommend themselves to even less than liberal minds today. Yet that authority rested on widespread popular support. Some of this loyalty to the Kirk derived from its continuing resistance to English influence. Further, the structures by which it operated were democratic ones and 'by the standards of the time it was a remarkably representative institution'.[11]

For all these reasons, the Kirk went through many troubled years. There were secessions in 1733 and 1759. The failure of the 1842 Claim of Right to bring an end to patronage led to the Disruption of 1843. Nearly five hundred evangelical ministers left to form the Free Church. Patronage was finally abolished, under pressure from remaining evangelicals, in 1874. It was not until 1929, though, that some reunification was achieved, with the return of the United Free Church. This followed years of negotiations, which had resulted in the "Auld Kirk" persuading the government to introduce the Church of Scotland Act 1921. Despite some dicta from the courts in this direction in the nineteenth century, for the first time since the Union the Kirk was now clearly outwith the jurisdiction of any civil authority in 'all matters of doctrine, worship, government and discipline'.

In the light of this long battle for sovereign control over its own affairs, it is easy to understand the support that has come from within

---

[10] As a result of legislation such as the Universities (Scotland) Acts 1858 and 1889 and the Education (Scotland) Act 1872.

[11] Bernard Crick, 'An Englishman in Scotland' in Owen Dudley Edwards ed *A Claim of Right for Scotland* (Edinburgh: Polygon Press, 1989) p 152.

the Church of Scotland for the 1988 Claim of Right for Scotland,[12] although it is by no means the only religious institution of a similar mind.[13] This Claim of Right was actually sponsored by the Campaign for a Scottish Assembly (now the Campaign for a Scottish Parliament) - a non-party organisation dedicated to gaining Scotland greater control over her own affairs. During the 1970s it had looked as if this was to come about. A Royal Commission[14] had recommended devolution and, after an abortive Scotland and Wales Bill, the Scotland Act had been passed. No Assembly resulted, though. The scheme had to be endorsed by a referendum. The legislation required the approval of 40% of the electorate. Although a narrow majority voted in favour, the target was not reached.

Some Scots, both of left and right, were against the Assembly in principle. Others had serious doubts about what was actually on offer.[15] Some were just apathetic, others openly sceptical about the chances of this new (like any existing) political institution improving

[12] See e.g. the Deliverance of the General Assembly of the Church of Scotland on the Report of the Church and Nation Committee in 1989: 'Reaffirm the tradition of theological reflection on constitutional matters outlined in the Report and its view that the Scottish people should be accorded a greater say in the government of Scotland through a democratically elected Assembly within the United Kingdom; and instruct the Church and Nation Committee to continue this reflection in co-operation with the other bodies which are discussing the constitutional future of Scotland, including the proposals set out in a "Claim of Right for Scotland"'. Also Professor T F Torrance's 1982 article 'Juridical Law and Physical Law'; and William Storrer, *Scottish Identity: A Christian Vision* (Edinburgh: Handsel Press, 1990).

[13] For example, the Chairman of the Executive Committee of the Scottish Constitutional Convention is Canon Kenyon Wright, of the Scottish Episcopal Church but nominated as a member of the Convention by an ecumenical grouping.

[14] Royal Commission on the Constitution (The Kilbrandon Commission): Report Cmnd 5460 and 5460-I, 1973.

[15] For example, the precise nature of the relationship between the Assembly and Westminster, the role of the Secretary of State for Scotland, the issue of *vires* and the fact that the method of constituting the Assembly seemed to give undue weight to the heavily populated, and predominantly Labour, Strathclyde Region.

their lot. Some registered electors, though moved or dead, were counted as against for the purposes of the 40% rule. Others - registered in two places but only allowed to vote once - were counted as against twice over or as both for and against. Whatever the reasons, the practical outcome was the repeal of the Scotland Act. The political manoeuvrings that went along with this led to the downfall of the Labour Government.

Despite earlier policy,[16] the new Conservative Government set itself against devolution. Yet the issue was far from dead. Of the 72 MPs returned for Scotland in 1983 only 14 were from the Conservative Party. Thatcherite ideas proved alien to the majority of Scots. Particular policies such as the closure of Gartcosh and the proposed introduction of the "poll tax" fuelled popular indignation. The SNP gained support. The Labour Party in Scotland began to offer a stronger commitment to constitutional change. With the 1987 General Election the number of Conservative MPs in Scotland was reduced to 10. Parties in favour of some kind of home rule gained 76% of the vote. Clearly, much of the reaction against the government could be accounted for in immediate and economic terms. The roots, however, would seem to go much deeper. Opposition to the poll tax, for example, was to be found amongst many who benefited from it financially. Yet one might have expected the doctrines of the "New Right", with their emphasis on competitive individualism, to have had a sympathetic reception in Scotland. For Calvinism emphasises self discipline and the virtue of work. Indeed the sociologist Max Weber

[16] In May 1970 the Scottish Conference of the Conservative party had endorsed the report of a committee chaired by the (then) Alec Douglas Home, recommending a directly elected "Convention" to carry out work previously conducted by Scottish Committees in the House of Commons. This became official policy, to be superseded four years later by an "Assembly" to be elected indirectly from among local councillors. In the aftermath of the October 1974 election, the Scottish Conservative leadership, although not the Party as a whole, gave their support to the proposals of the new Labour Government for a directly elected Aseembly. By 1979, however, views had changed. For a fuller account of the course of devolution, see Kellas, *The Scottish Political System* (cit ch I, n. 37) and for a detailed study of developments between 1885 and 1995, see James Mitchell, *Strategies for Self-Government* (Edinburgh: Polygon, 1996).

claimed a close connection between the Protestant ethic and the spirit of capitalism.[17] Anyway, not all Scots belong to the Calvinist tradition. Roman Catholicism and Episcopalianism survived alongside the Kirk and there are substantial ethnic minorities, particularly of the Islamic faith. It seems, anyway, to be a misreading of the Reformation in Scotland to see it as producing an individualistic philosophy. The Covenanting tradition was of people bound together in a common cause. A doctrine of **mutual** responsibility can be traced from the earliest days through to the work of the Church and Nation Committee in recent times.[18]

A similarly inclined approach is to be found in secular writings, particularly of the Enlightenment. Although these differ in many particulars, there is a shared belief in man's natural sociability. One finds the notion of natural sentiments, such as affection and sympathy, on which morality is made to rest. There is Carmichael's view that 'the right cultivation of social life consists in this: that each man so protect his right as to have due regard for all the rights which belong to other men in accordance with the assumption of natural equality.'[19] Rights occur in similar combination with duties in Reid's natural jurisprudence, where both exist under just systems of law and morals, setting 'the Bounds which I must observe respecting others, and the Bounds which others must observe respecting me.'[20] Again, Hutcheson wrote that:

> From a common bond of all with all, by which mankind are constituted by nature one great society, with some common laws binding them, there

---

[17] Max Weber, *Economy and Society,* ed G Roth and C Wittich (Bedminster Press, 1968) Vol 2, ch VI, pp 479, 587-8, 630.

[18] See, for example, the *Book of Discipline,* following on the 1560 Confession of Faith. Indeed it would seem to be of the very essence of Presbyterianism.

[19] Gerschom Carmichael, 1718, Supplements and Appendix to Pufendorf, *De Officio Hominis et Civis Juxta Legem Naturalem,* comp J N Lenhart, trans C H Reeves (Cleveland, Ohio: Lenhart, 1985) Supplement II xvii 62 and Appendix Thesis XI 514.

[20] Thomas Reid, 'Essays on the Active Powers' in *Inquiry and Essays,* ed Ronald E Beanblossom and Keith Lehrer (Indianapolis: Hackett, 1983) esp Essays 3 and 5.

> arise certain common rights not specially regarding the utility of any one, or a few, but that of all in general. . .[21]
>
> That the common interest of the whole body is the end of all civil polity . . .That civil power therefore alone is just which is naturally adapted to this end. . .[22]

Even Hume, for whom justice is an artificial virtue and one largely concerned with property rights, argues that it is ultimately natural to men and that the purpose of government is the distributing of justice.[23] Adam Smith, though usually regarded as the precursor of the New Right, sees human beings as forming moral judgments about their actions 'by endeavouring to view them with the eyes of other people, or as other people are likely to view them.'[24] The conception is one of human beings defining themselves by their relationships with others and in terms of shared understandings. It is found, too, in the thinkers who sought to explain law and morality in a historical context. Amongst them were Smith himself, Kames, Monboddo, John Millar and Dugald Stewart. The underlying approach is summed up in the words of Adam Ferguson:

> Man is, by nature, the member of a community; and when considered in this capacity, the individual appears no longer made for himself. He must forego his happiness and his freedom, where these interfere with the good of society. He is only part of a whole; and the praise we think due to his virtue, is but a branch of that more general commendation we bestow on the member of a body, on the part of a fabric or engine, for being well fitted to occupy its place and produce its effect.
>
> If this follows from the relation of a part to its whole, and if the public good be the principal object with individuals, it is likewise true, that the happiness of individuals is the great end of civil society: for in what sense

---

[21] Francis Hutcheson, *A Short Introduction to Moral Philosophy*, 1747, in *The Collected Works of Francis Hutcheson* (Hildesheim: Georg Olms, 1969) II 16 IV.

[22] Ibid, III 4 IV.

[23] David Hume, *A Treatise of Human Nature* 1739-40, Part II, I and II reproduced in D D Raphael ed *British Moralists 1650-1800* (Oxford: Clarendon Press, 1969) Vol II.

[24] Adam Smith, *Theory of Moral Sentiments* 1759 ed D D Raphael and A L MacFie (Oxford: Clarendon Press, 1976) III 1 2.

can a public enjoy any good, if its members, considered apart, be unhappy.[25]

The Enlightenment thinkers were not just concerned with abstract principles. The later ones, such as Millar and Stewart and Reid welcomed the French Revolution, at least in its early days. Stewart, in particular, was involved in the movement for reform at home, along with others, including a number of his former pupils. Also at the forefront was Henry Erskine, whose views became so unpopular with his fellow advocates that he lost his position as Dean of Faculty. Controversial though some of the arguments they put forward were,[26] these centred on change by constitutional means, especially on reform of the franchise.

Buckle, writing in the mid nineteenth century, regarded the Enlightenment thinkers as elitist. He argued that:

> the Scotch literature, notwithstanding its brilliancy, its power and the splendid discoveries of which it was the vehicle, produced little or no effect on the nation at large. That literature, by its bold and innovating character, seemed peculiarly fitted to disturb ancient prejudices, and to rouse up a spirit of enquiry. But its method, both of investigation and proof, was too refined to suit ordinary understandings. Therefore upon ordinary understandings it was inoperative.[27]

There is undoubtedly some truth in Buckle's view that Enlightenment thinking as a whole did not penetrate deep into Scottish culture, at least in the short term.[28] How far, though, this was because of the methods it adopted is open to debate. The neo-Marxist theorist Gramsci, for example, considers one of the main problems in interpreting contemporary society to be concerned with the relationship between the social ideas of intellectuals and popular

---

[25] Adam Ferguson, *An Essay on the History of Civil Society* 1767 (cit. ch I, n. 16) I, IX.

[26] Much of it conducted through the columns of the *Edinburgh Review*, founded in 1802, and under the editorship of Francis Jeffrey, an advocate.

[27] Henry Thomas Buckle, *On Scotland and the Scotch Intellect* ed H J Hanham (Chicago: University of Chicago Press, 1970) p 390.

[28] See George Davie, *The Democratic Intellect: Scotland and her Universities in the Nineteenth Century* (Edinburgh: Edinburgh University Press, 1961) and, more generally, Paul H Scott ed, *Scotland: A Concise Cultural History* (Edinburgh: Mainstream Pub. Co., 1993).

consciousness. Such a relationship is regarded as 'neither necessary nor automatic'.[29]

It may be, however, that some Enlightenment ideas, at least, should be understood in a different way. It is possible to regard them as an articulation, indeed an intellectualisation, of the "ancient prejudices" Buckle thinks they should have disturbed. The speculation that the underlying ethos of Scots culture is communalist rather than individualist is just that. If correct, though, it would do much to explain just why Thatcherite ideas were so alien to the majority of Scots.

That possibility aside, what certainly can be found, as a matter of long tradition, is a firm belief in constitutionalism and a strong sense of Scottish identity. This sense of identity can be traced from the Declaration of Arbroath, past the Union, through the 1880s (when the pressure for home rule began to reassert itself), through around two million signatures on the National Covenant in 1949,[30] to the present day.

Similarly, the belief in constitutionalism has had its expression in repeated demands for:

> a government which is not only freely chosen by the people but which conducts the business of government with respect to the freedom under the law of each citizen and all of them in such associations as they pursue.[31]

The most recent Claim of Right for Scotland, then, can be seen both as an aspect of contemporary politics and as fitting with long held attitudes and beliefs. Part of the Epilogue reads:

> The crucial questions are power and consent: making power accountable and setting limits to what can be done without general consent.
>
> These questions will not be adequately answered in the United Kingdom until that concentration of power that masquerades as 'the Crown in Parliament' is broken up.

---

29 A. Gramsci, *Letters from Prison* (London: Cape, 1975).

30 One of the main instigators of the Covenant was John MacCormick - also the MacCormick of *MacCormick* v *Lord Advocate* (see later this chapter) and sometime Rector of Glasgow University. See, too, J M MacCormick, *The Flag in the Wind* (London: Gollancz, 1955).

31 Neil MacCormick, 'Unrepentent Gradualism' in *A Claim of Right for Scotland* (cit n. 11) at p 100.

As a step toward achieving this, the signatories of the Claim of Right recommended the setting up of a representative Constitutional Convention. The recommendation was put into effect, the representation consisting of MPs, MEPs, selected councillors from local authorities, representatives from political parties, the churches, the trade unions and other organisations. Neither the Conservative Party nor the Scottish National Party has participated, the former holding by the Union in its present form, the latter by its policy of independence (though now 'in Europe'). Despite this the Convention still managed to reflect a very broad spectrum of Scottish opinion,[32] and its consultations were extensive.

Its work in establishing the framework for a future Scottish Constitution was effectively completed at the end of 1991, although it took until 1995 to reach consensus on the finer details of the system of proportional representation to be adopted. The main outcome was agreement on a Scottish Parliament within the United Kingdom, with power to legislate for Scotland, matters such as defence, major economic policies and social security only excepted. Its financing would be by way of assigned revenues from the UK Exchequer, together with a limited power to vary the rate of income tax. The legislation establishing the Parliament would be entrenched, as also a Bill of Rights.

High hopes were entertained for the outcome of the April 1992 General Election. In the event, however, both the Convention parties and the SNP failed to make the gains they had anticipated. The Conservatives actually increased their holding of seats to 11, including regaining one they had lost in a by-election only a few months earlier. In the course of the campaign the Conservative Party set its face firmly against any major reform, although the incoming government has accepted the possibility of a limited amount and placed a minister in the Scottish Office charged with its consideration.[33] The opposition

---

[32] Even if somewhat unevenly distributed.

[33] The main concession was sittings of the Scottish Grand Committee in Edinburgh and, since, in other parts of Scotland. The then Secretary of State for Scotland, Ian Lang, was clearly opposed to any major change. His successor, Michael Forsyth, has expressed similar opposition, indicating, however, that he would not expect a Conservative Government to attempt to abolish a Scottish Parliament if one were ever introduced.

parties found themselves in something of a disarray, those in the Convention calling on the government to organise a multi-option referendum - something which had previously only been the policy of the SNP. Various cross-party pressure groups, such as Scotland United, were established and rallies held. There were calls, too, for an unofficial referendum but this was idea rejected by the Labour Party and, initially at least, by the Liberal Democrats, and neither the Convention nor any other body with the capacity to organise one has taken the idea on board.

At the end of November 1995, the Convention presented its final scheme to the Scottish people and the Prime Minister offered Scottish MPs at Westminster more control over Scottish legislation. It seems unlikely that the issue will be laid to rest there. The Labour Party and the Liberal Democrats continue to support the Convention scheme.[34] In July 1996, the Prime Minister announced that, after seven hundred years, the Stone of Destiny was to be returned to Scotland. The Stone, captured by Edward I and placed in Westminster Abbey, may or may not have been the real coronation stone of the Scottish Kings. Recaptured in 1950 by a group of students, the stone eventually left in Arbroath Abbey and taken back to Westminster may or may not have been the one taken from it. Whatever the true history, the Stone remains a powerful symbol for the Scots and its return has been widely welcomed. Nonetheless, various pro Home Rule politicians have remarked that what is now needed is for the substance to following the symbol.

Significantly, many of the calls remain much the same as those for reform noted by the *Caledonian Mercury* in 1792:

> Even medals have been resorted to, on which are inscribed the political creed of the party at whose instance the die has been struck. To the people in this city the inscriptions are well known, but for the information of our readers in the country we shall mention them:
> On one -- 'Liberty, equality and an end to Impress Warrants'.

[34] Although the Leader of the former, narrowly endorsed by the Scottish Executive of the Labour Party, qualified this in June 1996 by stating that the legislation should be preceded by a referendum asking questions both about the establishment of a Parliament and its having tax-raising powers.

On the reverse side -- 'The nation is essentially the source of all sovereignty'. On another -- 'Liberty of Conscience, Equal Representation and Just Taxation'.

On the reverse -- 'For a nation to be free it is sufficient that it wills it'.[35]

Two hundred years on, the Convention is formally committed to the political view contained in the second of the inscriptions, namely that of the sovereignty of the Scottish people, and to the opinion that its scheme is what the nation would choose. The SNP holds the same in respect of independence. Recent examples from Eastern Europe suggest that there is political truth in the notion that freedom follows where the nation wills it - though often at a considerable price. From the legal point of view, however, it is the existing constitution in any state that determines the mechanisms of change.

On the face of it, the appropriate mechanism for putting any new framework into place in Britain is "the Crown in Parliament". Given a hostile majority at Westminster, then, even if little of it derives from Scotland, it would seem that there is no legally appropriate means of bringing a Scottish Parliament into being. This may be so, but the constitutional background is far more complex than it might at first appear.

It is widely assumed that one of the most significant features of the British Constitution[36] is the doctrine of the sovereignty of Parliament. According to Austin the doctrine means that Parliament can neither divide up nor limit nor part with its authority to make laws.[37] Despite challenges to this understanding, both historical and academic,[38] it has shown a remarkable capacity for survival. Yet even Austin's predecessor, Bentham, had a rather more sophisticated view. On the

---

[35] Edinburgh, 17 September, 1792. No 11091.

[36] In order to make the discussion as straightforward as possible, what is under consideration here is the Constitution of the United Kingdom of Great Britain and not that of Great Britain and Northern Ireland. Similarly, England should be read to mean England and Wales where appropriate.

[37] John Austin, *The Province of Jurisprudence Determined* (cit. ch I n. 12) p 225.

[38] See e.g. Geoffrey Marshall, *Constitutional Theory* (Oxford: Clarendon Press, 1971) esp ch III.

question of the limiting of legislative authority, for example, he wrote as follows:

> This respects the case where one state has, upon *terms*, submitted itself to the government of another: or where the governing bodies of a number of states agree to take directions in certain specified cases, from some *body* or other of members, for instance, appointed out of each.[39]

These later words seem to foreshadow the creation of the European Community. Clearly, Britain's membership of the Community does seem to cast some doubt on Austin's view, since its Regulations are directly applicable within the United Kingdom. Further, our courts are bound to construe legislation in conformity with its Directives, as, also, both Directives and Regulations in conformity with the jurisprudence of the European Court of Justice. Until recently this has been explained away in terms of authorisation by Parliament under the European Communities Act 1972.[40] That Act, it was said, could be repealed at any time. So, too, could any Act that attempted to entrench a Bill of Rights. For Parliamentary sovereignty means that Parliament cannot bind itself or its successors. It can, legally speaking, make any law it chooses, as and when it chooses. Further, no other body has authority to override its decisions.

A doctrine such as the sovereignty of Parliament, however, is concerned with what people are permitted to do. Sometimes people do things that are not clearly permitted (or even that are clearly not permitted!). The Supreme Court of the United States of America took the former line in *Marbury* v *Madison*,[41] when it read out of the Constitution its own authority to strike down legislation as unconstitutional. The House of Lords acted in much the same way in taking appeals from Scotland in civil cases after 1707. If such behaviour goes effectively unchallenged, then it is taken to be permitted. Similarly, it may become understood that what was once permitted is no longer permitted. If the change of attitude is significant enough, then it becomes clear that the original doctrine no longer holds. The least one can say about the doctrine of the sovereignty of

---

[39] Jeremy Bentham, *A Fragment on Government* (cit. ch II n. 1) ch IV, footnote to para 23.

[40] European Communities Act 1972 s. 2.

[41] 1803 1 Cranch 137.

Parliament is that, since 1972, it has become a lot less firm than it once was. In fact, following the European Court of Justice decision in *Factortame*, where an Act of Parliament was first suspended and then effectively voided for lack of conformity with Community law, it appears very shaky indeed. For, clearly, another body is regarded as having authority to override decisions taken at Westminster.[42]

It is worth noting that the term "doctrine" has two distinct meanings. First, there is the sense in which it is used by judges, as when they state 'it is a doctrine of the law that . . .'. In most such instances they might equally have said 'it is a principle of the law that . . .'. The term is used more particularly to refer to the principles by which they consider their own operations to be controlled. Thus, there is the doctrine of binding precedent beside that of parliamentary sovereignty. In the second sense "doctrine" is used for learned commentaries on the law. These offer the writers' interpretations of the state of the law. On the Continent they are highly influential. In Scotland, apart from the institutional writings, they have little real status, although they are occasionally cited in court.

Doctrine, in the second sense, then may question whether the doctrine (in the first sense) of the sovereignty of Parliament still holds. That is to say, it may question whether those involved in making and applying the law do actually operate on the basis that Parliament can legally speaking make any law it chooses, as and when it chooses, and that no other body has authority to override its decisions. It seems clear that our courts now are acceding to the view that they should not apply statutes that are even putatively contrary to Community law until

[42] *R* v *Secretary of State for Transport, ex parte Factortame* [1990] 2 AC 285. See also Case 213/89 [1990] ECR I-2433; Case 221/89 [1990] ECR I-3905. Further, decisions of the European Court of Justice following *Marleasing SA* v *La Comercial Internacional de Alimentación,* Case 106/89 [1990] ECR I-4135 and *Francovitch and Bonifaci* v *Italy,* Case 609/90 [1991] ECR I-5357 have indicated even more strongly the extent to which domestic courts are expected to give priority to Community law.

this issue has been resolved by the European Court of Justice.[43]

Doctrine in the second sense, though, can proceed well beyond this level of analysis. For doctrines, in the first sense, and rules and principles, as expressed by judges, are also simply interpretations of the state of the law. The fact that such interpretations are regarded as authoritative does not make them immune from criticism. There are, for example, grounds for questioning not just the current standing but also the original basis of the doctrine of Parliamentary sovereignty. With these run a challenge to the common doctrinal (in the second sense) assumption that Britain has no fixed constitution and, even, to the one that there is such a thing as the British Constitution. All of this turns on the status accorded to the Acts of Union of 1707 and the effects that they are deemed to have had. The most straightforward argument is between those who see them as pieces of legislation like any other and those who see them as creative of fundamental law and as providing a (partially) fixed constitution. A considerable body of modern Scots thinking inclines to the second view, contending that the authority of Parliament stems from the instruments by which it was set up and is limited by these instruments.[44]

Just what, then, did happen in 1707? Relations between Scotland and England were not markedly improved by the Union of the Crowns in 1603, when James VI of Scotland became James I of England. Apart from a brief space towards the end of the reign of Charles I, rule, whether under the Stuarts or Cromwell, became highly autocratic. In addition to war and periods of religious persecution, the era was also marked by attempts to achieve a full merger between the two

---

[43] The priority of Community law is not merely over ordinary legislation but may also be in respect of the actual Constitutions of Member States - see *Internationale Handelsgesellschaft*, Case 11/70 [1970] ECR 1125. Consider, for example, the criticism of the court in the 'Irish Rape Case' (*Attorney General* v *X and Others*) for its failure to prioritise the Treaty of Rome. See further in ch VI.

[44] For a full discussion of the issues, and some intriguing thoughts on them, see Michael Upton, 'The Marriage Vows of the Elephant: The Constitution of 1707' (1989) 105 *LQR* 39. See further in ch VII.

countries.[45] Another attempt was made after the Revolution Settlement, when William and Mary were invited to take up the Scottish throne, but foundered, largely on the matter of free trade, which the English were unwilling to concede. Matters reached crisis point with the accession of Anne to the throne, since she had no direct heirs. Opinion in Scotland was divided. Some wished to break the union of the crowns altogether and others to retain it only on highly favourable conditions. The Scottish Parliament managed to force legislation along the second lines past the Royal Assent. The English Parliament countered with an Act to block off Scottish trade. Commissioners were appointed from each side to negotiate a way out of the impasse. This was achieved by the Scots conceding union with England and the English conceding free trade with Scotland. It took only nine weeks to hammer out the details of the Treaty. Despite major public outcry once these were known, it was endorsed by the Scottish Parliament[46] with certain amendments, then by the English one and the union took effect from 1 May 1707.

The passing of the Acts of Union gave rise to allegations of bribery. Clearly, money did change hands, although it may be argued that some of it was already owed. If those involved did act from considerations of personal advantage, the wealth anticipated from improved trading conditions could have been as telling a factor. Fear of war as the alternative must have had some effect as well. Whatever the reality, many did see it as the barter of Scotland for financial gain. This view helped to foment the unsuccessful Jacobite risings of '15 and '45, as it still does nationalist feeling today. It is neatly expressed in the words, from later in the eighteenth century, of Robert Burns:

Fareweel to a' Scottish fame
Fareweel our ancient glory!
Fareweel even to the Scottish name,
Sae fam'd in martial story!
Now Sark rins o'er the Solway sands,
And Tweed rins to the ocean,
To mark where England's province stands;

---

[45] 1604 under James VI and I, 1652-1659 under Cromwell and 1667-70 under Charles II. Some would liken the attitude of the English more to that of persons engaged in a (hostile) takeover bid.

[46] Over 60 were in favour, with a majority in each of the three Estates.

Such a parcel of rogues in a nation!

What guile or force could not subdue,
Through many warlike ages,
Is wrought now by a coward few,
For hireling traitors' wages,
The English steel we could disdain,
Secure in valour's station,
But English gold has been our bane; -
Such a parcel of rogues in a nation!

O would, or had I seen the day
That treason thus could sell us,
My auld grey head had lien in clay,
Wi' Bruce and loyal Wallace!
But pith and power, till my last hour
I'll mak this declaration,
We're bought and sold for English gold:-
Such a parcel of rogues in a nation!

Rogues or not, it is clear that both the Commissioners and the members of the Scottish Parliament did make efforts to ensure that Scotland would not become a mere province of England, with particular emphasis on the protection of church and law. For example, the Scottish Parliament passed an Act securing the Protestant religion and Presbyterian Church government within Scotland, to be treated as a fundamental part of the union. This was confirmed by the English Parliament which, in ratifying the treaty, also passed its own equivalent for the Church of England.[47] Where the law was concerned a distinction was drawn between matters to be dealt with in common and those thought to be of purely Scottish significance.

Article XVIII provided that all laws not inconsistent with the treaty should remain in force, with the exception of those concerning the regulation of trade, customs and excises. In these cases the laws of Scotland were to become those applying in England. Otherwise pre-union Scots law was to be:

> alterable by the Parliament of Great Britain, With this difference betwixt the laws concerning publick Right, Policy, and Civil Government and those that concern private Right; That the laws which concern publick Right Policy and Civil Government may be made the same throughout the

[47] 6 Anne c.11.

> whole United Kingdom but that no alteration be made in Laws which concern private Right, except for the evident utility of the subjects in Scotland.[48]

Article XIX provided that:

> the Court of Session or colledge of justice do after the union and notwithstanding thereof remain in all time coming within Scotland as it is now constituted by the laws of that Kingdom and with the same authority and privileges as before the union subject nevertheless to such regulations for the better administration of justice as shall be made by the Parliament of Great Britain . . .

and similarly for the Court of Justiciary. In addition it was specified that:

> no causes in Scotland be cognoscible by the courts of Chancery Queen's Bench Common Pleas or any other court in Westminster Hall and that the said courts or any other of like nature after the union shall have no power to cognosce within Scotland or stop the execution of the same.

Certain parts of the Acts of Union have been repealed, being regarded as outdated. Those stated to be 'for all time coming' are, however, effectively untouched. Despite this the Westminster Parliament has a history of ignoring at least the spirit and, arguably, the letter of their provisions. This process started immediately, with 1707 seeing the abolition of the Scottish privy council and the introduction of the English system of justices of the peace,[49] the establishment of an exchequer Court in Scotland',[50] and, in 1708, the extension of the English law of treason to Scotland.[51] Further, in 1711, an Act was passed requiring the toleration of the Episcopal church in Scotland.[52] A more recent controversy concerned the community charge, which was introduced into Scotland a year earlier than

[48] The Article is quoted again and in full in chapter VII.

[49] 6 Anne c.40.

[50] 6 Anne c.53.

[51] 7 Anne c.21.

[52] 10 Anne c.10. Also regarded as objectionable were both the imposition of the Malt Tax and the Church Patronage (Scotland) Act, 10 Anne c.21, mentioned earlier in the chapter.

England,[53] although attempts to gain relief in this respect were unsuccessful in both the Sheriff Court and the Court of Session.[54]

Whether or not the Scots courts can, anyway, review Acts of Parliament for conformity with the terms of the union remains uncertain.[55] Whatever a court located in Scotland might decide on the matter, the chances are that it would be taken to the House of Lords. Article XIX, in listing the courts in which Scottish causes cannot be heard, did not expressly exclude the House of Lords since it was not one that sat 'in Westminster Hall'. Very shortly after the union the practice grew up of appealing matters in civil causes to the House of Lords (as the inheritor of similar powers held by the old Scottish Parliament).[56]

However the House of Lords were to decide in the event of the Scots courts attempting to avoid legislation regarded as contrary to the Treaty and Acts of Union, the situation would be one of constitutional crisis. To date one has not been precipitated. At the same time, however, the attitude of the Scots courts has run counter to one possible interpretation of the events of 1707. Namely that, while the Scottish Act of Union destroyed the Scottish constitution, the English Act had no effect other than bringing Scotland under the umbrella of the English constitution and giving the Scots a minority role to play in English constitutional processes. In *MacCormick* v *Lord Advocate*, Lord President Cooper stated:

> The principle of the unlimited sovereignty of Parliament is a distinctively English principle which has no counterpart in Scottish law. It derives from Coke and Blackstone and was widely popularised during the nineteenth century by Bagehot and Dicey, the latter having stated the

[53] The Abolition of Domestic Rates (Scotland) Act 1987.

[54] For a fuller discussion of these cases, see chapter VII. A similar attempt to gain relief from the imposition of tolls on the Skye Road Bridge was dismissed at Inverness Sheriff Court in March 1996.

[55] See e.g. *Minister of Prestonkirk* v *The Earl of Wemyss* Mor Appx; *Earl of Kinnoul* v *Presbytery for Auchterarder* (1936) 16 S 661; *Laughlan* v *Wandsbrough Paper Co* 1921 1 SLT 341; *Leonard* v *Paterson* 1944 HCJ (unreported) and, most recently, *Pringle, Petitioner* 1991 SLT 330.

[56] From *Greenshields* 1710-11 Rob. 12. Technically, though, the House of Lords does not decide Scots cases directly but refers them back to the Court of Session for it to alter its interlocutor where necessary.

> doctrine in its classic form in his *Law of the Constitution.* Considering that the Union legislation extinguished the Parliaments of Scotland and England and replaced them by a new Parliament, I have difficulty in seeing why it should have been supposed that the new Parliament of Great Britain must inherit all the peculiar characteristics of the English Parliament but none of the Scottish Parliament, as if all that happened in 1707 was that Scottish representatives were admitted to the Parliament of England. That is not what was done.[57]

Just what other interpretations might be put on the events of 1707 will be looked at later. At present it is sufficient to note that Scotland has a tradition of a certain kind of understanding of the purposes and limits of political power. This is not to contend that this kind of understanding has been either universal or unwavering - only that it is a consistently recurrent one. Nor is it in any way to claim that Scotland is unique in having that kind of understanding. There are, for example, marked similarities between both the Declaration of Arbroath and the Claim of Right of 1689, on the one hand, and, on the other, the following sixteenth century version of the Aragonese oath of allegiance to the king:

> We who are as good as you swear to you who are no better than we to accept you as our king and sovereign lord, provided you observe all our liberties and laws; but if not, not.

Rather, it is simply to acknowledge the importance of ideology for any attempt either to understand law or to bring out similarities and dissimilarities between legal systems.

Indeed ideology is one of the five different factors that the comparative lawyers, Zweigert and Kötz, consider critical for identifying the style of legal systems, by means of which they can be grouped into families.[58] As itemised in the Introduction, the other factors are their historical background and development; their predominant and characteristic mode of thought in legal matters; their especially distinctive institutions; and the kind of legal sources they acknowledge and the ways in which they handle them. The next chapter turns to a consideration of these aspects of the law of Scotland.

---

[57] 1953 SC 396 at p 411.

[58] Zweigert and Kötz, *Introduction to Comparative Law* (cit. Intro, n. 8).

IV

THE STYLE OF SCOTS LAW

History and Development

Before the Union

Even the briefest glance at its history and development shows present day Scots law to be of very mixed ancestry. Little is known about the customs of the indigenous Picts. Around 500 AD, however, settlement by the Scots of Ulster brought with it a range of Celtic laws and institutions, while similar settlement of Orkney and Shetland by the Scandinavians led to the introduction of Udal law.[1] This, probably largely in the form of the Code of King Magnus the Law Mender, remained operational in Orkney and Shetland at least until the ceding of the islands to Scotland in 1468-9. How far it survived beyond this date is a matter of dispute, as shown in the St Ninian's treasure case.[2]

It was Celtic law, though, that was the most influential for Scotland as a whole, at least until the reign of Malcolm Canmore (1058-1093). After that it began to be overtaken by other types of law. Even so, various aspects of it survived to much later dates. For example, the action of assythement, for wounding or slaughter, was not formally abolished until the Damages (Scotland) Act 1976, following its attempted revival in the case of *McKendrick* v *Sinclair*.[3]

---

[1] It also seems to have had some kind of standing in Caithness and Sutherland and, possibly, more generally in the coastal areas of the north east.

[2] *Lord Advocate* v *Aberdeen University and Budge* 1963 SC 533. See, for a general discussion of udal law, Sir Thomas Browne Smith's entries in *The Laws of Scotland: the Stair Memorial Encyclopaedia* (Edinburgh: The Law Society of Scotland/Butterworths, 1988) and, on its survival, Jane Ryder, 'Udal Law: An Introduction' in (1988) 25 *Northern Studies* 1.

[3] 1972 SC (HL) 25. I owe this example, as various other points on Celtic law, to Malcolm Waters.

Over time, unlike England, but along with most of continental Europe, Scotland developed her own version of the *ius commune*.[4] This involved a blend, unique to each area, of native custom with common elements of feudal law, the law merchant, canon law and Roman law. The feudal law began to come in under Malcolm Canmore and his Queen, Margaret, but was more directly introduced by David I in the mid twelfth century. It was largely imported from the England of the Anglo-Normans, although a number of differences developed.[5] Covering matters of land tenure, with its associated rights, and wrongs, "civil" or "criminal" issues were tried, according to level, by manorial courts, sheriff courts, the justiciary and the *curia regis*, the King's Council. Appeals lay, in some cases, by a procedure known as 'falsing of dooms'.

Two other types of arrangement existed, though. First, the King might by charter grant rights of judgment within a certain territorial area to one of his Lords. This could exclude the operations of sheriffs and justiciars and, even, his own jurisdiction, except over treason.[6] Second, towns, also by charter, might be granted the status of burghs. In these rules associated with land tenure took on a slightly different form and a local customary law developed. The courts were separately organised, too, with guild courts generally charged with administering the law merchant[7] and burgh courts operating in place of manorial and sheriff courts. Appeal was to the King's Chamberlain, although

---

[4] For a fuller discussion see O F Robinson, T D Fergus and W M Gordon, *An Introduction to European Legal History,* 2nd edn (London: Butterworth, 1994) especially, for Scotland, chs IX and XIV. Also D M Walker, *The Scottish Legal System* (cit ch II, n. 11) and W A Wilson, *Introductory Essays in Scots Law* 2nd edn (Edinburgh: W Green & Sons, 1984).

[5] Compare Glanville, *De Legibus et Consuetidinibus Angliae,* c 1190, with the *Regiam Maiestatem*, probably early fourteenth century. Also, for procedure, the *Quoniam Attachiamenta,* also fourteenth century.

[6] This was in the case of a grant 'in free regality'. There was also a lesser grant - 'in free barony'.

[7] Although with change of function, Dean of Guild Courts lasted in Scotland until 1975.

opinions on doubtful points might also be sought from the Court of the Four Burghs, over which he also presided.[8]

At the same time, canon law was being dispensed through the church courts. These operated under bishops but judicial power was usually delegated to a trained lawyer, called the official. Appeal lay to Rome.[9] A wide range of matters, both civil and criminal, was covered. The civil ones involved issues affecting church property and temporal matters regarded as having a spiritual aspect. These included marriage, succession, status and - a matter of argument - obligations involving oaths. Further, even in cases where issues would normally have been tried by the secular courts, a church court would deal with them if it regarded one of the parties as under its protection, as with clerics, widows and orphans. The criminal side involved crimes committed by or against clerics or against church property and offences against doctrine, such a blasphemy or witchcraft.

Procedure before the feudal courts initially followed the English pattern of specific writs, or *brieves*, for specific remedies. The remedies, though, seem to have been more general than the English ones and the *brieves* greater in number than the English writs. The *brieves* gave way over time to a simple summons to appear in answer to an allegation. It has been suggested that in the course of and following the Wars of Independence, 1286-1370, Scots law went into a "dark age" from which it did not recover until the seventeenth century.[10] The accusation rests in part on the appearance of a wide range of causes of action involving the simple allegation of a wrong and of judgments finding that the defender did "wrang" or "na wrang".

This is taken to imply a major lack of sophistication in the law. Certainly it is true that these were years of major political upheaval. It

8 Initially, Berwick, Edinburgh, Roxburgh and Stirling; then, following English occupation of Berwick and Roxburgh, Edinburgh, Stirling, Lanark and Linlithgow. Later most of the Burghs came to be represented, so that by the 1550s it had become a Convention of the Burghs. There is something of a contemporary parallel in COSLA (The Convention of Scottish Local Authorities).

9 Either in the form of appointed judges delegate in Scotland or to a tribunal in Rome (the *Sacra Romana Rota*).

10 Lord Cooper of Culross, 'The Dark Age of Scottish Legal History 1350-1650' in *Selected Papers* (cit. ch III, n.1).

is true, too, that dissatisfaction was expressed with the administration of justice.[11] More recent historical research has, however, cast doubts on the existence of a "dark age". Instead the period is seen rather as one of transition, a time of movement from unprofessional, unwritten law to the mature law that began to emerge in the fifteenth century.[12]

It would appear that procedure before the church courts had always avoided the restrictions imposed by limited forms of action. It may be, then, that the change from *brieve* to summons and, even, to general causes of action mark a partial adjustment to canon law ideas.[13] In any event, change is always subject to different appreciations. With the general causes of action, rather than a regression to the 'primitive notion that the chief task of a civil tribunal is not to enforce a right so much as to avenge a wrong,'[14] we may choose instead to see the beginnings of *Donoghue* v. *Stevenson.*[15]

Whatever the influence of canon law on secular law, there is no doubt that canon law, both in content and procedure, was heavily indebted to Roman law. It may be said, therefore, that canon law brought Roman law into Scotland "by the back door". Direct reception was limited and of a relatively late date. It had two main causes. First, there was the practice[16] of many Scots studying at continental universities, particularly in the Netherlands. On return they would cite Roman law, as absorbed by the *ius commune*, in pleadings before the courts. Second, whilst Roman law was used at first in a piecemeal fashion, to fill gaps and resolve conflicts between rules, it began to figure in the literature of the law. Eventually it was incorporated, as

---

[11] The Sheriff Court was a target up to the abolition of heritable jurisdictions in 1748, following the Heritable Jurisdictions (Scotland) Act 1746. For earlier times, see e.g. passages in Sir David Lyndsay's *Ane Satyre of the Thrie Estaits,* ed James Kinsley (London: Cassell, 1954).

[12] James J Robertson, 'The Development of the Law' in Jennifer M Brown ed, *Scottish Society in the 15th Century* (London: Edward Arnold, 1977).

[13] This idea is substantiated to the extent that the Court of Session adopted romano-canonical procedures from the outset.

[14] Lord Cooper, *Selected Papers* (cit. n. 10) at p 229.

[15] 1932 SC (HL) 1. The celebrated 'snail in the bottle' case.

[16] Dating mainly from the sixteenth century but occurring earlier too, as for example, in France during the days of the Auld Alliance.

considered appropriate, in the great systematisations produced by the institutional writers of the seventeenth and eighteenth centuries.

It would be a mistake, though, to imagine that all law in Scotland was formulated through the medium of the courts. The King in council, with or without the assistance of a wider parliament, would produce statutes. For example what Lord Cooper entitled 'The First Law Reform (Miscellaneous Provisions) Act.'[17] was enacted in the form of twenty nine Statutes of Scone in December 1318. Attempts to establish the first Scottish Law Commission can be identified as early as 1426, although this and later efforts never brought about the intended thorough overhaul of the law. The fifteenth century was, however, marked by a considerable number of acts making specific changes in procedures or in substantive law.

It has to be admitted, however, that centralised power was not strong. Acts were framed in general terms and sometimes, it would seem, more in hope than expectation of conformity. Certainly there were repeat enactments, as illustrated by the following example from 1487:

> Anent the matter of the inbringin of bulyeoun and keping of gold and silver within the realme and punycioun of the merchandice that bringis nocht in bulyeoun, and als the punycioun of thame that has gold and silver furth of the realme, it is statute and ordainit that the actis and statutis of parliament made tharoppoun of before be put to scharp execucioun.[18]

Although such measures were nominally acts of parliament, the real decisions relating to them were taken by a Committee, the Lords of the Articles, for whose views parliament itself was effectively a "rubberstamp". In similar vein was the gradual transfer by both council and parliament of their increasing judicial business to specially appointed members.[19] By the second quarter of the sixteenth century there was a body of Lords of Council whose sole function was the decision of civil causes. This group, with the founding of the College of Justice in 1532, formed the basis of the now distinct Court of Session.

---

[17] *Selected Papers* (cit. n. 10) at p 88.

[18] Acts of the Parliament of Scotland, ii 182 c. 11. For another example, see the Act of 1540/1 on feu farm tenure (APS ii 376 c. 35) which, preamble apart, was identical with an Act of 1503/4 (APS ii 253 c. 35).

[19] Variously Parliamentary auditors and Lords of Council.

Important features of the court were a strong clerical influence - more than half the original members and the first four Lords President were churchmen - and its power to regulate its own procedures,[20] which it did along romano-canonical lines. Whilst clerical influence began to decrease after the Reformation, it did so slowly. There was relatively little impact on procedure or on the substance of private law, except in relation to prohibited degrees of marriage and to divorce.[21] The main change was structural, with a division of the functions of the church courts between Kirk sessions and commissary courts, with the Commissary Court in Edinburgh having the exclusive right to deal with questions of marriage and status.[22]

Despite the upheavals that followed the Union of the Crowns in 1603, Scots law continued to develop, particularly in relation to landholding and trade. Legal literature flourished too. Compilations of court decisions or *Practicks* were already well established. These began to take on the form of digests[23] and other comprehensive works started to appear. These included Welwood, *The Sea Laws of Scotland*, 1590, Craig's *Ius Feudale*, 1603, published 1655, Skene's edition of the *Regiam Maiestatem* and the *Quoniam Attachiamenta* 1609, and, most influential of all, Stair's *Institutions of the Law of Scotland*, 1681.

The *Institutions* was a remarkable work, not only in its content but for the circumstances in which it was produced. Stair's judicial office, latterly as Lord President of the Court of Session, was twice interrupted by his refusal to forswear the right to take up arms against the King. He completed the *Institutions* shortly after the second of these occasions, before departing to exile in the Netherlands. This

---

[20] Conferred by the College of Justice Act 1540 APS ii 371 c. 10. An interesting aspect of the procedure was the practice of a judgment being given by the whole court. This remains the continental model but tends to be found in Scotland today only in the Court of Criminal Appeal.

[21] The courts granted divorce for adultery straight away and began to do so for malicious desertion. The latter practice was recognised by statute in 1573, c. 55: Anent thame that divertes fra uthers being joyned of befoir in lauchfull Mariage.

[22] Appeal lay to the Court of Session.

[23] Commencing with Balfour in the 1570s.

lasted until his return with, and later reinstatement under, William of Orange.

For Stair, law should be seen as 'a rational discipline, having principles from which its conclusions may be deduced.'[24] Exempting Duarenus and Grotius from the criticism, he wrote:

> There is little to be found among the commentaries and treatises upon the civil law arguing from any known principles of right, but all their debate is a congestion of the contexts of the law: which exceedingly nauseates delicate engines therein finding much more work for the memory than judgment in taking up and retaining the Lawgiver's will, rather than searching into his reason.[25]

Stair's object was to offer a comprehensive restatement of Scots law, set out in accordance with the principles of natural law, equity being at the apex. The content was drawn mainly from the existing laws and customs of Scotland but elements of feudal, canon and Roman law as found in the *ius commune* and in the writings of continental jurists are interwoven into the whole. These are taken selectively, however, on the basis that men 'are most happy whose laws are nearest to equity and most declaratory of it'.[26]

Just which other writers, and even which of their writings, count as institutional is not wholly agreed. Craig's *Ius Feudale*, Bankton's *Institute* 1751-3, Erskine's *Institute* 1773 and Bell's *Commentaries*, 1804, are clearly treated as such for the civil law[27] while Mackenzie's *Law and Customs* 1678 and Hume's *Commentaries* 1797 are so for the criminal.[28] What makes the classification of some importance is the significance attached to the writings that are regarded as institutional.

---

[24] I i 16.

[25] I i 17. Some law students may feel that little has changed. Compare, too, Hume's 'The Law . . . appear'd nauseous to me' and Alasdair MacIntyre's comment 'Hume's view of the study of law as quite other than that of philosophy marks . . . a break with the dominant Scottish tradition'. *Whose Justice? Which Rationality?* (London: Duckworth,1988) p 283. (I am indebted to John Tasioulas for this reference).

[26] I i 15.

[27] More doubtful are Mackenzie's *Institutions* 1678, Erskine's *Principles* 1754 and Kames *Principles* 1760.

[28] There is some uncertainty over Alison, both *Principles* 1832 and *Practice* 1833.

T.B. Smith, for example, has argued that these have the same status as 'a decision by a Division of the Inner House of the Court of Session',[29] while Lord Normand has suggested that 'the court will pay as much respect to them as to a judgment of the House of Lords, though it is bound to follow a judgment of the House of Lords whatever the institutional writers may have said.'[30]

Since the Union

Craig, Stair and Mackenzie apart, the institutional writers post-date the Treaty and Acts of Union. Despite the separate standing still accorded to Scots law, it became subject to new influences. The practice of appealing matters in civil causes to the House of Lords contributed to this, particularly since only sixteen direct representatives of the Scottish peerage sat in it. Accordingly questions of Scots law were liable to be determined by men who, if trained in law at all, as they later came to be, were trained in English law. It was not until 1876, when salaried Lords of Appeal were appointed, that Scots judges came to have one, and more usually two, customary places in Scotland's highest civil court. In any case involving five judges, however, they will necessarily be in a minority. In fact, there is no requirement that they are even involved in every decision affecting Scots law. In fairness, though, it should be added that, since 1876, a number of unfortunate decisions would appear to have been concurred in by at least one Scots judge.[31] Also in modern times, at least, it would seem unlikely that an English majority would decide a case against the concerted opinion of their Scottish bretheren.

It is possible to list a considerable number of instances in which alien doctrines have been introduced into Scots law through the House of Lords. The most notorious was that of "common employment"

---

[29] *A Short Commentary on the Law of Scotland* (Edinburgh: W Green, 1962) p 32.

[30] 'The Scottish Judicature and Legal Procedure' (Address to the Holdsworth Club 1941).

[31] e.g. Lord Robertson in *Cameron* v *Young* 1908 SC (HL) 7; Lord Dunedin in *Dumbreck* v *Addie & Sons (Collieries) Ltd* 1929 SC (HL) 51; and (in the writer's opinion, though not all Scots lawyers would agree) Lord Reid in *White & Carter (Councils) Ltd* v *Macgregor* 1962 SC (HL) 1.

which formed part of the law of Scotland from 1858 following the reasoning of Lord Cranworth: 'But if such be the Law of England, on what ground can it be argued not to be the law of Scotland?',[32] until its abolition by statute in 1948.[33] Similarly, the English distinction between "invitee, licensee and trespasser" formed part of Scots law from *Dumbreck* v *Addie* in 1929[34] until its similar removal in 1960.[35] This example is a particularly interesting one, since it also affords a more recent glimpse at the House of Lords failure to distinguish between its English and Scottish roles. *British Railways Board* v. *Herrington*[36] was arguably the first case in which the Lords fully used its power, reclaimed in the Practice Statement in 1966, to depart from its own decisions. What exercised the court in this case was whether it should depart from its decision in *Dumbreck* v. *Addie*. The question never seems to have been raised as to whether, since *Dumbreck* was a Scottish case and *Herrington* an English one, it was an appropriate point of departure.[37]

Besides these examples, one may cite the introduction of the *scienter* rule in relation to animals,[38] the influence of the English

---

32 *Bartonshill Coal Company* v *Reid* 1858 3 Macq 266, establishing that an employer was not vicariously liable where one of his employees injured another in the course of employment.

33 Law Reform (Personal Injuries) Act 1948.

34 (cit. n. 31).

35 Occupiers Liability (Scotland) Act 1960 s. 2.

36 [1972] AC 877.

37 According, however, to Lord President Inglis in *Virtue* v *Alloa Police Commissioners* 1873 1R 285, it would be an error in constitutional law to do so since, in his opinion the House always sat in one character, 'as the House of Lords of the United Kingdom'. He does not, though, explain the basis of his opinion and it appears not to have found favour more generally with the Scottish judiciary.

38 *Fleeming* v *Orr* 1855 2 Macq. 14, to the effect that strict liability for injuries caused by domestic animals only arose where that animal was known to have dangerous propensities. Now removed by the Animals (Scotland) Act 1987.

doctrine of privity of contract,[39] of a separate category of negligence[40] and of the law of mistake[41] - all in the area of obligations. These have run counter to a tradition, still found in the French civil code, of viewing the law of obligations as a coherent whole with *culpa* or fault at its core. Striking though this point may be, a cautionary note should be added. Insufficient research has been done on the whole range of House of Lords decisions in Scots cases to make a fair assessment of its influence on Scots law as a whole. It needs to be said, too, that a considerable amount of anglicisation has been brought about from within Scotland, by use of English precedents in Scottish courts,[42] or by statute, notably in the area of commercial and consumer law.[43] Despite Scotland's affinity with continental systems, U.K. membership of the European Community has, paradoxically, led to pressures for greater assimilation of Scots commercial law with the English variety.[44]

At the same time, it is possible to overstate the extent to which Scots law has been affected. As shall be seen later, Scots private law retains many distinct features. Also, unlike the Court of Session, no appeals developed from the High Court of Justiciary to the Lords and, matters such as treason and road traffic apart, criminal law remains distinct. It is also largely a matter of case law rather than statute - for example neither the Infant Life Preservation Act 1929 nor the Obscene

---

[39] Approximately, the restriction of rights and obligations arising from a contract to the parties to it. As discussed in T B Smith, 'The Common Law Cuckoo: Problems of "Mixed" Legal Systems with Special Reference to Restrictive Interpretations in the Scots Law of Obligations' in *Studies Critical and Comparative* (Edinburgh: W. Green, New York: Oceania, 1962).

[40] Ibid.

[41] See T B Smith, *A Short Commentary* (cit. n. 29) p 809f.

[42] See T B Smith, 'English Influences on the Law of Scotland' in *Studies Critical and Comparative* including his reference to D M Walker 'A Note on Precedent (1949) 61 *Juridical Review* and the finding that 25% of the cases cited in the Court of Session since 'Hitler's war' were English. More recent research suggests a similar level.

[43] e.g. Sale of Goods Act 1979.

[44] See e.g. Neil Gow QC, 'Can Scotland's Separate Legal System Survive?' *The Law Magazine* 22 January 1988.

Publications Act 1959 have Scottish counterparts. Equally, much in the area of public law is separately enacted for Scotland. There have always been purely Scottish procedures for judicial review[45] and a distinct Scottish flavour to the decisions reached.[46] Also, the influence has not all been all of England on Scotland.[47] Further, the changes should be seen in the light of a more general "growing together" of the common law and civilian traditions.[48]

Scots law, then, has to be classified as belonging, in part at least, to the common law tradition. It does so in the sense that its content does not depend entirely on legislation, as would be the case in a codified system. That said, the notion of common law in Scotland is far broader than in England, since it covers all non-statute law. In addition, such common law owes much to its civilian and canonical roots. The best one can say, therefore, is that Scotland has developed into a particular type of "hybrid" or "mixed" jurisdiction. It remains still to be seen how justified was Levy-Ullmann's claim that:

> Scots Law as it stands gives us a picture of what will some day be the law of the civilised nations - namely, a combination between the Anglo-Saxon system and the Continental system.[49]

Modes of Thinking

The very broad survey above of the development of Scots Law has already indicated some of the features that will be found where the

[45] Now Rule of Court 58; formerly Rule 260B. In particular, under Scots Law there is no need for leave to apply.

[46] Particularly in relation to scope: see e.g. *West* v *Secretary of State for Scotland* 1992 SLT 66.

[47] For example, England may be said to have followed Scotland in allowing the possibility of rape within marriage. See *S* v *H M A.* 1989 SLT 469 and then *R* v *R* [1992] AC (HL) 599.

[48] See e.g. B Markesinis ed, *The Gradual Convergence* (Oxford: Clarendon Press, 1994); P de Cruz, *Comparative Law in a Changing World* (London: Cavendish, 1995); R Jagtenberg, E Örücü & A de Roo eds, *Tranfrontier Mobility of Law* (The Hague: Kluwer Law International, 1995); but, also, contra P Legrand, 'European Legal Systems are not converging' (1996) 45 *ICLQ* 52.

[49] Quoted in Lord Cooper of Culross, *Selected Papers* (cit. n. 10) at p198.

second aspect of Zweigert and Kötz criterion of "style" is concerned. In respect of distinctive modes of legal thinking they write of the differences between the civilian and common law approaches as follows:

> On the continent lawyers think abstractly, in terms of institutions, in England concretely, in terms of cases, the relationship of the parties, "rights and duties". On the continent the system is conceived as being complete and free from gaps, in England lawyers feel their way gradually from case to case. On the continent lawyers delight in systematics, in England they are sceptical of every generalisation. On the continent lawyers operate with ideas, which often, dangerously enough take on a life of their own; in England they think in pictures; and so one could continue.[50]

A E Örücü, in comparing common law, civilian and socialist legal systems has argued that each has a different internal logic, at least at "Day One".[51] Whether mixed jurisdictions have a separate kind of internal logic of their own has yet to be established. This issue is complicated by the fact that there would seem to be few, if any, entirely pure jurisdictions and that they can be mixed in a number of different ways. For example, they can be mixed historically, in the sense that they have absorbed different kinds of law over time and adapted them to a greater or lesser extent. Sometimes the process will have been gradual. Sometimes the introduction will have been abrupt. It may have been the result of willing reception, at least by those in power, as happened with Turkey[52] earlier in this century and with

---

[50] Zweigert and Kötz, *Introduction to Comparative Law* (cit. Intro, n. 8) at p 70.

[51] 'The Internal Logic of Legal Systems' (1987) 7 *Legal Studies* p 310.

[52] With Turkey this included a Civil Code from the Swiss Civil Code and Code of obligations; a Penal Code from the Italian Code of 1889; and a Commercial Code, from the German Code of 1887 and the Italian Code, all in 1926, and then, in 1927, the Code of Civil Procedure from the Swiss Canton of Neuchatel, followed by, in 1929, three more codes, including a Code of Criminal Procedure from the German Code of 1877. On this, see Esin Örücü, 'Turkey: Change under Pressure' in Örücü, Attwooll and Coyle ed *Studies in Legal Systems: Mixed and Mixing* (cit ch II, n. 32).

Japan in the late nineteenth,[53] or by way of imposition in the course of some type of colonial rule.[54] Jurisdictions may, however, be mixed contemporaneously, in the sense that different bodies of law can apply to the same group of people depending on the area of life concerned, as with canon law and feudal law in Scotland of the middle ages or with the Quebec of today, where a civil code sits beside what is largely an all Canadian criminal law. Equally, one jurisdiction may treat different bodies of law as applicable to different groups of people, although the area of life concerned is the same. One may cite, for example, the different rules of family law applying to those of the Jewish faith and those of other (or no) religious faith in Israel and the development in Zimbabwe of what is effectively an internal "private international law" to cope with the various different tribal laws operating there.

Just how the mixing has occurred and how fully will obviously have effects for its style in general and the mode of thinking employed in particular. First impressions of Scots Law, however, suggest that its greater affinity is with the continental approach. The historian Buckle, who saw Scots thinking as under the malign influence of the clergy and who believed that only the English inductive approach could allow real scientific thought and proper intellectual development, wrote:

> In Scotland . . . men have always been deductive; even the most original thinkers being unable to liberate themselves from the universal tendency, and being forced to accept a method which time had consecrated, and which was interwoven with all the associations of the national mind.[55]

It is, however, rash to make generalisations about national characteristics - just as it would be to suggest that there is **a** method of

---

[53] With Japan, reception of German law began in the 1880s, although the Criminal Code of 1882 was French in basis and the Civil Code of 1898 was influenced by both systems. The Japanese Constitution, however, was the result more of imposition although endorsed by the Parliament - see e.g. Setsuko Sato in 'The Validity of a Constitution Established through a Revolution: The Case of Japan' in E Attwooll ed, *Shaping Revolution* (Aberdeen: Aberdeen University Press, 1991).

[54] Amongst many possible examples, by the British on the native peoples in Quebec and Australia and by the French in Algeria.

[55] *On Scotland and the Scotch Intellect* (cit. ch III, n. 27) at p 243.

judicial decision making. One does not need to read many judgments to see that judges, at least from the way in which they frame their opinions, arrive at their decisions in different ways. Some even appear to vary their approaches from case to case. That said, they can still to a fair extent be classified as favouring a deductive or an empirical approach. This classification, though, does not necessarily follow nationality. For example, (the Scottish) Lord Reid was in the finest tradition of common law judges, whilst (the English) Lord Scarman would seem to share the continental lawyers' thinking 'in terms of institutions' and 'delight in systematics'.

All that said, however, and despite many instances to the contrary, the ethos of Scots Law and, at its best, of the Scots judiciary is arguably a deductive one.[56] Indeed, one may add a caveat to Zweigert and Kötz's view that English lawyers think in terms of 'rights and duties'. They do, perhaps, but only as a consequence of the existence of remedies. For the Scots lawyer, on the other hand, rights and duties are to be discerned from the substantive law, and, where they exist, a remedy should be made to follow. Similarly, Dworkin's claim that a legal system contains principles as well as rules caused something of

---

[56] For the claim - by a Scot - that legal reasoning generally is, partially at least, a deductive process see Neil MacCormick, *Legal Reasoning and Legal Theory* (Oxford: Clarendon Press, 1978) especially chs II and III, responses to this by Alida Wilson, 'The Nature of Legal Reasoning: A Commentary with regard to Professor MacCormick's Theory' (1982) 2 *Legal Studies* 269, followed at p 286 by MacCormick, 'The Nature of Legal Reasoning: a brief reply to Dr Wilson' ; and by Bernard Jackson, *Law, Fact & Narrative Coherence* (Merseyside: Deborah Charles Publications, 1988) esp ch III and, in response, MacCormick, 'Notes on Narrativity and the Normative Syllogism' (1991) 4 *International Journal for the Semiotics of Law* 163 and further exchanges in (1992) 5 *International Journal for the Semiotics of Law*. See also the revised Foreword in the 1994 paperback edition of *Legal Reasoning and Legal Theory*.

a stir in England.[57] It moved most Scots lawyers only to comment, if somewhat belatedly, on a point they had simply taken for granted.[58]

Another way in which Scots law fits with continental systems rather than the common law one is in the contrast made between antiformalism and formalism. Although this has already been touched on in the discussion of historical development, the lack of division between law and equity bears repetition. An example of this is the *nobile officium* of the Court of Session which allows it to do what justice demands in cases where no remedy is available through ordinary procedures.[59] With this can be contrasted the situation under English law, where there were separate courts of law and equity until 1875 and where it has been argued that 'though they run in the same channel, they run side by side and do not mingle their waters'.[60]

In private law, Zweigert and Kotz argue, antiformalism 'shows itself in consensualism, that is, the rule that agreement creates contractual obligations, no matter how it is expressed.' The approach in Scots law has been, and remains, mixed. Traditionally, some obligations can

[57] R M Dworkin, 'Is Law a System of Rules' in R Summers ed, *Essays in Legal Philosophy* (Oxford: Blackwell, 1968). See the response by Colin Tapper, 'A Note on Principles' (1971) 34 *Modern Law Review* 628. See also, R M Dworkin, *Taking Rights Seriously* (London: Duckworth, 1977) esp ch 2.

[58] See e.g. N MacCormick '"Principles" of Law' 1974 *Juridical Review* 217. And, for a contrary view, R H S Tur 'Positivism, Principles and Rules' in E Attwooll ed, *Perspectives in Jurisprudence* (Glasgow: Glasgow University Press, 1977).

[59] Also, there is the power of the High Court of Justiciary, in exceptional cases, to declare behaviour criminal although it was not, or not clearly, so before. See Baron Hume's *Commentaries on the Law of Scotland Respecting Crimes* and the case of *Bernard Greenhuff* 1838 2 Swin 236. For comment and further references see Lindsay Farmer, '"The Genius of our Law . . .": Criminal Law and the Scottish Legal Tradition' (1992) 55 *Modern Law Review* 25.

[60] From W Ashburner, *Principles of Equity* (1902) p 23 but this view was rejected by Lord Diplock in *United Scientific Holdings Ltd* v *Burnley Borough Council* [1978] AC 904 at pp 924-5, where he stated that 'this metaphor has become mischievous and deceptive. . . If Professor Ashburner's fluvial metaphor is to be retained at all, the waters of the confluent streams of law and equity have surely mingled now'.

only be constituted in writing, whereas with others - for instance, concerning the lease of property for less than one year - a verbal agreement is sufficient. Before the Requirements of Writing (Scotland) Act 1995 certain of the obligations that needed writing could only be constituted by "solemn writing", that is by writing fulfilling certain formal requirements.[61] This category of *obligationes literis* has now disappeared, although actual writing may still be needed, particularly for certain types of property transfer, and a degree of form is required in other cases, too, largely as a result of statute.[62] By contrast, the 1995 Act has introduced greater formalism in relation to unilateral voluntary obligations. Unlike the English recognition only of promises made under seal, these used to require no particular form for their constitution. They now have to be in writing, unless undertaken in the course of business.[63]

The final aspect of mode of legal thinking mentioned by Zweigert and Kötz is what Ihering called the "struggle for law". It is regarded as a feature of Western law generally that 'it is the duty of a person, owed both to himself and to the idea of law itself, to fight for his rights'.[64] This is in contrast with the Far Eastern approach where resort to law is a sign of failure to act in a civilised manner. Properly, harmony should be restored by means of the parties reaching their own agreed settlement. Clearly, Scots law fits within the Western model. It must be said, though, that the Western model is itself changing to some extent, with an increased use of less formal procedures for dispute resolution and a renewed emphasis on self regulation.[65]

Distinctive Institutions

The discussion so far has not really indicated the existence of any especially distinctive institutions - Zweigert and Kötz's third aspect of style. There is an ambiguity in the term "institution" in that, in

[61] Also, until this Act (s. 11), proof of some less formal agreements had to be by writ or oath. Now it may be by any means.

[62] e.g. the Consumer Credit Act 1974 s 60.

[63] s. 1(2)(c).

[64] *Introduction to Comparative Law* (cit. n. 50) at p 65.

[65] For more detail on both of these see ch V.

ordinary parlance, we may use it for some kind of building where a distinct activity is carried on by a particular body of people for some particular social purpose. This is especially so for prisons and hospitals. Sometimes we think of courthouses in the same way. Where we use the term institution for a building, however, we are really just transferring to the bricks and mortar the notion that it houses some kind of organisation that has been set up or "instituted" to serve certain of our ends. At that level, the institution is not the building, nor even the people that it contains, but the activities involved and the rules, principles, policies and practices by which they are conditioned. In this sense, we may also use the term institution to cover any kind of social arrangement that is initiated, conducted and terminated according to such rules, principles, policies and practices. Where these are, in whole or in major part a matter of law, we are justified in calling the institution legal.[66] Typical examples would be contract and marriage.

One thing that is thought to be unique to the Scottish jurisdiction satisfies the notion of institution in the organisational sense. This is the Children's Hearing System.[67] Here a panel of lay people, after appropriate training, decide what steps should be taken in respect of children referred to them. The referral is done by Reporters, who look into the background, decide whether to proceed and organise all the relevant paperwork. Grounds for referral include the child having committed an offence, being involved in solvent or drug misuse,[68] truanting or being the subject of abuse or neglect. Where an offence is involved the panel does not "try" the child. If the child has not admitted committing the offence, this must first be established before the Sheriff. The Panel's only concern with any ground of referral is with what should be done in the best interests of the child. This may involve the child being looked after by the local authority, social work supervision and, in some cases, no further action.

---

66 See D N MacCormick, 'Law as Institutional Fact' (cit. ch II, n. 7).

67 Set up following the Kilbrandon Report (Cmnd 2306) under the Social Work (Scotland) Act 1968. See now the Children (Scotland) Act 1995.

68 The former initially in consequence of the Solvent Abuse (Scotland) Act 1983; now see the Children (Scotland) Act 1995 s. 52(2)(k). The latter, under s. 52(2)(j) implements the UN Convention on the Rights of the Child.

The Children's Hearing System, then, is clearly a legal institution, to be placed alongside courts, tribunals and other similar bodies. It is equally clearly, however, a legal institution with a distinctive approach. It is goal oriented, with panel members using their discretion as to the best means of achieving that goal in particular cases. In this it differs - at least where their overt function is concerned[69] - from the standard Western models and fits more comfortably with the kind of internal logic found in socialist systems.

In writing of institutions, however, Zweigert and Kötz are not so much concerned with law making and law applying organisations as with the social arrangements sense of the term and even with certain aspects of these. Thus they instance, amongst other things, agency, the requirement of consideration in contracts, and trusts for the Common Law and *negotiorum gestio,*[70] the requirement of cause in contracts, and abuse of right, for the Romanistic family. Scottish Law provides a considerable list of such features, some of which show affinity with the common law tradition, some of which show affinity with the civilian one and some of which show neither.

In criminal law, the best known is the "not proven" verdict[71] but one might also cite: the 110 day rule limiting detention before trial; the declaratory power of the High Court[72] and the role of the Crown Office in practically decriminalising or recriminalising activities by its attitude toward prosecuting them;[73] the lack of opening speeches by prosecution and defence; the judge's charge to the jury, much narrower in its scope than its southern counterpart; and the limited revival of

[69] See, however, the views expressed by J A G Griffith, *The Politics of the Judiciary* 4th edn (London: Fontana, 1991) and the implication that judicial decision making is always goal oriented.

[70] Administering the affairs of another without authority but in circumstances where it is reasonable to do so.

[71] Currently under review, although the weight of opinion seems to be in favour of its retention.

[72] See n. 59.

[73] As homosexual behaviour between the passing of the (English) Sexual Offences Act 1967 and the Criminal Justice (Scotland) Act 1980.

judicial examination on remand.[74] Also there is the existence of a well developed public prosecution system,[75] of majority verdicts,[76] and the emergence through case law of the defence of diminished responsibility[77] all of which have had some recent impact in England.[78] One might also mention that 'wicked recklessness' as well as intention has long been treated as sufficient *mens rea* for murder and that Scots law has a flexible approach to problems of insanity, untrammelled by the McNaghten rules.

In family law one may contrast the very early introduction of judicial divorce for adultery and malicious desertion with the lack of any proper procedures for adopting children prior to 1930. There is, too, the Scots notion of the irregular marriage, although the only form that still survives is that of "cohabitation with habit and repute" and the Scottish Law Commission has recently canvassed opinion concerning its abolition too.[79] Another old Scots institution that has effectively disappeared following the Commission's activities is the distinction between minors and pupils (those under 18 but over 14 for boys and

---

[74] Criminal Justice (Scotland) Act 1980 s. 6. See also the effects of the Criminal Justice (Scotland) Act 1995 s. 10.

[75] Prosecution began to be placed in the hands of the Lord (then the King's) Advocate in the latter part of the sixteenth century. The system is currently adminstered through the Crown Office in Edinburgh but operates largely through locally based Procurators-Fiscal. Private prosecutions by injured persons are still possible but these are very rare indeed and cannot take place without either the concurrence of the Lord Advocate or the consent of the High Court.

[76] 15 jurors, with 8 being sufficient for a majority.

[77] Including *H M A* v *Dingwall* (1867) 5 Irv. 466; *H M A* v *Savage* 1923 JC 49; *H M A* v *Braithwaite* 1945 JC 55.

[78] i.e. respectively, the introduction of the Crown Prosecution Service; of majority verdicts (though on a 10-2 basis); and of diminished responsibility by the Homicide Act 1957 s. 2.

[79] 'Family Law: Pre-consolidation Reforms'. Scot. Law Com. Discussion Paper No 85, 1990, paras 2.1-2.19.

12 for girls) with the latter having had considerable legal capacity.[80] A particular view of family obligation is also shown by the fact that Scots law has traditionally not allowed complete freedom of testamentary disposition, with spouses and children counting as creditors against the deceased's moveable property.[81]

In the area of contract English law has been influential, particularly in the areas of error (or mistake) and of damages. Nonetheless, in certain aspects Scots law remains distinct. As mentioned earlier, it does not have any developed doctrine of privity of contract. Indeed the existence of a *jus quaesitum tertio* (the right of a third party for whose benefit the contract was made to sue on it) argues in the opposite direction. Scots law has no doctrine of consideration. Neither, at least explicitly, does it have any doctrine of cause.[82] In quasi-contract, however, and, indeed, in the whole area of recompense, roots in the *ius commune* are obvious and there are marked similarities of principle with modern French law. The traditional basis of delict (or tort), *culpa* or fault, includes both intention and negligence. This has, of course, been eroded by the development of strict liability but, even so, traces of the Roman law of quasi-delict remain. Similarly, with the *actio injuriarum*, for insult or affront,[83] damages may be awarded even where there is no financial loss. Such *solatium* may be awarded, too, following other delictual actions and in addition to damages for financial loss - for example, for grief and suffering at the death of a relative. On the other hand, land law in Scotland remains feudal in its genesis. Indeed, until 1974 it was common for owners of houses to

[80] The Age of Legal Capacity (Scotland) Act 1991 introduced a statutory regime in which 16 has become the relevant age for both sexes for most purposes. There are, however, certain exceptions and see also the Children (Scotland) Act 1995 which confers certain rights at the age of 12.

[81] Ius relicti, ius relictae and legitim.

[82] Very crudely, the doctrine of consideration means that an agreement is only binding if for value, that of cause means that any party to an agreement or undertaking must be able to gain some legitimate satisfaction from it. Cause is, therefore, a much wider notion than consideration, covering, for example, the invalidity of contracts made for immoral purposes.

[83] It has been argued that this might be utilised to afford a right of privacy under Scots law. See David L Carey Miller 1980 *SLT* (News) 109.

have amongst their expenses an annual feu duty, payable to their feudal superior.[84] The situation is, however, gradually changing and the Scottish Law Commission has recommended total abolition of the system.[85]

All these examples, with the exception of those concerning criminal law, involve aspects of the substantive law governing relations between members of society. Parallel instances can be found in the substantive law that governs relations between members of society and "the state" and in adjective law, particularly in the rules of evidence and procedure. Of considerable importance for the latter is the self regulatory power of the courts - as with the introduction of new procedures by Act of Adjournal or of Sederunt.[86] For example, a new Small Claims Procedure was introduced in Scotland at the end of 1988. Although originally provided for in general terms by the Law Reform (Miscellaneous Provisions) (Scotland) Act 1985, the actual implementation was by the Act of Sederunt (Small Claims Rules) 1988. While accounts of the law, in relation to common law systems and mixed jurisdictions at least, give a prominent place to the courts, this aspect of their activities is sometimes rather neglected.

This turns our attention to the fourth aspect of style identified by Zweigert and Kötz - the kind of legal sources acknowledged and the way they are handled. The situation in Scotland is examined in the next chapter.

[84] The Land Tenure Reform (Scotland) Act 1974 made redemption of feu duty (if allocated) compulsory on sale.

[85] See Robert Rennie, 'The Feudal System - Going, Going, Gone?' 1995 *Juridical Review* 321.

[86] For the Court of Session. The equivalents in the High Court of Justiciary are Acts of Adjournal.

V

THE STYLE OF SCOTS LAW CONTINUED

Sources and how they are handled

How, then, does Zweigert and Kötz's fourth aspect of style - the kind of legal sources acknowledged and the way they are handled - operate in Scotland? Here something needs to be said about what is meant by a source of law. Sometimes the term "source" is used in a historical sense, referring to the different elements that have contributed to the development of the law, as with canon law and feudal law. Sometimes it is used to refer to the bodies that are regarded as generating the law, such as Parliament, the courts and, on some accounts, the people. Sometimes it is used to refer to the places one needs to look in order to find out what the law is, such as statutes, reports of judicial decisions, institutional writings. Sometimes it is used to refer to the factors that may legitimately be considered in establishing the law on a given matter, such as rules of statute law, judicial precedents, authoritative statements, principles, equity and custom, even policies.

This rather mixed usage can cause confusion, particularly since the last two senses, particularly, are often mingled. For present purposes, the final sense will be the one used, although with some reservations. The reservations arise on two main grounds. First, in looking to what may legitimately be taken into account on establishing the law on a given matter, it is sometimes assumed that this must mean what may legitimately be taken into account **by the judiciary**. Even if this is a convenient way of looking at matters, it is not altogether satisfactory. For it is far from the case that all applications of law are through the medium of the courts. There is, on the contrary, an increasing use of non-court based methods of resolving disagreements with a legal content. Second, since what a court may legitimately take into account is actually a matter of some dispute, there are problems in producing a definitive list of such sources. Further, there are clearly matters that a court may legitimately take into account in reaching a decision, namely the facts, or, arguably, in establishing some rule - for example, the repercussions of this for future decisions[1] - that are not sources of the specified kind.[2]

The role of non-judicial bodies

Their activities are usually lumped together under the heading of alternative dispute resolution or ADR for short. ADR itself, however, takes on various forms. Some of it is scarcely "alternative", in the sense that it has still been generated from within the existing legal system, usually by Act of Parliament or, at least, under statutory authority.[3] What largely distinguishes it from the normal judicial process is either or both of less formal procedures (and, often, surroundings) and a much greater degree of lay participation. Within the judicial process members of the public are normally found only as jurors or witnesses.[4] The less formal procedures found with ADR, however, are intended to allow the parties in dispute to conduct their own cases. This is reinforced by the fact that Legal Aid is not available to them. Similarly, non lawyers figure widely amongst the decision takers. Most typically, two lay people sit with a legally qualified chairman, although with the Children's Hearing System the Panel is drawn entirely from the general public.[5]

Whether participation in such ADR is "lay" in the fullest sense of the term must, however, be open to doubt. First, while the procedures may just about be straightforward enough to allow parties to conduct their own cases, the legislation with which they have to grapple often

---

1 For an argument concerning the proper limits of such consequentialist reasoning, see MacCormick, *Legal Reasoning and Legal Theory* (cit. ch IV, n. 56) especially chs V and VI.

2 See further, on this issue, the distinction made by Joseph Raz between a theory of law and a theory of legal adjudication, 'The Problem about the Nature of Law' in 1982 *Contemporary Philosophy*, vol 3.

3 For example, industrial tribunals were originally set up under the Industrial Training Act 1964.

4 Justices of the Peace in the District Courts apart.

5 At present the majority of the Reporters, who bring the cases to the Panel, also lack legal qualification. This, though, particularly now traineeships can be done through the Reporters' Department, seems to be changing.

is not. Many employ lawyers despite the lack of Legal Aid. For example in 1994/5 47.3% of employers and 24.4% of employees coming before Industrial Tribunals in Scotland had legal representation.[6] Further, even where lawyers as such are not involved, the assistance of trade union officials, CAB workers, Welfare Rights officers and so on, is regularly sought. Such "para-legals" may develop a very high level of expertise in the area concerned.

Equally, with the decision makers, absence of legal qualification does not imply that no training is offered in the area of law concerned. Not only that, but the lay members tend to be appointed because they are regarded as having a special expertise in the aspect of life to which that area of law particularly relates. Thus, with industrial tribunals, one of the two lay members will have come from a group appointed following nominations by employers organisation, the other from a group similarly appointed following nominations from trade unions. With Disability Appeal Tribunals the lay members are expected to have a special knowledge of the problems of the disabled; with Medical Appeal Tribunals, the "lay" members are doctors in general practice.

Other factors, too, may affect the composition of tribunals in ways which mean that the lay membership tends to be drawn from particular sectors of the community, rather than reflect a cross section. For example, the fact that lay members of Social Security Appeal Tribunals do not receive any pay requires them to have some other source of income. In practice it largely means being in receipt of a pension, with obvious consequences for the average age of those involved. All in all, then, whilst the membership of tribunals is clearly more diverse than that of the judiciary - acronymically described as MACERS, or male, affluent, caucasian, elderly and remote[7] - the circle remains relatively closed and establishment based.[8]

There is another respect, though, in which the operation of such bodies may differ from that of the courts. On each issue before it, a

---

[6] Industrial Tribunals in Scotland - Fact Sheet 1994/5.

[7] Coined by Lord McLuskey in 'Law, Justice and Democracy' *The Reith Lectures 1986* (London, 1987).

[8] Although the greater participation of women, particularly within the Children's Hearing System, should be noted.

court will find for one party and against the other - there is rarely any in-between.[9] By contrast, a Rent Assessment Committee may give neither the landlord nor the tenant quite what he or she is seeking. Its function is rather to ascertain certain facts about the property and, since the Housing (Scotland) Act 1988,[10] determine in consequence what is the appropriate market rent, irrespective of what the landlord is asking for or the tenant is willing to pay. Although the decision-making of the Rent Assessment Committee is still probably still to be classified as a form of adjudication, the distance there may be between the outcome and the initial position of both parties more closely resembles what may happen in the event of disputed planning applications. The Planning Committee of the District (or Highland or Island) Council, having considered the views of various officials and, perhaps, having granted a hearing to both the applicant and the objectors, may grant the application subject to various conditions.[11] Neither side gets quite what it wanted - the developer has to pay an additional "price", the objector is placated by the lessening of the expected nuisance or the provision of an additional amenity, and the Council makes a "planning gain" in the form, for example, of some desired development, such as a new road or additional shops. That said, though, there is a stark contrast between the operations of the Rent Assessment Committee, whose hands are effectively tied by the legislation, and of the Planning Committee, whose operations, in this context, are "extra-statutory".

Another form of dispute resolution with acknowledged legal standing is arbitration. Here the matter is referred to some named person or body for decision, according to informal procedure. The award of the arbiter is binding on the parties but is not enforceable without recourse to the courts. Only in rare circumstances can it actually be challenged. Some arbitrations take place because that is the method of resolving the dispute presumed by statute.[12] Others do so as a matter of contractual agreement. This is a longstanding feature

---

[9] Contributory negligence is one such exception.

[10] s. 25.

[11] See Jeremy Rowan-Robinson and EricYoung, *Planning by Agreement in Scotland* (Edinburgh: W Green & Son, 1989).

[12] e.g. Agricultural Holdings (Scotland) Act 1949 s. 68.

of contracts between businesses and is increasingly provided for in consumer contracts. For example, the Association of British Travel Agents provides an independent low cost Arbitration Scheme limited to smaller claims, as an option for dissatisfied clients. "Compulsory" arbitration under standard form contracts, on the other hand, has been restricted under recent legislation.[13]

Most of these processes - at least, where there is no appeal - have the effect of concluding the dispute for the parties concerned, in the sense that the decision or award is a binding one.[14] By contrast investigation of complaints of maladministration by the Parliamentary or the Local Government Commissioner for Administration can result only in findings as to whether or not such complaints are justified, together with recommended course of action.[15] Compliance on the part of the authorities remains voluntary. The remedy afforded the complainant may be no more than an apology. Rather more powers are accorded to the Equal Opportunities Commission and the Commission for Racial Equality. If on investigating complaints of sexual or racial discrimination respectively they become satisfied that an employer is behaving unlawfully, they may issue a non discrimination notice. If the employer wishes to dispute the notice he or she has six weeks in which to appeal the matter to an industrial tribunal. If the notice is confirmed, or if there is no appeal, and there is any repetition of the unlawful practice within five years, the EOC and the CRE may obtain an interdict against the employer at the Sheriff Court to prevent its being continued.[16] These bodies, however, appear to have made only sparing use of such powers.

So far as mediation and conciliation are concerned, the terms tend to be used interchangeably. If they are to be distinguished, though, it seems best to see the mediator as a "go between" or an "honest broker"

---

[13] Consumer Arbitration Agreements Act 1988. For a comprehensive account of arbitration in Scotland see R Hunter, *Law of Arbitration in Scotland* (Edinburgh: T & T Clark, 1987)

[14] Although, as mentioned in the text, recourse may still be needed to the courts for enforcement purposes.

[15] Respectively, the Parliamentary Commissioner Act 1967 and the Local Government (Scotland) Act 1975 Part II.

[16] Sex Discrimination Act 1965 s. 71; Race Relations Act 1976 s. 62.

and the conciliator as a "bringer together". Besides the way communication is achieved between the parties, though, it is also possible to separate out mediation and conciliation by reference to their aims. Both seek to produce a solution that is acceptable to each side. With mediation, however, this may be limited to the parties becoming resigned to accepting half a loaf rather than risking no bread at all. Typical examples, found even once the judicial process is underway, are "out of court settlements" and "plea bargains". Conciliation, on the other hand, is directed to finding a way forward that both parties can accept as fair or just or reasonable. This is, for instance, the role played by Family Conciliation Services in relation to questions of residence and contact on divorce. The object is to get the parents to find a scheme which they can agree to be in the best interests of their children, irrespective of all the other factors which set them at odds with one another.

Mediation and conciliation, however classified, tend to have a limited role within the officially constructed framework of dispute resolution. Generally speaking, the existence of such processes outside it is regarded as irrelevant. For example, whilst the decisions of arbiters cannot normally be challenged in the courts, the recommendations that follow conciliation proceedings - such as those afforded to customers with complaints by the Radio, Electrical and Television Retailers' Association - are just that. They are no bar to those who remain dissatisfied seeking a judicial decision instead.

On the other hand there is, of course, the role played by Conciliation Officers from the Advisory, Conciliation and Arbitration Service (ACAS) in the early stages of cases brought before industrial tribunals. The fact that only about 40% of such cases actually come to a hearing suggests a high rate of success.[17] Recently, too, a new rule of court has allowed sheriffs to refer couples in dispute over residence or contact

[17] Even if some of the "fallout" is accounted for by failure of nerve, taking the line of least resistance and so on. See Cosmo Graham and Norman Lewis, 'The Role of ACAS in Equal Pay and Sex Discrimination Cases' EOC, June 1985.

to the local Family Conciliation Service.[18] To some this is seen a a sensible acknowledgement of the fact that the courts are not the best bodies to deal with this kind of problem. To others it is, rather, yet another example of law attempting to colonise relations in the wider social world.

By contrast, there are clear attempts, particularly within the business part of that social world, to keep dispute resolution outwith the officially constituted framework. Apart from the tendency to increased (and sometimes enforced) self regulation and the growth of internally promoted mechanisms for resolving customer complaints,[19] firms are seeking ways to avoid litigation, and even arbitration, between themselves. This is shown by the steady growth in membership since its launch in the UK in November 1990 of the - originally American - non-profit making Centre for Dispute Resolution (CEDR), which uses techniques such as "the mini trial" or mediation to facilitate negotiated settlements, as also by the developing programme of voluntary based Mediation UK.

As far back as 1963 Stewart Macaulay questioned the extent to which business relations are, anyway, conducted in terms of contract law.[20] Pursuing some of these ideas in 1990, Britt-Mari Blegvad wrote:

> What is often desired in modern business is not application of a past-oriented rule granted on legal entitlement but a future-oriented solution where the disputing parties are defined as parties to a shared situation and where co-operative means rather than legal constraints are needed. If this description is plausible, it is easier to understand the present role of the Danish Maritime and Commercial Court. The court continues to serve the societal need for regulation. Dispute settlement based on the *relations* between the parties has become the core of its work, displacing to a degree dispute settlement based on formal rules.

[18] Rules 170B(15) and 260D(10) in the Court of Session and Rule 132F in the Sheriff Court. It should be noted that while reference to the service may be thought of as compulsory, a conciliated outcome cannot be so. Further, even where the conciliation does work, the agreement still has to be endorsed by the Sheriff.

[19] See later in this chapter.

[20] Stewart Macaulay, 'Non-Contractual Relations in Business: A Preliminary Study' (1963) 28 *American Sociological Review* 55.

> Equity, rather than predictability of outcome, will be given pride of place and compromises will be the result.[21]

It is clear then, even from this far from comprehensive account, that there are various different approaches to the settlement of disputes. Whilst the law is sometimes thought of as confining itself to "courts" and "adjudication", it is capable of employing a much greater variety of techniques. That said, it can be argued that much of this kind of ADR, through certain fixed procedures and an increasing orientation towards precedents, has become far more court-like than desirable.[22] Those who look to reform disagree about the best approach. Some would restructure the system completely, seeking genuine informality and/or rules allowing wide discretion to the decision makers. Others would promote the training and use of para-legals, so as to allow those who cannot afford lawyers greater access to the necessary expertise. Others still would argue for the extension of legal aid to tribunals, with the object of making legal representation the norm. Whichever of the above is favoured, it seems clear that there is a sufficient variety of internally generated dispute resolution processes to make an exclusive concentration on the judiciary inappropriate for the purpose of determining what the law is on any given matter.

The range of sources

As indicated earlier, the second ground for having reservations about proceeding by looking to what the judiciary (or even all official dispute resolvers) may legitimately take into account arises from the existence of disagreement, one, as to just what this encompasses and, two, as to which of the things that they may take into account actually form part of the law.

---

[21] Britt-Mari Blegvad, 'Commercial Relations, Contract and Litigation in Denmark: A Discussion of Macaulay's Theories' (1990) 24 *Law and Society Review* 397 at p 409.

[22] For example, there has been recent criticism of the degree of formality with which, in some courts at least, the small claims procedure has been conducted. See Alan A Paterson and T St John Bates, *The Legal System of Scotland: Cases and Materials* (Edinburgh: W.Green/Sweet & Maxwell, 1993) pp 13-20 and also *Kulinski* v *Hassell* 1993 SLT (Sh Ct) 23.

On the first point, for example, is it regarded as - and should it be regarded as - legitimate for judges to take policy considerations into account? On the second point, does the law consist of everything that judges may take into account or only of those items that they **must** take into account? Or, perhaps, is it comprised only of the ones that, whether judges must - or merely may - take them into account, involve the imposing of duties or the granting of rights?

Legislation and judicial decisions. What does at least seem to be relatively uncontroversial is that, where Scots law is concerned, both legislation and judicial decisions have to be considered and, for those involved in the application of the law, followed within certain bounds. Legislation in this context includes both Acts of Parliament and delegated legislation, that is statutory instruments issued by Ministers, for example in making detailed regulations under an Act or bringing the whole or parts of it into effect. Besides what comes from Westminster, such rules of statute law include Acts of the Scottish Parliament before 1707 and, since 1972, the legislation of the European Communities. The collection of the old Scottish statutes is incomplete. In consequence they are a defective source in the sense of a place one can look to find out what the law is. Scots statutes are, anyway, subject to desuetude - that is tacit repeal through long term contrary usage[23] - and may thus turn out to be no longer counted as law. They have, therefore, a very limited role as a source of law. By contrast, Regulations and Directives issuing from the European Communities have an increasing one. Community law apart, statute law has priority as a source of law, in the sense that it prevails over all other sources of law. One striking illustration of this is the *Burmah Oil Case*,[24] in the course of which it was made known to the judges that, if they decided in favour of Burmah Oil, Parliament would legislate to alter the law in retrospect. The judges did decide in favour of Burmah Oil and Parliament did so legislate, in the form of the War Damages Act 1965.

The priority given to statute law has not, however, diminished the role of the judiciary. Most areas of law are mixed - from the criminal law, where statute has only made limited inroads, to sale of goods,

---

[23] See *Brown* v *The Magistrates of Edinburgh* 1931 SLT 456.

[24] *Burmah Oil Company* v *Lord Advocate* 1964 SC (HL) 117.

where the basis is almost entirely statutory.[25] Statutes are, of course, anyway in need of interpretation and such interpretations themselves form part of the case law. Case law itself offers a strong source of law in the shape of precedents. These are previously decided cases regarded as raising substantially the same issues as the case presently under consideration. By custom judges consider themselves bound to follow an earlier case unless they can find some fact or factor that allows them to distinguish the present case from it or to overrule the earlier case. Just what it is in the earlier case that judges are bound to follow has been the subject of a great deal of jurisprudential discussion.[26] It is broadly agreed to be the *ratio decidendi* but numerous explanations have been offered as to what is meant by the term. It is, perhaps, most clearly understood as the legal ground offered by the judge as justification for finding in favour of one party rather than another.

Finding the *ratio* is, however, complicated by the fact that, in the course of their opinions, judges may appear to offer a number of possible grounds or may not state clearly what the ground is. Further, in cases where several judges are involved, those in the majority may be offering different grounds for coming to the same conclusion. The *ratio* of case A, therefore, has in effect to be established by the judge in case B. It becomes whatever formulation of the state of the law he takes to have been crucial to the determination of case A. Thus, in the early days after *Donoghue* v. *Stevenson* its *ratio* was taken to have been that a manufacturer owes a duty of care to the ultimate consumer of his goods where there is no possibility of intermediate inspection.[27] Nowadays the *ratio* can be more generously interpreted in terms of the "neighbour principle" enunciated by Lord Atkin.[28]

It appears, then, that the operation of precedential decision-making is such as to allow the judge elbowroom in determining whether, if

---

[25] Even if, initially at least, largely consolidatory of the existing common law.

[26] See e.g. 'Precedent' in the *The Laws of Scotland: Stair Memorial Encyclopaedia* (cit. ch IV, n. 2) Vol 22, p 92.

[27] *Grant* v *Australian Knitting Mills* [1936] AC 85.

[28] *Donoghue* v *Stevenson* 1932 SC (HL) 31 at p 44, although with the exclusion of causing pure economic loss.

only on the facts, a previous case needs to be followed in the particular instance and, if so, what is actually involved in following it.[29] Certain other features may also weaken the effect of precedent as a source of law. Previous cases do not all have the same standing. Apart from those that have been overruled by a higher or later court, some will have been distinguished so often as to be regarded as relevant only to their own particular facts. Where the decision was located in the hierarchy of courts can also make a considerable difference. In Scotland, in addition, the tradition is that no decisions by a single judge are binding on any other single judge, irrespective of the status of the court,[30] though they may be regarded as highly persuasive. Despite some recent decisions giving effect to a contrary view, however, this is still probably the case where the civil law is concerned.[31] More generally, the doctrine of binding precedent was a mid-to-late nineteenth century development and it has never obtained quite the same grip as in England. Admittedly, decisions of the Inner House of the Court of Session[32] and of the High Court of Justiciary Court of Criminal Appeal are binding on the lower courts and the Court of Session always defers to the opinion of the House of Lords. The Inner House of the Court of Session, however, unlike the House of Lords between 1898 and 1966[33] and the English Court of Appeal,

[29] This would seem to be an example of what Ronald Dworkin calls 'weak discretion' - see *Taking Rights Seriously* (cit. ch IV, n. 57) p 31ff.

[30] So a Sheriff is neither bound by the decision of any other Sheriff (except those of his own Sheriff Principal) nor, it is argued, by that of a Lord Ordinary in the Outer House of the Court of Session.

[31] See *Jessop* v *Stevenson* 1988 SLT 223 and, subsequent to it, *Farrell* v *Farrell* 1990 SCLR 717; *Chalmers* v *Trustees of Peterhead Harbour* 1990 SCLR 387; *Cromarty Leasing* v *Turnbull* 1988 SLT (Sh Ct) 62; *Wright* v *Frame* 1992 GWD 8-447. Also T B Smith, 'Precedent in the Sheriff Court' 1988 *SLT* (News) 137; G Maher, 'Precedent, the Sheriff Court, and Colleges of Justice' 1988 *SLT* (News) 209; S C Styles, 'Jessop' 1990 *Juridical Review* 110.

[32] This is mainly an appeal court, although it does have a limited jurisdiction at first instance, for example to hear certain petitions.

[33] From the case of *London Street Tramways* [1898] AC 375 until the Practice Direction by the then Lord Chancellor, Lord Gardiner [1966] WLR 1234.

has never regarded itself as bound by its own decisions.[34] Further, acceptable grounds for departing from earlier decisions include such broadly defined factors as social change.[35]

Custom and Institutional Writings. Besides statute and case law, judges also look to custom and to the authoritative formulations of the law found in the institutional writings.[36] To a large extent these need to be considered together, since much of the writings consist in the reporting of customary law. For the institutional writers custom fell into two types - ancient and recent. Ancient custom was notorious, while the existence of more recent custom needed proof.[37] Some custom was native, some consisted in what had been adopted and adapted from the feudal, canon and civil law. Some was general, some local. Some derived directly from the community, some had been refined by court decisions and/or by formulations in legal literature.

It is important to note that, for the institutional writers, custom, whether ancient or recent, native or of foreign origin, general or local, written or unwritten, was clearly law. In the words of a later German jurist, custom was seen as 'the badge and not a ground of origin of positive law.'[38] Indeed for Stair custom, as declaring equity, was a more valuable kind of law than that to be found in the statutes. In the present day, custom has a more limited role, since much of it will have been overtaken by statute or been incorporated, often via the institutional writers, into case law. Even so, it still does occasionally have a direct bearing on the decision of cases.[39]

It is worth adding that judicial practices themselves - the priority given to statute law, at least where it expressly overrides case law or

---

[34] Although it will only overturn them following consideration by a full court. See, for an example, *Morgan Guaranty Trust Co of New York* v *Lothian Regional Council* 1995 SLT 299.

[35] See e.g. *Beith's Trustees* v *Beith* 1950 SC 66. Also on the maxim *cessante ratione legis cessat ipsa lex*, see *Commerzbank AG* v *Large* 1977 SC 375; 1977 SLT 219.

[36] See previous chapter.

[37] Stair, *Institutions* I i 16; Erskine, *Institute* I i 44.

[38] F K von Savigny, *Traité de droit romain* trans Ch. Guenoux (Paris: Firmin Didot Frères, 1840)

[39] Here it should be distinguished from custom of trade.

custom; the rules of statutory interpretation; the treatment of precedents and so on - are arguably forms of customary law. Certainly, such practices are more than mere habits, since judges consider themselves bound to follow them.[40] They involve an acceptance that there are certain things that not merely may but actually **must** be taken into account in deciding cases and that they must be so in certain defined ways. On this basis, the things that judges consider they must take into account, such as statutes and prior judicial decisions, are sometimes referred to as formal sources of law.

This is, however, rather misleading. Unless one takes the view, sometimes said to be that of the American Realists, that only the courts create law, what the judges must take into account are not sources of law but actual laws. In consequence, they are better referred to as formal sources of judicial decision-making. It should be noted, too, that, unless judicial practice of the kind mentioned above is itself regarded as a kind of customary law, we are more or less forced into the position of saying that the rules judges follow in determining what the law is are not legal but only social ones.[41]

Equity. Another source of judicial decision-making treated as formal in Scots law is equity. It is, however, difficult to detect distinct rules of equity. The role of equity has, in the main, been that of influencing the development of the common law,[42] the Court of Session, for example, exercising a general equitable jurisdiction as well as a special residual one or *nobile officium.* In consequence, a number of equitable principles can be read out of the more detailed rules of the common law and are regularly cited in judicial decisions. Those include the principles of natural or procedural justice, by which a party is regarded

[40] See H L A Hart's distinction between habits and rules in *The Concept of Law* 2nd edn (Oxford: Clarendon Press, 1994) esp pp 55-60.

[41] This is a point on which I am unclear about Hart's ideas. See ibid p 97, where, in discussing the idea of rules of adjudication, he argues that 'Besides identifying the individuals who are to adjudicate, such rules also define the procedure to be followed' but it seems far from certain that all of the practices amount to rules of adjudication. Many seem more like aspects of the rule of recognition, the status of which as a legal or social rule itself seems to be uncertain, see ibid pp 109-112.

[42] See Lord Kames, *Principles of Equity* 3rd edn (Edinburgh: Bell & Creech, 1778) p 26.

as entitled to a fair hearing of his case.[43] They also include principles of substantive justice such as that "no man ought to profit from his own wrong".

On the basis that judges clearly consider themselves bound to take them into account, it may be argued that equitable principles, at least, should be counted among the formal sources of judicial decision-making and, hence, as part of the law. This claim, too, may be made for other moral and political principles that have become similarly embedded in custom and the cases. It does not, however, find favour with those who believe that law consists only of particular rules that have been "posited" or laid down by statute or in the form of the binding part of a judicial decision. A similar problem arises out of the existence of codes of practice and of various forms of self regulation.

Codes of Practice and Self-Regulation. As with alternative forms of dispute resolution, some codes of practice are generated from within the system. They may, first, be issued by government ministers under powers delegated to them by statute. An example is the code of practice on 'Picketing' under the Employment Act 1980.[44] Others, though still subject to Parliamentary approval may, second, come from statutory bodies. Examples of these include the various ACAS codes, such as 'Disciplinary practices and procedures in employment'; 'Disclosure of information for collective bargaining purposes'; and 'Time off for Trade Union duties and activities'.[45] Similarly, the Health and Safety Commission may issue codes of practice relating to health and safety at work - for instance, that on 'Safety Representatives',[46] as well as approve codes on the same subject drafted by other organisations.

---

[43] e.g. *audi alteram partem* (both sides of the case should be properly heard); *nemo iudex in re sua* (noone should be judge in his own cause).

[44] Originally established under the Employment Act 1980, now under the Trade Union and Labour Relations (Consolidation) Act 1992 s. 203. For another example, see the Environmental protection Act 1990 ss. 2, 3 & 4.

[45] Respectively, replacing s. 17 of the Industrial Relations Act 1971; under s 17 of the Employment Protection Act 1975; and under s. 199 of the Trade Union and Labour Relations (Consolidation) Act 1992, previously ss. 27-32 of the Employment Protection (Consolidation) Act 1978.

[46] With the consent of the Secretary of State. See Health and Safety at Work Act 1974 s. 16.

Sometimes legislation requires such codes to be drafted. In other cases it is a matter of discretion for the minister or body concerned. Occasionally, instead, as with the Fair Trading Act 1973,[47] the statutory body has the function of encouraging various groups to regulate themselves by drafting their own codes of practice. Following that Act, a fair number of trade associations have produced such codes, including those involved with laundering and drycleaning, the sale and repair of electrical goods, double glazing, sales of photographic equipment and film processing, package holidays and funerals. A further group of codes are generated directly by the organisations concerned, either to avert the threat of legislation or to preempt any such threat. Examples of these are, respectively, those issued by the Press Complaints Commission, the Advertising Standards Authority, the Independent Committee for the Supervision of Telephone Information Services[48] and the code of professional practice issued by the Law Society of Scotland.

Whoever is reponsible for producing them, such codes of practice have a distinctive role. With certain exceptions - which are codes of practice in name rather than nature[49] - they do not require people to follow them nor provide the basis for civil actions or criminal charges. On the other hand, they are admissible in evidence before courts and tribunals and account must be taken of them in the decision. Thus, in the case of health and safety at work, someone complying with the code of practice cannot successfully be prosecuted under the legislation to which it relates.[50] By contrast, failure to comply with the code will be treated as sufficient to prove that an offence has been committed unless the accused can show that he or she has done what the law requires in some other, but equally effective, way.

Although, by and large, they have similar effects, there are, clearly, differences in status between the codes. This is particularly so in respect of those codes that are statutory in basis and are effectively

---

[47] s. 124(3).

[48] I am indebted to my colleague David Goldberg for this example.

[49] e.g. the Immigration Rules under the Immigration Act 1971.

[50] The Health and Safety at Work Act 1974 s. 17; the Health and Safety Regulations 1977. Similarly, compliance with the Highway Code operates to help establish the standard of the reasonable defender in delict actions.

imposed on the people affected by them and those that are matters of self regulation, whether entirely voluntary or not. The first kind may conveniently - if sometimes rather misleadingly - be classified as a type of delegated legislation. They can, accordingly, be seen as "posited", even though there is controversy surrounding the fact that the procedures do not always allow for proper Parliamentary scrutiny. In consequence, doubts about their status as law are confined to those who would insist that law must be immediately directed to the imposing of duties or the conferring of rights.

The category into which voluntary codes should be put, however, can be seen as presenting more of a puzzle. Thus, in the English case of *R* v *Panel on Takeovers and Mergers*[51] Sir John (now Lord) Donaldson M R opened his judgment with the following words:

> The Panel on Takeovers and Mergers is a truly remarkable body. Perched on the 20th floor of the Stock Exchange Building in the City of London, both literally and metaphorically it oversees and regulates a very important part of the financial market. Yet it performs this function without visible means of legal support.[52]

After considering the position of the Panel and of the City Code on Takeovers and Mergers which it administers more fully, though, he concluded 'Invisible or indirect support there is in abundance'.

As part of such support, he identified the Stock Exchange (Listing) Regulations 1984,[53] the Prevention of Fraud (Investments) Act 1958 and the Banking Act 1979. Thus, he considered:

> The picture which emerges is clear. As an act of government it was decided that, in relation to takeovers, there should be a central self regulatory body which would be suppported and sustained by a periphery of statutory powers and penalties wherever non statutory powers and penalties were insufficient or non existent or where EEC requirements called for statutory provisions.[54]

Accordingly, one way in which conformity with the City Code is maintained is through the fact that membership of the organisations represented on the Panel can be a condition of following a particular

---

[51] *R* v *Panel on Takeovers and Mergers, ex parte Datafin plc and another (Norton Opax plc and another intervening)* [1987] 1 All E R 564.

[52] at p 566.

[53] SI 1984/716.

[54] at p 574.

occupation - for instance, being a stockbroker. Anyone attempting to carry on that occupation once membership is withdrawn is liable to fall foul of the criminal law. This applies, too, in relation to other types of occupation, such as law and medicine. The professional bodies concerned establish rules and codes for the conduct of their members and disciplinary procedures that become operative in the event of non compliance. As the courts will only intervene in respect of such procedures in very limited circumstances - for example, where the requirements of natural justice have not been met - the professional bodies create what could be regarded as mini legal systems for their members. Even where carrying on the occupation does not involve a criminal offence, it may still be practically impossible, as happens in the case of trade union closed shops or of bans imposed by professional sports organisations.

Self regulation, then, whether through codes of practice or by other means, may exist in conjunction with "posited" law and gain indirect support from it. Equally, it may be generated by it, as happened with the Financial Services Act[55] and the establishment of the Securities Investment Board and its delegees, the Investment Management Regulatory Organisation (IMRO), the Life Assurance and Unit Trust Regulatory Organisation (LAUTRO) and the Financial Intermediaries, Managers and Brokers Regulatory Association (FIMBRA). Self regulation is, of course, not a new idea. It contributed heavily to the development of the law merchant, through the operation of guilds, as monitored by the Dean of Guild Courts.

Clearly, then, judicial (and other legal) decision-making is informed by the existence of codes of practice and by forms of self regulation in general. The way in which the decision-making is informed, however, is very much dependent on the circumstances of the particular case. It may vary from an assessment of the facts in the light of the code and its role to a refusal to interfere with the consequences of its operation. Such codes may, however, have been established by means that have no connection or only an indirect connection with statute law. The same holds for other forms of self regulation. Equally, these are not something produced by the judiciary, only given a measure of recognition by it. Nor do the codes of practice necessarily operate to

---

[55] 1986.

impose duties or to grant rights. Often their effect is, rather, to confer a measure of immunity.

For these reasons, some people have difficulty in counting codes of practice and self regulation as law, even though they are matters that judges may, and often **must**, take into account in deciding cases. Sometimes the problem is resolved by labelling them "soft law". Codes of practice and self regulation, however, are not the only things which raise questions as to their status.

The next chapter will consider more of them.

VI

AND SO TO IDEOLOGY

Sources continued

International treaties and conventions. These only take effect within the domestic law of the United Kingdom where they are expressly incorporated by Act of Parliament. The European Convention on Human Rights has not been incorporated in this way.[1] In consequence, citizens of the United Kingdom cannot seek redress for alleged breaches of their rights under the Convention in the courts of the United Kingdom. Indeed, it is only relatively recently that the English courts have taken its provisions into account at all in reaching their decisions. To date, the Scots courts have not followed suit.[2] It may, of course, be argued that they are bound to do so, if it is accepted that, although initially separately established, the contents of the Convention have been absorbed as fundamental principles by European Community Law. Certainly, that Community law can be a powerful instrument in this way is shown by the acceptance on the part of the Irish Supreme Court that even a Constitutional ban on abortion could not be given effect so as to prevent travel abroad for the purpose of obtaining abortion services.[3]

Even so, it is by no means clear that all the rights guaranteed by the Convention have been brought into our domestic law through Community law, while the Convention, qua Convention, remains

---

[1] The European Convention for the Protection of Human Rights and Fundamental Freedoms, of 4 November 1950, which entered into force on 3 September 1953; at the present time it has been ratified by twenty-eight of the thirty-one members states of the Council of Europe. Ten protocols have been added, the first dated 20 March 1952 and the most recent dated 25 March 1992. That, and the previous one, dated 6 November 1990 have not yet entered into force.

[2] J L Murdoch, 'The European Convention on Human Rights in Scots Law' (1991) *Public Law* 40.

[3] *Attorney General* v *X* (Sup. Ct., Feb 17, 1992); [1992] 2CMLR 277; [1992] ILRM 401. See also Articles 59 and 60 of the Treaty of Rome.

largely outside it. There is, therefore, something of a puzzle about its status. For, if one requires law to have been laid down by Parliament or in the course of judicial decisions; or directly to impose duties or confer rights with remedies attached; or, even, if one would confine law to those matters that judges **must** take into account in reaching their decisions, the legal standing of the Convention is in considerable doubt. At the same time, it is clear that some citizens, at least, within the United Kingdom do regard it as applicable law.

While the Convention may not be justiciable in our courts, the government allows a right of individual petition to the European Commission and Court of Human Rights in Strasbourg. A significant number of people every year do seek redress for perceived violations of their rights through this machinery.[4] This has covered matters as diverse as corporal punishment, union membership, telephone tapping, prisoners' rights and registration of birth. Admittedly, favourable decisions of the European Court of Human Rights do not have any direct effect. Full vindication remains dependent on an actual change in domestic law or administrative practice. Even so, there would seem to be something odd in ruling out even the possibility of counting the Convention as law where citizens in the United Kingdom are concerned.

Further, despite the fact that Treaties are claimed to require express incorporation, customary international law receives a degree of direct recognition. For example, in the English case of *Trendtex,* Lord Denning took the following view:

> Seeing that the rules of international law have changed - and do change - and that the courts have given effect to changes without any Act of Parliament, it follows to my mind inexorably that the rules of international law, as existing from time to time, do form part of our English law.[5]

Even if this view is not a universally accepted one, it does again indicate the complexity of the problem that the status of international law poses for legal theory in the United Kingdom. This can be contrasted with the situation in the Netherlands. There no treaty can be

---

[4] In 1994, 2944 applications were registered of which 236 were from the United Kingdom.

[5] *Trendtex Trading Corporation* v *Central Bank of Nigeria* [1977] 1 All E R 881 at pp 889-890.

ratified until it has received the approval of the States General. This is in contrast with the United Kingdom, where ratification is a matter of government decision. In contrast with the United Kingdom, too, is the fact that, once ratified and published, the provisions of the treaty take precedence over domestic law.[6] In certain circumstances, too, law making and applying powers may be conferred directly on international organisations.[7]

Administrative decisions. Here the problem of status arises at much more local level. Sometimes officials are left to their own interpretation of what the law requires. Where a Public Entertainment Licence is sought, for example, conflicting instructions concerning the standards to be met may be offered by two people working in different local authority departments, or even in the same one. At other times instructions to officials are issued by way of directions or guidelines, for example, the guidelines issued by Her Majesty's Inspectorate of Pollution under the Environmental Protection Act 1990 to local authorities concerning the issuing of licences to firms using lesser types of pollutant.[8] While directions are mandatory, guidelines are advisory and intended to indicate the parameters within which discretion should be exercised. Even so, there is evidence to suggest that they have sometimes been treated as mandatory and interpreted accordingly.[9]

The extent to which administrative decisions may be challenged is rather limited. Sometimes, as with the Social Fund, there is no appeal to any outside body.[10] Sometimes an appeal will only be successful

---

[6] Articles 65 & 66 of the Constitution.

[7] Article 66.

[8] s. 36(3).

[9] *R* v *Secretary of State for Social Services, ex parte Stitt* [1991] COD 68. See also *R* v *Social Security Fund Inspector, ex parte Sherwin; ex parte Roberts* The Times July 5, 1990.

[10] The review of determinations under ss 138-140 of the Social Security Contributions and Benefits Act 1992 is dealt with by s 66 of the Social Security Administration Act 1992. The stages of challenge are to a second Social Fund Officer; then to a Social Fund Inspector. Inspectors need not be appointed from within the Department of Social Security. Whilst limited by s 140(1)(a)-(e) of the Act and directions and guidance issued under it, they seem to have some scope for independent action.

where it can be shown that the decision-taker has used the discretion in a highly unreasonable way. There is now a well developed case law concerning the level such unreasonableness must reach.[11] At other times, however, the attack may be based on a point of law, in terms of the interpretation made of the statutes, statutory instruments or cases, whether directly or by way of the directions or guidelines issued. Successful challenges in Scotland have covered such diverse matters as the retirement rights of a prison officer,[12] fish farming[13] and the distribution of air traffic.[14]

Outside such successful challenges, however, administrative decisions, like various forms of self regulation, have the same kind of effect as law for those to whom they apply. This is illustrated very clearly by the situation relating to adoption. Under the Adoption (Scotland) Act 1978, a minimum age of 21 is specified generally for adopters.[15] There is no mention in the Act of any maximum age. Placement for adoption is, however, put by the Act in the hands of agencies,[16] which have developed their own guidelines. While these differ slightly from local authority to local authority, it is virtually impossible for couples around the forty years of age mark to adopt babies or young children unless and sometimes even when they already have blood ties with them.[17] The government has put adoption legislation under review because of dissatisfaction with this and other

---

[11] From *Associated Provincial Picture Houses* v *Wednesbury Corporation* [1948] 1KB 223 and known as "Wednesbury unreasonableness" . See for Scotland, *West* v *Secretary of State for Scotland* 1992 SLT 636.

[12] *Jackson* v *Secretary of State for Scotland* 1992 SLT 572.

[13] *North Uist Fisheries* v *Secretary of State for Scotland* 1992 SLT 333.

[14] *Air 2000* v *Secretary of State for Transport* (No 2) (OH) 1990 SLT 335.

[15] Adoption (Scotland) Act 1978, s. 14(1) (adoption by a married couple) and s. 15(1) (adoption by one person). A minor exception exists in the case of a married couple, where the one who is the parent of the child need only be 18, provided that the other is 21.

[16] Ibid, s. 11, which provides for restriction on arranging adoptions and placing of children.

[17] Hence the recourse by many couples who can afford it to overseas adoptions. See also *R* v *Secretary of State, ex parte Luft* [1991] Imm AR 382.

aspects of its operation. As things stand, however, since it seems unlikely that the courts would find the guidelines sufficiently unreasonable to sustain a challenge to them, an upper age limit does, to all intents and purposes, exist.

Another major example here is that of a considerable number of extra-statutory tax concessions. The Revenue itself acknowledges over 200 cases where statutes are read in ways that help the taxpayer if they would otherwise impose hardship or lead to results that were not foreseen by the legislation in respect of particular cases. Where employees are concerned, for instance, certain benefits - such as the provision of transport for late night travel to and from work, long service awards and attendance on external training courses - are not subjected to tax. Another instance of a concession in this area relates to s. 155 of the ICTA 1988 and the provision of meals in a canteen where these are available to all employees. The concession is to the effect that the canteen need not be on the employer's premises and that a ticket or token system can be used.[18] Judges have expressed varying views about the merits and legitimacy of such concessions.[19]

Policies. Since guidelines of the above kinds are the expression of policies, this brings their status as such into consideration. According to Ronald Dworkin policies should be understood as 'that kind of standard that sets out a goal to be reached, generally an improvement in some economic, political or social feature of the community. . .'[20] Again, 'Arguments of policy justify a political decision by showing that the decision advances or protects some collective goal of the community as a whole'.[21] Dworkin claims that policies as such should not be taken into account when deciding cases. Yet it is clear that Scottish judges do take things they call policies, particularly public policy, into account and that they consider themselves entitled to do

---

18 It must, it seems, be a canteen, though, and not a public restaurant.

19 Compare *Vestey (No 2)* v *IRC* [1979] 2 All ER 225 and *R* v *IRC, ex parte Fulford-Dobson* [1987] QB 978. My thanks are due to John Brown and Mervyn Lewis for pointing me towards these examples.

20 *Taking Rights Seriously* (cit ch IV, n. 57) p 22.

21 Ibid at p 82.

so. This is particularly obvious in the criminal law,[22] as shown in the case of *Smart* v *H M Advocate*,[23] where the accused, who had been charged with assault, substantially admitted the charge as libelled, but alleged that the complainer had agreed to a "square go". In holding that consent was not a defence, Lord Wheatley said:

> We are only too aware of the prevalence of what is alleged to be a "square go" in one form or another always leading to serious results. Accordingly . . . it is in the public interest . . . that it should be decided and made known that consent to a "square go" is not a defence to a charge of assault based on that agreed combat[24]

On some accounts policies, or at least political values, are - in hard cases at least - the determining factor in judicial decision making.[25]

There is, however, an argument that principles and policies cannot be distinguished in the way Dworkin suggests - in the first of the two quotations anyway. Policies, according to MacCormick, do not set out goals but, rather, consist in courses of action intended to secure existing goals. The example given is that of a government which, having the goal of "reducing the rate of inflation" - introduces an incomes policy.[26]

On this basis, to say that judges implement policies is to say that they adopt approaches to decision-making intended to secure goals

---

[22] And even more so in relation to special defences - see e.g. the case of *Carraher* v *H M Advocate* 1946 JC 108, 1946 SLT 225, where proof of psychopathic personality was considered inadequate to ground the special defence of diminished responsibility and the subsequent evidence of Lord Cooper to the Royal Commission on Captial Punishment: 'At the time of the Carraher judgment the lawyers had become alarmed at the flood of psychological or psychiatric evidence introducing, or attempting to introduce, as new special defences, all kinds of psychological or mental abnormalities . . . It was in reaction to that, I think, that the Carraher decision was pronounced'. (Q. 5468). For a more recent example, see *Brennan* v *H M Advocate* 1977 JC 38, which is discussed in chapter VII.

[23] 1975 JC 30; 1975 SLT 65.

[24] 1975 JC 30 at p 34; 1975 SLT 65 at p 67. See now also *R* v *Brown* [1994] 1 AC 212 ("the sado-masochism case").

[25] See J A G Griffith, *The Politics of the Judiciary* (cit. ch IV, n.69).

[26] MacCormick, *Legal Reasoning and Legal Theory* (cit. ch IV, n. 56) at p 262. See also especially the excursus to ch IX.

regarded as legally appropriate. Accordingly, references to policies, policy arguments or policy considerations are used as ways of pointing to a link between the circumstances of a given case and such goals. This is illustrated by the dictum of Lord Denning in the English case of *Miliangos* v *Geo. Frank*:

> It would seem very hard on the Swiss supplier that, instead of receiving Swiss francs worth over £60,000, as the contract required, he should get sterling worth £41,000. It would mean that the English company could be taking advantage of their own wrong.[27]

The policy argument in this example, as in many others, becomes simply the assertion that a particular principle is of relevance to, and must be taken account of, in the decision. Further, formal justice requires that following it or discounting it in this decision means doing so in all like decisions. Of course, judges may disagree about what the outcome of implementing the principle would be for any given goal, but this does not mean that there need be any disagreement about the goal as such.[28]

If, on the other hand, policies are identified with goals, to say that judges decide cases on the basis of policies is to say that they decide them so as to make the outcome fit with some predetermined goal. This does not mean, however, that judges can adopt whatever goals they choose or use any methods they please for achieving them. Both need to be validated by some existing rule or principle. Thus, in the *Kay* case the Lord Ordinary, on appeal, was said to have gone 'far outwith the judicial role . . . in giving a decision in favour of one party on a ground of his own devising . . .' namely as to how an overdose of penicillin might have materially contributed to deafness following on meningitis.[29]

On the other hand in the English case of *Duke* v *GEC Reliance Ltd*,[30] the goal of protecting employers from liability for unfair dismissal for operating discriminatory retirement ages was felt to be

---

[27] *Miliangos* v *George Frank (Textiles) Ltd* [1976] QB 487 at p 500.

[28] As, for example, whether or not a particular decision would "open the floodgates". See e.g. *Bourhill* v *Young* 1942 SC(HL) 76.

[29] *Kay's Tutor* v *Ayrshire and Arran Health Board* 1986 SLT 435, per Lord Emslie at p 440.

[30] [1988] 1 All E R 626.

compatible with the terms of the Equal Pay Act 1970 and the Sex Discrimination Act 1975 and with the fact that employers were not directly liable under Community law. A policy argument, in the first sense discussed, was also brought in to link the circumstances of the case with the interpretation arrived at:

> It would be most unfair to the respondent to distort the construction of the 1975 Sex Discrimination Act in order to accommodate the 1976 equal treatment directive as construed by the European court in the 1986 *Marshall* case. As between the appellant and the respondent the equal treatment directive did not have direct effect and the respondent could not reasonably be expected to reduce to precision the opaque language which constitutes both the strength and the difficulty of some Community legislation. The respondent could not reasonably be expected to appreciate the logic of the Community legislators in permitting differential retirement pension ages but prohibiting differential retirement ages.[31]

It might, of course, have been the goal of giving women equal treatment with men that was given priority. Such a goal is clearly compatible with the statutes as construed according to the Equal Treatment Directive, as required by Community law. In this case the policy argument, in the first sense discussed, might have run:

> It is most unfair on the appellant that she should have been forced to retire at the age of 60, to have been deprived of an occupation which she might have enjoyed for five more years, as well as an appreciably higher income. . .

What is clear, however, about policies - whether they are understood as courses of action or as goals - is that they are different in character from all the other things mentioned to date of which judges may take account. Unlike statute law, precedents, authoritative statements, principles, equity and custom - even guidelines and codes of practice - they do not of themselves set standards to which human behaviour ought to conform. Instead they are considerations that influence, within defined limits, the selection, interpretation and application of such standards.

The extent to which any course of action or goal ought itself to be pursued is, of course, a matter of debate. Some goals, internal to the law, such as certainty and the treatment of like cases alike, are clearly regarded as respectable. Various well entrenched courses of action directed toward achieving them may take on a normative status as

[31] At p 627.

doctrines. Thus, a simple practice of considering earlier cases, in pursuit of goals such as certainty and formal justice, may develop gradually to a stage where a doctrine of binding precedent becomes adopted. At the same time, certainty and predictability can be set against other goals regarded as internal to the system, such as that of doing substantive justice. Pursuing such a goal may lead to a policy decision to overrule a previous decision. Again in *Miliangos* v *Geo. Frank*, the following quotation from Lord Simon of Glaisdale illustrates his desire to reconcile the two by means of adopting a course of action involving prospective overruling:

> Overruling Havana [1961] AC 1007 involves that the law must be deemed always to have been as my noble and learned friends now declare it. This may affect the vires of some Rules of Court; but beyond this there has been, so far as I have seen, no consideration of what consequences the retrospective alteration of the law (for, let us face it, that is the reality) may have. I would be more ready to go along with my noble and learned friends if the decision had prospective effect only. One of the several reasons why radical law reform is in general more appropriately carried out by Parliament is that a statute can (and usually does) operate prospectively. I venture once again to plead that consideration should be given to the various forms of prospective overruling such as obtain in some other common law systems.[32]

It is for this kind of reason that policies are central to the understanding of Zweigert and Kötz's fifth and final aspect of style - the ideology of a system.

Ideology

The terms "ideology" and "ideological" are often used pejoratively so as to imply a partial, and by implication distorted, view of the way things are or ought to be. They are often used in political debate, along with other key words, in a derogatory fashion. Nigel Harris identifies some of them, and alternative formulations, as follows:

> *the idéologist* (that is, the person with whom the speaker disagrees) is *dogmatic* (loyal to his beliefs), *doctrinaire* (uncompromising, clear), *rigid* (principled), *aggressive* (keen, enthusiastic) *Messianic* (hopeful of a final solution), *apocalyptic* (fears a final disaster), *totalitarian* (beliefs are coherently unified and relatively comprehensive), *brainwashed*

[32] [1976] AC 443 at p 490.

(persuaded), *devoted to myth and illusion* (believes what he believes), and so on.[33]

In a neutral sense, however, "ideology" means simply a (relatively) coherent set of ideas, whether apparently of fact or value, about the nature of the world and of those who inhabit it.

Looked at in this way, the ideology of a legal system consists of a particular set of ideas. Some of these ideas can be classified as specifically legal. Others, however, are ones that the system has taken on board out of the more general set of ideas informing the society in which it operates. Our entire criminal law, for example, is based on the premise that human beings are possessed of free will and so are able to choose whether or not to engage in behaviour deemed to be criminal.[34] For Scots law, as with most of the western systems, many of the ideas in this more general set stem originally from Graeco-Roman culture and from the Judaeo-Christian tradition. They have, of course, been conditioned by developments in scientific, philosophical and religious thought. They have taken on a form which, in some cases, is individual to Scotland. The adopting of a particular type of Protestantism, together with associated views as to the role of the church, offers a clear example. Various aspects of its impact - from constitutional understandings to the law of divorce - have already been mentioned.

Any attempt to give an account of the ideology of a legal system in terms of the more general set of ideas by which it is informed is, however, complicated by the following considerations. First, and most daunting, there is the extent of the exercise. Second, there is a problem about coherence. As mentioned in the first chapter, there are arguments to the effect that our ideas are determined for us. They are already built in to the structure of reality as it is or as it is for us, whether they come from God or result from the character of our minds or brains, alone or in interplay with nature, or are the offshoot of material factors, such as the modes of production. Even if these arguments are accepted, the notion that the ideas themselves will fit together presupposes two things. First, that the structure of reality is itself coherent. Second, that all of the more general ideas upon which the law rests reflect the same

33 *Beliefs in Society: the problem of ideology* (Middlesex: Watts, 1968) p 26.

34 Consider, for example, the whole notion of *mens rea* and the existence of defences such as involuntariness and insanity.

level of understanding of reality or the same stage of development within it. Equally, on other arguments, our ideas are simply things that we, as human beings, happen to have developed. In which case any coherence between them can only be a matter of accident or, perhaps, of gradual approximation over time. It follows that, whichever the philosophical approach, it is by no means clear that the ideas we identify will form an even relatively coherent set - other, perhaps, than as a result of deliberate attempts at their manipulation within limited areas. Yet, unless all of them are included, the account will be an ideological one in the pejorative sense.

Third, there is the problem of location. The notion of ideology implies that the ideas concerned are shared ones. While having some shared ideas is obviously a precondition for social co-existence, it is flying totally in the face of the evidence to suggest that anything near uniformity is required.[35] There clearly are competing ideologies within most, if not all, societies, whether evidenced by the existence of deviant sub-groups or a plurality of political parties or a variety of religious sects or differences in occupational ethos or whatever. The existence of such competing ideologies manifests itself regularly within the legal process. The English case of *Gillick* provides a striking example.[36] This concerned a DHSS circular on family planning which recognised that, in exceptional cases, it might be appropriate for doctors to prescribe contraceptives to patients under the age of 16 without consulting their parents. Mrs Gillick sought to establish that not only consultation but actual parental consent was required.

Lord Fraser of Tullybelton considered the extent of the legal capacity to be accorded to a girl under 16, the purpose of parental rights, and the appropriate scope for the exercise of clinical judgment by doctors. He concluded that such capacity could include the capacity to consent to contraceptive treatment, that parental rights did not exist for the benefit of the parent but for the benefit of the child and that

[35] cf. Charles Taylor's point in 'Interpretation and the Sciences of Man' in *Philosophy and the Human Sciences* (cit. Intro, n. 7) p 15, esp p 46ff, that ideology can be seen as providing a set of shared social meanings that provide the framework within which disagreement is possible.

[36] *Gillick* v *West Norfolk and Wisbech A H A and another* [1985] 3 All E R 402.

there might be circumstances in which the doctor 'is a better judge of the medical advice and treatment which will conduce to a girl's welfare than her parents.'[37] He reached this conclusion partly on the basis of an assessment of the existing cases and statutes; partly on the basis of reflections on the nature of child development, changing social attitudes to parental authority and the likely practical effects of a parental veto; and partly on a judgment as to which course would best serve the welfare of the child.

Lord Scarman, too, found against Mrs Gillick but, in doing so, sought to look beyond the details of the law, which might be appropriate only to their own time, to identify the underlying principle. In this case he found it to be that 'parental rights are derived from parental duty and exist only so long as they are needed for the protection of the person and property of the child'[38] and that 'parental right yields to the child's right to make his own decisions when he reaches a sufficient understanding and intelligence to be capable of making up his own mind on the matter requiring decision'.[39] Lord Scarman also took the view that the Court of Appeal had been wrong to favour a fixed limit at the age of 16, since as 'nature knows only a continuous process, the price would be artificiality and a lack of realism in an area where the law must be sensitive to human development and social change.'[40]

On the other hand, Lord Templeman, dissenting, doubted whether 'a girl under the age of 16 is capable of a balanced judgment to embark on frequent, regular or casual sexual intercourse, fortified by the illusion that medical science can protect her in mind and body. . .'[41] He similarly doubted whether a doctor, acting without the views of the parent, could know enough of the circumstances 'to form a "clinical" or any other reliable opinion that the best interests of the girl require the provision of contraceptive facilities.' He felt, rather, that the parent was 'entitled to exercise parental rights of control,

---

[37] at p 412.

[38] at p 420.

[39] at p 422.

[40] at p 421.

[41] at p 432.

supervision, guidance and advice,'[42] and that only where the parents and doctor together failed to prevent the girl from participating in sexual intercourse should contraception be considered.

Contrary to Lord Fraser, Lord Templeman thought that the various statutory provisions taken together did indicate that an unmarried girl under 16 was not competent to decide to practice sex or contraception. Nor did Lord Templeman consider that, short of a direct pledge, confidentiality would be breached if a doctor disclosed to parents that their child had sought contraceptive advice. By contrast, the issue for Lord Fraser was whether abandoning confidentiality might 'cause some of them not to seek professional advice at all, with the consequence of exposing them to "the immediate risks of pregnancy and sexually transmitted disease"'.[43]

Clearly, then, the outcome of the case rested, at least in part, on a decision as to which of various non-legal understandings of the world should be given priority and thus become the legal one. On some accounts the priority given by the law will always be to the ideology of the dominant social group.[44] This does something to resolve the problem of location, provided that it can be shown to be true. There are, however, dangers inherent in such attempts. We can become involved in circularity by identifying the dominant group through the ideological understandings inherent in the law while identifying the law by reference to the ideological understandings of the dominant group. We are also likely to have particular difficulty in respect of the fourth problem that besets anyone trying to give an account of the more general set of ideas by which the legal system is informed. This is the problem of bias. It arises out of the fact that all ideologies consist of interpretations of reality. Since these ideologies actually exist, however, they too are part of reality. In consequence, offering an account of some particular ideology will involve a further interpretation of reality. Such an account must then itself be ideological.

---

[42] at p 433.

[43] at p 412.

[44] See later chapters, especially ch XI, with reference to critical legal studies and feminism.

This does not of itself mean that it will be ideological in the pejorative sense of giving a partial and distorted view of what the ideas actually are. There are, however, risks of misunderstanding and these grow greater the less we share in and approve of the ideas concerned. Equally, on the other hand, where we do share in them and approve of them, we may be so accustomed to that particular way of looking at the world that we do not realise that it *is* just a way of looking at the world and as much a matter of ideology as any other. For example, much black letter law teaching proceeds on the assumption that what is being taught is the law and not the law from a certain point of view. Further, simply because we do approve and disapprove of certain sets of ideas, it is difficult to avoid making our accounts of them value laden. Consider, thus, the following reports offered by meetings that took place in Scotland at the time of the French Revolution: first, from the Association of the Friends of the Constitution at Dundee:

> *lst* That it is the great object of this Society to obtain by constitutional means, *a reform* in the present *inadequate state* of the *representation of the people* and also a more *limited duration* of Parliaments. We doubt not that these two important improvements will furnish the means of correcting the glaring abuses which have been and are at this time justly complained of.
>
> *2d* We disclaim every design of attempting to injure the *British Constitution*. Our aim is to ameliorate its present form and restore its original purity. When notorious abuses remain uncorrected they must in the end necessarily produce the most unhappy convulsions. We cannot therefore avoid regarding as truly inimical to our happy Constitution, the conduct of those men who obstinately resist every proposal for *Reform*, and we account the timely removal of abuses the only method of preserving the excellent form of our Government.
>
> *3d* That we publish the intention of our Association, and call on such of our fellow citizens as venerate the constitution of this Kingdom, to unite with us and other similar societies, to obtain that *Reform in our Parliamentary Representation*, which we have avowed to be our great object, and which has long been the desire of the enlightened and public spirited men of the *Nation*.[45]

---

[45] Extracted from the Caledonian Mercury, No 11903, meeting dated 17 September 1792. In issue 11101, dated 22 October, a correction is offered to the report, including the substitution of the words 'to perfect and establish it' in place of 'ameliorate its present form'.

Second, from Culross, less than three months later:

> The Heritors and Inhabitants of this parish, taking into their serious consideration the dreadful consequences to be apprehended if an early check is not given to the attempts of Levellers and Republican incendiaries, who, under the mark of Reform, are doing their utmost to reduce this country to the situation of now barbarous France. . . , struck with the contrast between the present state of Britain and France, and grateful to God for the blessings we enjoy. . .we will support and defend our present Constitution. . .
>
> We earnestly recommend to such of our countrymen as are advocates for a reform, or more properly speaking an alteration in our Parliamentary representation, and who are not affected with the principles of Republicanism or Equality, that they would join with us and other good subjects in securing to ourselves, with God's assistance, the measure of blessings we at present enjoy, and postpone every reform, except the necessary reformation in our own lives and conduct, until it has pleased God to remove the dark cloud which now hangeth over the nation.
>
> We again repeat our abhorrence at such attempts as have or may be made by wicked individuals or Gallician organised seditious societies, to create distrust, sow discord and weaken that unanimity which should reign in the hearts and prevail in the councils of Britons. . .[46]

Given all these complications, it seems wise to abandon an attempt to look at the more general set of ideas upon which the ideology of the legal system rests and to confine ourselves to that ideology as such. Unfortunately, this does not make any of the problems disappear. For instance, even if, instead of considering the whole set of ideas articulated within Scots law, we were just to look at the pattern of values it expresses, the task would still be a daunting one. First, a full account of such values could not be derived from the substantive rules and principles of Scots law alone. Reference would need to be made to the goals pursued by legislators, judges and other practitioners of the law, as well as to the practices and doctrines directed to achieving them. Admittedly, such values can, in large measure, be found by reference to written sources - statutes, reports of judicial decisions and

[46] Extracted from the Caledonian Mercury No 11124, meeting dated 13 December 1792. Signed by the Earl of Dundonald, Lord Cochrane,Sir Charles Preston of Valleyfield Bart, Mr Dundas of Blair [plus 9 others], the Magistrates, Town Council and Town Clerk of the Burgh of Culross and by a very numerous meeting of the burgesses of Culross, Tenants and Inhabitants of the Parish.

so on - but this does not mean that they are always fully spelt out in them.

Second, it would be a mistake to suppose that the law reflects a uniform pattern of values. Those introduced into the law by legislation will differ according to the political complexion of the government in power. Such values will, over time at least, be made by the judiciary and other legal functionaries to adjust to other values within the system or to factors outside it, such as social change. Further, the values found in one area of law may differ from those found in another. In consequence, for example, a foetus is not regarded as a person in respect of the law relating to abortion but is so where antenatal injuries are concerned, at least where criminal liability is concerned.[47] The position is considerably less clear where civil liability is at issue.[48]

Even in a particular and quite narrow area, values may come into competition. Indeed, this is largely what makes a case a hard one. In the case of *B* v *F*,[49] for instance, the clash was between "freedom" and "security". One form in which the value of freedom finds expression is in the principle that no one ought to be detained without due process of law. At the same time, the law is concerned, among other things, with offering protection to and from people who may be a danger to themselves or others. In this case, because of a deterioration in the petitioner's condition, the doctors involved felt that it would be irresponsible to discharge him from mental hospital. The time for which they were entitled by statute to detain him had, however, elapsed. One of the doctors stated:

> Faced with a choice between protection and care of the patient, and abiding by the letter of the Mental Health Act, I chose the former option

---

[47] See *McCluskey* v *H M Advocate* 1989 SLT 175; 1988 SCCR 629.

[48] See *McWilliams* v *Lord Advocate* 1992 SLT 1045, contra *Hamilton* v *Fife Health Board* 1992 SLT 1026, as successfully reclaimed at 1993 SLT 624. For the position in England now see the Congenital Disabilities (Civil Liability) Act 1976; *McLaughlin* v *McLaughlin*, unreported.

[49] *B* v *F* 1987 SLT 681; 1987 SCLR 504. The decision of the 2nd Division was affirmed on appeal to the House of Lords, reported as *B* v *Forsey* 1988 SLT 572, *B* v *F* 1988 SCLR 504.

- a decision that was arrived at after very careful consideration, and which I felt to be ethically imperative.[50]

At first instance it was found that the continued detention was justified at common law. On appeal, though, it was held that the common law power to confine someone mentally disordered was now limited to private persons. Doctors and hospital managers could only do so as permitted by the mental health legislation. The Lord Justice Clerk added that the situation was a most unfortunate one and that he hoped that Parliament would alter the law so as to give medical practitioners some power to detain mentally disordered patients in similar circumstances.[51]

Again, in *White and Carter (Councils) Ltd* v *McGregor*,[52] two values clashed. The representative of a garage proprietor had entered into a contract for a display of advertisements for the garage on litter bins. The same day the proprietor sent a letter to the contractors, asking them to cancel the contract. They refused to do so and five months later began to display the advertisements. The garage proprietor declined to pay. The contract stipulated that, if any instalment remained unpaid for four weeks or if he was in any way in breach of contract, the balance due for the whole three years advertising became immediately payable. The law conforms to the view that promises ought to be kept. It is, accordingly, a well established rule 'that repudiation by one party does not put an end to a contract. The other party can say: "I hold you to your contract, which still remains in force"'.[53] At the same time, it is also well established, as an equitable principle, that a party offended by a breach of contract has a duty to minimise his or her loss.

By a majority of 3-2, the House of Lords considered the first of the two to have priority. In doing so they reversed the earlier Scottish case of *Langford & Co* v *Dutch*[54] in which, in very similar circumstances,

---

[50] *B* v *F* 1987 SLT 681, at p 681.

[51] 1987 SLT at p 690. See now the Mental Health (Detention) (Scotland) Act 1991.

[52] 1962 SC (HL) 1.

[53] In the words of Lord Morton of Henryton, dissenting, with Lord Keith of Avonholm, at p 16.

[54] 1952 SC 15, at p 18.

the Lord President had stated that 'the only reasonable and proper course, which the pursuers should have adopted, would have been to have treated the defender as having repudiated the contract and as being on that account liable in damages'. In *White and Carter*, Lord Reid expressed doubts as to what principle the Lord President had in mind and claimed 'It might be, but it never has been, the law that a person is only entitled to enforce his contractual rights in a reasonable way'. It would, he argued, 'create too much uncertainty to require the Court to decide whether it is reasonable or equitable to allow a party to enforce his full rights under a contract. The Lord President cannot have meant that.'[55]

Yet the courts had for years been deciding whether some contracts as such were unenforceable - namely those in restraint of trade. Of course, it is possible to reconcile the two approaches on an economic basis, since it may be argued that the repudiation of the contract was restricting the trade of the advertisers. Even so, it is interesting to speculate whether the decision in *White and Carter* - although not itself involving a contract of that kind - would have gone the same way had it come after, rather than before, the consumer protection legislation of the 1970s and 1980s.[56]

It seems clear, therefore, that, even if one were to confine oneself to looking at what are uncontroversially regarded as the formal sources of judicial (and other legal) decision-making in Scotland - legislation, judicial precedent, equity and authoritative statements of the law - an account of the values articulated by Scots law would be long and involved, contain a large number of uncertainties and be in constant need of updating. It would also, equally clearly, fail to tell the whole story. Whatever the status to be accorded to custom, to principles, to guidelines, to codes of practice and to various forms of self regulation, to doctrines and to policies, they are undoubtedly of relevance to the formulation of law in the cases. So, too, may be treaties, conventions, customary international law and - not previously mentioned - decisions

---

[55] 1962 SC (HL) 1, at p 14.

[56] For example, the Consumer Credit Act 1974, the Supply of Goods (Implied Terms) Act 1973, the Unfair Contract Terms Act 1977, the Consumer Protection Act 1987, the Consumer Arbitration Agreements Act 1988, and, in part the introduction, in the first mentioned, of a "cooling off" period in which withdrawal could be made without penalty.

and rules from other jurisdictions. Decisions from other common law jurisdictions are regularly cited in the courts, treated as law and regarded as being of persuasive force. Rules of foreign law are often central to the outcome of cases in private international law, even though such rules are normally regarded as matters of fact, rather than matters of law.[57] Even so, their influence is shown, for example, by the extent to which courts in the United Kingdom have recognised polygamous marriages and the Talaq form of divorce.[58]

Nor, by confining oneself to the formal sources of judicial (and other legal) decision-making, would one really solve the problem of location - that is, of whose articulation of the values is to count. One would, for example, expect the legislature's to do so. Yet the values embodied by a statute may be refined in the course of its operation. The extent to which this has happened cannot always be established by reference to the activities of the higher courts. For instance, it was in Hamilton Sheriff Court that use was first obviously made of the provision in the Family Law (Scotland) Act 1985[59] allowing pension rights to be taken into account as part of matrimonial property for the purpose of its

---

[57] *Sanderson* v *Armour* 1922 SC (HL) 117, per Lord Dunedin at 127; *Colville* v *James* (1862) 1M 41; *Campbell's Trs* v *Campbell* (1905) 5F 366, 373; *Emerald Stainless Steel Ltd* v *South Side Distribution Ltd* 1982 SC 61, 64 - although they are identified as questions of fact 'of a peculiar kind', see *Parkasho* v *Singh* 1968 P 233 at p 250.

[58] On the Talaq divorce *Russ* v *Russ* [1964] P 312, [1964] 3 WLR 430; followed in *Qureshi* v *Qureshi* [1972] Fam 173, [1971] 2 WLR 518 - but see now the Family Law Act 1986 s 44(1) which covers both jurisdictions and effectively precludes recognition of non-procedural divorces. On the recogntion of polygamous marriages in England see *Radwan* v *Radwan* (No 2). Scots law has traditionally been unsympathetic to the idea although the position is unsettled. See now, however, the Matrimonial Proceedings (Polygamous Marriages) Act, s. 2 of which applies to Scotland and provides for recognition of such marriages for the purpose of certain consistorial remedies; and the Private International Law (Miscellaneous Provisions) Act 1995, ss. 5 & 6 in relation to England, s. 7 in relation to Scotland.

[59] s. 10(5).

division on divorce.[60] Admittedly, the Sheriff's decision was sustained by implication in a case taken before the Court of Session in the following year.[61] Yet, even if this had not happened, other Sheriffs might well have been persuaded to follow suit and the practice, now routine, still have developed of solicitors advising clients to take pension rights into account in reaching their own agreements.

There seems to be a question, too, about the status of the provision in the four years before *Muir* was heard. There is no doubt that that particular understanding of what fairness requires was to be found in the statute law - but how fully can the value be said to have entered into the ideology of the law as a whole? Nor, just because some value can be found within the formal sources of judicial (and other legal) decision-making, can it be guaranteed that that value remains part of the ideology of the law. The Sexual Offences Act 1967 decriminalised homosexual acts between consenting adult males in private - but only for England. The parallel legislative change for Scotland did not come for another thirteen years, with the Criminal Justice (Scotland) Act 1980. On the other hand, in 1972, there was a direction to Procurators Fiscal from the Crown Office not to prosecute in such circumstances. There must accordingly be some doubt that homosexual activity of the kind concerned did still count as a *malum* in Scots law prior to the Act. A similar ambiguity existed in relation to a 1991 direction from the Crown Office, which limited prosecution in most cases where those involved were over the age of 18, rather than the statutory age of 21, until it, too, was overtaken by legislation.[62]

Although relating to a different type of behaviour, a similar example is found in a Crown Office Circular from January 1980. In 1974 the Government had tried to deal with the problem of travelling people setting up unauthorised encampments by reimbursing local authorities, initially in part and later in full, where they provided suitable and

---

[60] *Muir* v *Muir* 1989 SLT (Sh Ct) 20. Although see now *Gillon* v *Gillon (No 3)* 1995 SLT (OH) 678 to the effect that an agreement not taking pension rights into account will not automatically be unfair.

[61] *Little* v *Little* 1990 SLT 785, before the First Division.

[62] Crown Office Circular, No 2025/1, issued December 1991. (HC Debates, Vol 218, 844W), superseded by the Criminal Justice and Public Order Act 1994. Re-enacted for Scotland by the Criminal Justice (Scotland) Act 1995.

properly serviced sites in their own areas. A number of local authorities, however, failed to provide what was regarded as an acceptable number of sites. The Trespass (Scotland) Act 1865 provides that:

> Every person who. . .occupies or encamps on any land, being private property, without the consent and permission of the owner or legal occupier. . .shall be guilty of an offence.[63]

It could be regarded as inequitable, however, for prosecutions to take place in circumstances where the local authority concerned, particularly in the light of the incentives offered, had not taken steps to provide alternative sites. The Crown Office Circular accordingly required Procurators Fiscal to inform the Lord Advocate of cases of unauthorised encampment reported to them by the police, so that a decision whether or not to prosecute could be taken on all the circumstances, including the availability of local sites.[64]

Four main conclusions can be drawn from all of the above. First - and unsurprisingly - that accounts of the values articulated by the law will differ according to what is accounted law for this purpose. Second, that someone attempting to formulate a general statement of what the law on any particular subject is - whether as student, teacher or commentator - may well need to look beyond what is uncontroversially regarded as law, such as statutes and judicial decisions. Either that or admit that any statement of the law, defined in such terms, needs to be supplemented by a statement of various non-legal, but relevant, rules, principles, policies and practices, before anything like a full picture emerges.

Third, that those concerned with formulating the law in the context of a particular case - whether by way of prediction in the instance of a legal adviser, by way of persuasion in the instance of a pleader, or by way of decision in the instance of a judge and the like - will almost certainly look beyond what is uncontroversially regarded as law. In the first two instances this is because judges simply do do so: in

---

63 s. 3.

64 Normally, where no alternative sites had been provided, the Procurator Fiscal would be instructed not to prosecute. Where they had been, prosecution might be expected. In other words, the non-harassment policy was limited to,cases where the local authority's "pitch targets" had not been reached. (I am grateful to Iain Dyer for this example).

consequence, the adviser cannot advise well unless she or he anticipates how the judge will do so; the pleader cannot plead well unless she or he can do more than merely repeat the words of the relevant statute or previous decisions. The judge will simply do so because, unless the case is one where there is nothing to be determined but the facts, she or he will not be able to judge well - or even at all - without looking beyond what is uncontroversially regarded as law. For at least one of the parties must be arguing that this is inadequate for the purposes of determining the case concerned.

Fourth, and finally, whatever the data base used, one thing will hold good, no mattter whether the statement of the law is being formulated generally or in the context of a particular case. That is, the exercise will involve an interpretation of whatever it is - be they rules or principles or policies and, in the context of a particular case, the facts - that are under consideration. It is with problems associated with interpretation that the next chapter is concerned.

VII

MATTERS OF INTERPRETATION

In chapter III it was mentioned that, where the status to be accorded to the Treaty and Acts of Union of 1707 is concerned, the most straightforward argument is between those who see them as pieces of legislation like any other and those who see them as creative of fundamental law and as providing a (partially) fixed constitution. The possible interpretations of their constitutional effect cover a much wider range than that though.[1] The first - that, while the Scottish Act of Union destroyed the Scottish constitution, the only effect of the English Act was to give the Scots a minority role to play in English constitutional processes - and its rejection in *MacCormick* v *Lord Advocate* have already been discussed.

Second, it may be suggested that the Acts of Union destroyed the existing Scots and English constitutions and established a new unitary constitution for the two nations. They did so, however, only to the extent of specifying that there should be one Parliament for both of them. In this case only Article I (instating the new Kingdom) and Article III (instating the new Parliament) are of any real legal significance. Indeed, they sometimes seem to be regarded as fixed - usually by opponents of moves towards home rule - in a way that other parts of the Acts of Union are not.

It is worth remarking here that both the first and second interpretations have interesting implications for talk about the Scottish and English legal systems. For some legal theorists take the view that laws can only be regarded as belonging to the same system if they can be traced to the same source. According to the first interpretation, from 1707 the source of all law - either by active enactment or tacit acceptance - was the English Parliament. It follows that the Scots "legal system" has to be seen as a sub-system of the English legal system. On the second interpretation, on the other hand, there are no separate Scottish and English systems - both are sub-systems of the

---

[1] For a full discussion of the underlying issues see Upton, 'The Marriage Vows of the Elephant: the Constitution of 1707' (cit. ch III, n. 44). This is also rich in its citation of other sources.

British system. The same would follow from the third suggestion - that the Acts of Union destroyed both the existing constitutions and established a new unitary one for both nations which placed limits on the powers of their single Parliament.

Fourth, it may be suggested that the Acts of Union did not destroy either of the existing Scots and English constitutions but merely amended them. The effect was not only to limit the powers of the new Parliament but also to establish it in the context of a federal or quasi-federal British constitution. On this account the new Parliament was to be seen both as continuing the old Scots and English Parliaments and as a new institution, with functions for the whole of Britain. Although staffed by the same personnel in all three cases, their capacities remained distinct. The Scottish and English legal systems stayed in place but were joined by a third - the British.

Fifth, it may be suggested that the Acts of Union left the Scottish and English constitutions intact and simply delegated the functions of the pre 1707 Parliaments to a new body - the Parliament of Great Britain. That Parliament, within the limits set by the Acts of Union, was to act as a Scottish Parliament or an English Parliament as the occasion demanded. Sometimes it was to act as both at once. On the source of laws approach to identifying legal systems, it follows that there is no British Constitution, no British legal system and no British law - except as a shorthand term for laws with the same content that are applicable in both Scotland and England.

Just which of these views one takes seems to depend largely on how one understands the interpretive process. One of the problems with interpreting a legal document - or any written text at all for that matter - is in deciding just how its meaning ought to be established. Should the person doing the interpreting try to determine what the author had in mind or should he or she attempt to make the best possible sense of the text according to his or her own lights? Statutory interpretation in Britain theoretically adopts the author approach. What the judges frequently say they are doing is seeking "the intention of Parliament".

This is, though, necessarily a fiction. First, normally at least, some members of Parliament will have voted for and some against the measure. Of course, it can be argued that those who voted against passed through the "Noes" lobby in the knowledge that they were engaging in law making activity and that, in doing so, they intended any change voted upon by the majority to count as law. Acknowledging its status in this way, however, clearly does not involve making some commitment with the "Ayes" to its specific content. To claim that it does is as absurd as to argue that those who voted for the opposition parties in the 1992 General Election intended - a few highly devious tactical voters apart - to return a Conservative government. Insofar as those voting against a measure can be said to have any intention in relation to its content at all, this can only be that it should be understood in a way that is most sympathetic to their view that it should never have been passed in the first place. Second, it is possible that few - perhaps even none - of those voting for the measure were themselves "of the one mind" as to what they were trying to achieve. For example, those voting for the Employment Acts 1980 and 1982 were clearly in favour of curbing trade union power. How many of them, however, had any real awareness of the extent to which the words they used would permit of this being done?[2]

In consequence, the question the judges are really asking is not 'What did parliament intend?' but 'What should we deem Parliament to have intended?' The process is very similar to that in precedential decision-making, as considered in chapter V, where the judge, in the course of deciding case B, formulates a ratio for case A. In interpreting both statutes and previous judicial decisions, the judges are actually attempting to make the best possible sense of the text according to their own lights. According to these lights, however, their freedom to make this "best possible sense" is limited. For their role remains that of constructing a meaning that can plausibly be attributed to the author, the legislature. Just how much leeway they regard themselves as having in this respect depends on their inclination to the literal (or "conservative") or to the "liberal" method. Procedurally, at least, they normally begin with the former, looking first to the ordinary meaning - or, where appropriate, to the technical meaning - of the words in the

---

[2] See, for example, *Dimbleby & Sons* v *NUJ* [1984] 1 All E R 751; [1984] ICR 386.

statute.[3] Even this leaves room for disagreement, though, particularly where value laden words such as "fair" or "reasonable" are used.

It is accepted, too, that sense cannot be made of any section or subsection simply by taking its words in isolation, and rules have been developed about the way they should be read in context. For example, there is the *noscitur a sociis* rule, to the effect that the meaning of a vague word should be found from that of the words with which it is "keeping company". Equally, according to the "golden rule" of statutory interpretation, the statute may be construed so as to avoid 'any manifest absurdity or repugnance'.[4] The English case of *Federal Steam Navigation Co Ltd* v *Department of Trade and Industry* provides an interesting example of this in respect of a majority decision to the effect that the word "or" in a statute was being used inclusively, that is to mean "and", and not in an alternative or exclusionary sense, thus allowing both the owner and the master of a ship to be prosecuted for an offence.[5]

With the literal method, too, judges do not always attempt to make sense of a statute from what is found within its "four corners" alone. It is, for instance, quite permissible to look at other statutes in the same area and the way in which they have been interpreted to see if a word has taken on some technical legal sense, as opposed to the ordinary, everyday one. It is at this stage that the second main problem in deciding how the meaning of any text should be established begins to make itself apparent. This requires making a choice between those who would argue that any text can be "decoded" from internal evidence alone and those who maintain that it has to be understood in the context of some external reality. In the case of references to statutes in the same area it is, of course, still possible to argue that the

[3] It is suggested in by D Neil MacCormick and Robert S Summers in D Neil MacCormick and Robert S Summers eds, *Interpreting Statutes: A Comparative Study* (Aldershot and Vermont: Dartmouth, 1991) at p 533 that 'In all the systems studied here, the linguistic aspect of interpretation has the greatest prominence in the sense of nearly always coming first in order of consideration'.

[4] *Becke* v *Smith* 1836 2 M & W at 195.

[5] [1974] 2 All E R 97; [1974] 1 WLR 505. Although this sense of "or" is commonplace amongst logicians, it is not so often encountered in ordinary langauge.

text is being internally decoded. It is just that the text has been broadened. A literary parallel would be that of understanding a passage from Lewis Grassic Gibbon's *Grey Granite* not merely as part of a chapter in that novel nor even as part of the novel as a whole but as part of the whole trilogy that goes to make up *A Scots Quair*.

Even with references to other statutes, though, the text remains a relatively closed one. It is limited not just to the area of law concerned but also to one particular source of judicial decision-making within it. The text can, however, be opened up in other ways - to include Parliamentary debates as recorded by Hansard or Government White Papers or reports of Royal Commissions and so on. An opening up of this kind has been taking place in practice in recent years, with the most significant departure being regarded as that of *Pepper* v *Hart*, which allowed reference to a statement made by a Minister on a matter of taxation.[6] For some, however, the last, at least, involves too much of a concession to the liberal method. Although still concerned with decoding legislation "from the text", this method admits of two possibilities. First, the text may be broadened to take in other sources of judicial decision-making, formal and less formal, such as precedents not directly in point to the statute concerned and general principles. The words are then interpreted systemically, so as to make the best fit with another aspect or aspects of the law or with the legal system as a whole.[7] On some views, this results in too great a move away from authorial or legislative intention. Second, the words are again interpreted systemically, but on a genetic or historical basis, so as to make sense of them in terms of the "mischief"[8] the statute is there to remedy or the social and political role it, or allied legislation, has come to play.

---

[6] *Pepper (Inspector of Taxes)* v *Hart* [1992] 3 WLR 1032, making reference to Parliamentary proceedings before the passage of the Finance Act 1976. See Neil Walker, 'Discovering the Intention of Parliament' 1993 *SLT* 121. The Right Hon Sir Nicholas Lyell QC MP, '*Pepper* v *Hart*: The Government Perspective' (1994) 15 *Statute Law Review* 1.

[7] For more detail on this and later points see Zenon Bankowski and D Neil MacCormick, 'Statutory Interpretation in the United Kingdom' in *Interpreting Statutes* (cit. n.3).

[8] *Heydon's Case* (1584) Co Rep 7a at 7b.

Just what these are, however, is still supposed to be read out of "the text". What can be read out will, of course, depend on just how open or closed the text is taken to be and the direction in which it is extended. For those seeking to make the best possible sense in terms of authorial intention, it is clear that this direction must be a Parliamentary one. The argument then becomes one between those who would confine scrutiny to legislation alone and those who would extended it to recorded Parliamentary dealings of other kinds, even to certain ministerial pronouncements.[9] As put by Bankowski and MacCormick:

> sometimes, but rather rarely in the UK, the reference is to an actual historically formed aim or purpose of the legislators, discoverable from sources other than or additional to the text of the statute itself. . . the historical genesis of legislation is taken to justify imputing to the legislature as a legal institution the actual subjective motivation of leading legislators, or draftsmen, or participants in the preparation of legislative proposals or in legislative debate.[10]

On some accounts, however, this kind of activity is not a matter of broadening the text at all. It is, rather, one of making sense of the statute in the context of an external reality. On such accounts it is a mistake to believe that the meaning of a text can be established by identifying various possible readings and choosing the one that fits best into some internally coherent whole. If judges claim to be doing this they are misleading not only others but also themselves. For such an understanding of the interpretive process misses an important point about language. Language is located in the physical world. In consequence the meanings that it is used to express must bear some kind of relationship to that world.

A simple command like 'Shut that door!', for instance, has meaning only in a particular context. This includes: there being some object of the kind we call "a door" within range; of it having been left in the position we call "open"; the speaker desiring it to be in the position we call "closed"; and the speaker having the belief that uttering the

---

[9] Besides *Pepper* v *Hart*, other examples of recent inroads into what has been the more restrictive of the two views, as adopted in the UK, are offered by the cases of *Pickstone* v *Freemans plc* [1989] AC 66 and *Owens Bank Ltd* v *Bracco* [1992] 2 AC 443.

[10] *Interpreting Statutes* (cit. n. 7) at p 387.

words should (or at least may) cause some other person to make the physical movements that will cause it to be in the desired position. Accordingly, we cannot grasp the meaning of 'Shut that door!' simply by understanding "shut", "that", "door" and "!" and the grammatical roles they play. We have to take on board certain notions about physical objects, modes of action, psychological states and power relationships. One obvious difficulty with this approach is that it could bring in, in principle at least, the totality of our experience. In consequence, those who adopt it but still see law as having some kind of independent existence have to acknowledge that its content is being partly determined by outside factors. This is effectively Kelsen's position in the *Pure Theory of Law* where he sees the legal norm as a framework within which judges make political decisions.[11]

The idea that these factors form part of some external reality to be identified with the physical world is, however, regarded as a contentious one. For many would argue that language, as itself located in the physical world, is only sets of noises and patterns of ink on paper. It should, instead, be understood as part of the social world, as a means of communication. As such it reflects ways in which we perceive the world, rather than the world itself. Indeed, it does not just reflect the ways in which we perceive the world, it actually conditions them. On this kind of understanding it follows that law is not being adjusted to reflect reality as such. It is being adjusted to make it fit with extra legal conceptions or constructions of reality. All such constructions are at least open to question. Certainly few, if any, are universally agreed. Some of them contradict others. Not all are internally coherent. In addition, only selected aspects of some particular constructions of reality will be brought to bear in any given case. The selection of these aspects will itself be influenced by factors such as the interpreter's own experiences, by certain beliefs about the role he or she is playing and about the nature of the task in hand. As well as being questionable in general terms, then, the approach will also be partial and value laden. In consequence, interpreting some text so as to fit with it may introduce distortions of a serious nature. The outcome will be ideological in the pejorative sense.

[11] *The Pure Theory of Law* (cit. ch I, n. 2) ch 8.

The fact that judges, both in Scotland and the U.K. as a whole, are predominantly MACERS thus gives rise to serious concern. For the content of the law will come heavily to depend on the conceptions of extra legal reality that this one social group are prepared to accept or reject. How they may do this is illustrated very clearly by returning to the common law and considering the case of *Brennan* v *H.M. Advocate*.[12] A man had consumed 20-25 pints of beer, a microdot of LSD and, on some reports, a glass of sherry. Subsequent to this he had a quarrel with and stabbed and killed his father. He was charged with and convicted of murder. Murder in Scots law requires the physical act to be accompanied by a guilty mind or *mens rea*. This involves either deliberate intention to kill or wicked recklessness. A person who was insane at the time of a crime is deemed incapable of having had the necessary *mens rea*. Where someone is found to be of diminished responsibility, the quality of the crime is reduced from murder to culpable homicide.

At the appeal, it was argued for the accused that the trial judge had been wrong a) in not allowing the jury to consider the special defence of insanity and b) in directing them that the accused's state of intoxification did not entitle them to reach a verdict of culpable homicide. On the first point, it was held that the meaning of the term "insanity" for the purpose of the defence had nothing to do with the popular view. Neither was it to be established on the basis of medical opinion:

> It is, on the contrary, a question which has been resolved by the law itself as a matter of legal policy in order to set, in the public interest, acceptable limits upon the circumstances in which a person may be able to relieve himself of criminal responsibility. It would be a very dangerous and a very sad thing indeed if it ever came to be laid down as a principle of law that a man was not responsible for his actions because he had brought himself to a state like that of a madman by pouring a quantity of alcohol down his throat . . . The law holds that the man who brings himself into that state by drinking alcohol is responsible for what he does when he allows himself to get into such a fury that he acts like a madman and inflicts injuries on others.[13]

---

[12] 1977 SC (JC) 38.

[13] at p 44.

On the issue of diminished responsibility the court held - despite certain cases arguing in a different direction - that it was not necessary to consider the question of intention. For:

> Self induced intoxification is itself a continuing element and therefore an integral part of any crime of violence, including murder, the other part being the evidence of the actings of the accused who uses force against his victim. Together they add up or may add up to that criminal recklessness which it is the purpose of the criminal law to restrain in the interests of all the citizens of this country.[14]

Thus, in disposing of the first ground of appeal, the court clearly took a view to the effect that insanity and drunkenness are not the same thing. This conception of reality they considered to have been embedded in the law since the time of Hume's *Commentaries* in the eighteenth century. It could be argued, therefore, that an internal approach to interpretation was being maintained. Disposing of the second ground was, however, rather trickier. The way in which it was done seems explicable only in terms of an attempt to avoid the implications that would follow from taking certain extra legal conceptions of reality on board. For neither our ordinary nor our scientific understandings would encourage us to argue that someone who had consumed that amount of drink and drugs would have any kind of normal awareness of the nature of what he was doing - or be capable of exercising any normal kind of control over it. The court implicitly acknowledged as much by bypassing the problem.

Instead of locating the necessary *mens rea* in intention, they did so in wicked recklessness. It is not quite clear whether they "backdated" the beginning of the criminal act to the stage when (presumably) the accused started to drink too much; or whether they regarded this as the onset of the state of recklessness which continued in being until the stabbing took place, so that the criminal act occurred only at the point when the state of recklessness and the use of force came together. The quotation above seems to support the second understanding better than the first. Whichever understanding is adopted, however, both seem to rest on certain "purpose built" constructions of reality, set at some distance from our everyday conceptions of what "the act" and "recklessness" involve. Yet, implicitly justifying this kind of contrivance was the court's perception - whether or not well founded

---

[14] at p 51.

- of the dangers that would flow from allowing people to be regarded as less responsible for their actions when drunk. The later case of *Ross*, however, suggests that a different attitude may prevail in cases where someone is genuinely unaware of what he or she is consuming, as with a drink spiked with drugs.[15]

Clearly then, if the second view of the nature of the interpretive process is correct, there is room for considerable variation in outcome, dependent on the understandings of the wider social and physical world by which it is informed. Such variation can occur even within the "internal decoding" approach, though, given the range of what may be counted as part of the text. This is particularly apparent if one considers the difference between the literal method and that advocated by Ronald Dworkin. He insists that it is the duty of the judge to give people their rights according to the law, understood initially in the narrow sense of statutes and precedents and so on. What is significant is the contribution that the judge must make in "hard cases" to ensure that she or he is giving people their rights. This involves resolving conflicts or filling gaps in the black letter of the law by constructing and/or applying the appropriate principle. This principle should reflect what may be termed the "positive political morality" of the community, for if:

> some case arises as to which the rule book is silent, or if the words in the rule book are subject to competing interpretations, then it is right to ask which of two possible decisions in the case best fits the background moral rights of the parties. For the ideal of adjudication, under the rights model is that, so far as is practicable, the moral rights that citizens have should be made available to them in court.[16]

In his later *Law's Empire* he likens the interpretive process to that of writing a chain novel. He argues that:

> the most abstract and fundamental point of legal practice is to guide and constrain the power of government in the following way. Law insists that force not be used or withheld, no matter how useful that would be to ends in view, no matter how beneficial or noble these ends, except as licensed

[15] *Ross* v *H.M. Advocate* 1991 SLT 564; 1991 SCCR 823. Note, however, the restrictions subsequently specified in *Sorley* v *HMA* 1992 JC 102 and *Ebsworth* v *HMA* 1992 SCCR 671.

[16] Ronald M Dworkin, *A Matter of Principle* (Oxford: Clarendon Press, 1986) p 16.

> or required by individual rights and responsibilities flowing from past political decisions about when collective force is justified.[17]

The central notion is that of law as integrity which, he claims 'supposes that law's constraints benefit society not just by providing predictability or procedural fairness, or in some other instrumental way, but by securing a kind of equality among citizens that makes their community more genuine and improves its moral justification for exercising the political power it does'.[18] Unlike the mere de facto community, where people regard themselves as having no special responsibilities to one another, and the "rulebook" one, where they merely 'accept a general commitment to obey rules established in a certain way that is special to that community',[19] in this more genuine community people 'accept that their fates are linked together in the following strong way: they accept that they are governed by common principles, not just by rules hammered out by political compromise'.[20] In consequence:

> Members. . . accept that their political rights and duties are not exhausted by the particular decisions their politicial institutions have reached, but depend, more generally, on the scheme of principles those decisions presuppose and endorse. So each member accepts that others have rights and that he has duties flowing from that scheme, even though these have never been formally identified or declared. Nor does he suppose that these further rights and duties are conditional on his wholehearted approval of that scheme; these obligations arise from the historical fact that his community has adopted that scheme, which is then special to it, not the assumption that he would have chosen it were the choice entirely his.[21]

Under such circumstances 'each citizen respects the principles of fairness and justice instinct in the standing political arrangement of his particular community, which may be different from those of other communities, whether or not he thinks these the best principles from a utopian standpoint'.[22]

---

[17] R M Dworkin, *Law's Empire* (London: Fontana Paperbacks, 1986) p 93.

[18] Ibid pp 95-6.

[19] Ibid p 210.

[20] Ibid p 211.

[21] Id.

[22] Ibid p 213.

At the stage where integrity is brought in as an adjudicative principle it 'instructs judges to identify rights and duties, so far as possible, on the assumption that they were all created by a single author - the community personified - expressing a coherent conception of justice and fairness'[23] and requires each judge 'to test his interpretation of any part of the great network of political structures and decisions of his community by asking whether it could form part of a coherent theory justifying the network as a whole'.[24] In consequence of all this it can be argued that what Dworkin has done is broaden the text of the law so as to include within it at least the well entrenched political morality of the community. Insofar as accessing this morality is genuinely feasible for the judge, his approach does apparently get round the problem of decision-making which is ideological in the pejorative sense. For, whichever one's understanding of the interpretive process, judicial discretion is kept to the minimum.

There are, however, considerable difficulties with notion of law as integrity. Not least of these is whether it can accommodate cultural pluralism to the extent that Dworkin seems to believe.[25] Similarly, there seems to be an underlying assumption that the scheme of principles, the coherent conceptions of justice and fairness and the network of political structures and decisions that have established themselves do actually secure the 'kind of equality among citizens that makes their community more genuine and improves its moral justification for exercising the political power it does' - something that members of disadvantaged groups in general and feminists in particular may be moved to doubt.[26] For such principles, decisions and networks are seen not as the outcome of 'debate about which principles the community should adopt as a system, which view it should take of justice, fairness and due process' but of an operation by which the powerful have succeeded in planting 'the flag of [their] convictions over as large a domain of power and rules as possible'.[27] In which case,

[23] Ibid p 225.

[24] Ibid p 245.

[25] Ibid p 213.

[26] Vide, ibid pp 204-5.

[27] Ibid p 211. Consider in this context, the ideas of Jürgen Habermas (see ch XII).

adjudicative integrity looks set, if not to perpetuate the situation, at least to countenance only the slowest of moves away from it.

Ultimately, then, the understanding one has of the interpretive process depends on the view one takes in relation to much wider debates. Significant amongst these is that as to whether law is some kind of rational construct or the product of other forces. Further, if it is a rational construct, according to what principles (rationally) should it be constructed - ones already built into the structure of reality or ones that are peculiarly its own or ones that are designed to reflect extra legal understandings of the world? Equally, if law is the product of other forces, just what kind of forces are they? Do they - be they human instincts or economic modes of production or political power structures - have some life of their own, independent of human understanding and control? Equally, if law is the product of such forces, can it have any life of its own?

Just how the different approaches to interpretation can produce different effects can be seen from their application to the Acts of Union. The cases in the Sheriff Court concerning the poll tax[28] were raised under Article XVIII, which reads:

> That the Laws concerning Regulation of Trade Customs and such Excises to which Scotland is by virtue of this Treaty lyable to be the same in Scotland, from and after the Union as in England and that all other laws in use within the Kingdom of Scotland do after the Union and not withstanding thereof remain in the same force as before (except such as are contrary to or inconsistent with this Treaty) but alterable by the Parliament of Great Britain with this difference betwixt the Laws concerning publick Right Policy and Civil Government and those which concern private Right, That the laws which concern publick Right Policy and Civil Government may be made the same throughout the whole United Kingdom but that no alteration be made in Laws which concern private Right except for the evident utility of the subjects within Scotland.

Interesting issues were canvassed concerning whether taxation was to be concerned as only a matter of public right or of private right also, whether the article required or only permitted laws concerning public right to be made the same and whether if a law did concern private right the question of its evident utility was justiciable within the Scottish courts.

[28] *Stewart* v *Henry* 1989 SLT (Sh Ct) 34 and *Fraser* v *MacCorquodale* 1989 SLT (Sh Ct) 39.

For present purposes, however, most important is what was made of of the first part of the article. In his judgment in *Stewart* v *Henry* the Sheriff stated:

> I agree with senior counsel for the defender that the word "excises" in the context of Art. XVIII has the restricted meaning of a tax on commodities, rather than referring to general taxation. Thus it cannot refer to the community charge. In any event, as senior counsel for the defender submitted, the community charge is not a tax to which Scotland is made liable "by virtue of this Treaty". On both these grounds this part of the pursuers case is therefore irrelevant.[29]

"A tax on commodities" is clearly a justifiable interpretation of "excises" in this context, even if no argument was afforded to support it, given that it conveys the ordinary meaning of the term. If, however, the article is read in conjunction with Article VI, a different understanding of its effect may perhaps be generated. It runs as follows:

> That all parts of the United Kingdom for ever from and after the Union shall have the same allowances, encouragements and drawbacks, and be under the same prohibition and restrictions and regulations of trade and liable to the same customs and duties on import and export.

The words 'the same allowances, encouragements and drawbacks' can readily be taken to embrace taxation generally, with the later part of the article illustrating the areas which were the subject of particular concern. In that case the words in Article XVIII 'Laws concerning Regulation of Trade Customs and such Excises to which Scotland is by virtue of this Treaty lyable' could just be interpreted as covering all forms of taxation. This is made more plausible if a prospective reading is given to Article XXV (see below). On the other hand, if a historical view is taken, it does seem more likely that Article XVIII was strictly concerned only with indirect taxation, given that different systems of land taxation and poor relief persisted for a very long time after the Union. Yet again, can such a distinction readily be made, given that the Acts were passed at a time when personal taxation, such as that involved in income tax or the community charge, was scarcely known?

Indeed once one moves from a literal to a liberal reading, it seems possible to take the goal of *either* total *or* partial uniformity out of the financial provisions of the Acts as a whole. Clearly those that did

---

[29] at p 37.

maintain differences were mainly transitional ones. In consequence, one may question the implications of the view 'that the community charge is not a tax to which Scotland is made liable "by virtue of this Treaty". Is this meant to indicate that the 'Laws concerning Regulation of Trade Customs and such Excises to which Scotland . . . is lyable' are confined, despite the words 'from and after the Treaty' to those in force at the time of the Treaty? Or, perhaps, to the sorts of regulation of trade or forms of customs and excise then in vogue? If so, would the introduction of VAT a year earlier in Scotland than England been regarded as compatible with the Acts of Union?

By contrast, *Pringle, Petitioner*,[30] the case taken to the Court of Session, rested on the wording of Article VI. The petition did not mount a challenge to the legality of the Abolition of Domestic Rates (Scotland) Act 1987 or to regulations made under it. Instead it involved an appeal to the *nobile officium* of the Court of Session to relieve the petitioner of the burden of the sum paid for the community charge during the year that it had not been in operation in England. Their Lordships did not consider that this would be an appropriate exercise of their equitable power, since, given that the petitioner had not had to pay rates during that year, it had not been established that there has been any inequity involved. As it was not in direct point to the decision of the case, two of the three judges, the Lord President and Lord Weir, reserved their judgement as to whether any challenge to the legality of the Act could have been successfully mounted in terms of the Acts of Union.[31]

Further, even though it is possible to make direct sense of Articles VI and XVIII either on their own or in combination with one another or with other articles or with the provisions of the Acts as a whole, this is not the case with Article XXV. This reads:

> That all Laws and Statutes in either Kingdom, so far as they are contrary to, or inconsistent with, the Terms of those Articles, or any of them, shall from and after the Union, cease and become void, and shall be declared to be, by the respective Parliaments of the said Kingdoms.

The article is usually taken to refer to pre-Union Laws. Yet, on closer inspection, its ambit is unclear. This is particularly the case if one takes the view that the effect of the Union was to abolish the respective

[30] 1991 SLT 330, before the First Division.

[31] at p 333.

Parliaments. For non existent bodies cannot set about declaring that any kind of laws have become void. Of course, the wording can be explained away as a careless reproduction in the Acts of the terms of the Treaty and the "golden rule" of interpretation used to get round the difficulty. The Article could then be read as saying 'shall from and after the Union cease and become void, and it is hereby declared by the respective Parliaments of the said Kingdoms that they shall be so'.

Even with this much reconstruction, though, the article remains ambiguous. In consequence it is necessary to abandon attempts at a purely literal reading and to try to establish, on a genetic or historical basis, the goal to which it was directed. It is perfectly possible to take this to have been the abolition, prospectively and conditionally, of all pre-Union laws inconsistent with the Union. Again, those inclined to the second type of understanding of the interpretive process would ask to just what aspects of the wider social world at the time this could be made to relate.

Did the existing members of both Parliaments have some shared desire to save the new Union Parliament the trouble of legislating to the same effect? Was there some doubt as to whether the new Union Parliament would have the authority to invalidate pre-Union law inconsistent with the Union? Did members of one or other or both Parliaments lack trust in the new Union Parliament, believing that it might - despite the other provisions of the Acts of Union - leave in place laws operating to the disadvantage of people in the Kingdom they represented. Or was it just to ensure that aspects of the law only indirectly covered by the Acts were done away with too.

On the other hand, the article can be read as fully prospective. 'All laws and statutes, so far as they are contrary to or inconsistent with the Acts of Union or any part of them, shall from and after the Union cease and become void'. On this reading, the goal to which the article is directed, or at least was directed at the time, is transparent. Both Parliaments, in declaring laws contrary to the Acts of Union to be void, were attempting to bind the Union Parliament as their successor. Again, those inclining to the second approach to interpretation will be moved to ask to just what aspects of the wider social world this could be made to relate.

In the case of the Scots Parliament one may readily suggest a fear of English domination and a desire to erect barriers against their numerical superiority in the Union Parliament.[32] For the English Parliament, however, it is difficult to detect any similar basis for concern. Indeed all the Articles affording protections do so for the Scots. It seems likely, therefore, that different meanings can be taken out of the Scots and English Acts. The puzzle comes when they are read together, as happens, too, when parties have agreed the wording of a contract, but with very different ideas as to what that wording has committed them to.

Further, interesting though it may be to speculate as to how the Acts of Union should be read in the context of 1707, what is in more direct concern is their present day legal significance. For example, to which (if any) of the five different types of constitution - the English umbrella, the minimal unitary, the unitary limited, the (quasi) federal or the delegated - have they actually given rise? On a literal view of their wording, only the last three seem at all plausible. Yet, it may be argued, these bear little resemblance to how and where power is actually exercised. Even if law and politics can be separated, their relationship at this level is so close that a meaningful account of one cannot be given without reference to the other.

Clearly, to look at the wording of the Acts of Union alone is, for the purpose of establishing their significance today, far too narrow a procedure. For whichever method of, or approach to, interpretation is adopted, it will be coloured by contemporary understandings. It is better that these are made explicit. In consequence, the text must be broadened to include the whole body of law that has a bearing upon the Acts of Union. In terms of the literal method, if it is relevant at all at this level, the broadening would, one imagines, be confined to that part of the law in which the terms of the Acts have been directly defined - namely, decided cases. With a more liberal method, however, various levels of legal development could be taken into account.

Broadening the text also allows a measure of response to those adhering to the second understanding of the nature of the interpretive process. For what we are looking at is how the Acts of Union have really worked. Rather than saying we are "broadening the text", we could say that we are taking the Acts of Union and interpreting them in the light of how people have actually behaved with regard to them.

[32] That this continued to be a matter of sensitivity is evidenced by Bentham in *A Fragment on Government* (cit. ch II, n. 1) ch IV para 37 note 1.

Admittedly we are confining ourselves to the ways in which they have developed the law. But, since we are happy to admit that the law does reflect power relationships, there is no real quarrel between us. In fact looking at the law may tell us a great deal about how those relationships are structured.

The trouble is that, once we do start looking at legal developments, we find that they point in different directions. For example, one might cite the transfer of Admiralty prize jurisdiction in respect of Scottish waters to an English court applying English law in support of the English umbrella interpretation. The occasions on which the House of Lords have decided Scots cases on the basis of English law fit with this too. On the other hand, the marked constitutional changes that have taken place since 1707, including the widespread acceptance of the doctrine of Parliamentary sovereignty, lend most support to the minimal unitary interpretation.

Yet again, the facts that - matters such as the Universities (Scotland) Act 1853 honourably excepted - there has been no direct legislative breach of the Articles of Union and that some of the indirect ones have been repaired, argue for the unitary limited one. Similarly, the (quasi) federal interpretation gains ground when one considers that Bills are passed separately for Scotland, for England and Wales and for the United Kingdom of Great Britain. Equally, the delegation interpretation is assisted by the fact that there is no court established to apply the law of Great Britain, even though the House of Lords sometimes behaves as if it is so, particularly in matters of taxation.[33]

Needless to say there is room for disagreement as to just which rules, principles, conventions and practices should be read as part of the text/what legal developments should be counted as evidence. Certainly there are far more possibilities than the examples given above. There is even more room for disagreement as to the significance that should be attached to them. Nor is it all a matter of purely academic interest. To date the Scots courts have never attempted to strike down legislation of the Union Parliament as *ultra vires*. There have, however, been some broad hints that they might

[33] See, for example, *Lord Advocate* v *Earl of Moray's Trustees* 1905 7F (HL) 116; *Inland Revenue* v *Glasgow Police Athletic Association* 1953 SC (HL) 13. My thanks are due to Martyn Jones for the point and the references.

consider themselves as entitled to do so. A time may come when the issue has to be faced head on.[34]

Further, on the basis of at least two of the interpretations of the constitutional situation, it is possible to construct arguments to the effect that a Scottish Parliament could be established by non-revolutionary means outwith the normal Westminster processes. Whether any such course could be envisaged as a matter of practical politics is a very real question. Yet the answer depends, in some measure at least, on whether it could be convincingly portrayed in legal terms as "constitutional" or legitimate. From what has been said before, it is not difficult to imagine the form the counter arguments would take.

Equally, there are those who would regard all this constitutional analysis as, at best, of incidental interest. For they would rest their case for Scottish self government on the doctrine of the sovereignty of the Scottish people. Yet, there is a question about the nature of this doctrine. If it is to be regarded as a legal one then it must be shown to be so by means of arguments related - at some level at least - to the state of the law. Otherwise all that is involved is a claim of political or moral right.

What the discussion to date has clearly shown, though, is that there is by no means complete agreement as to the basis on which law should be identified and, thus, as to what actually count as arguments to do with the state of the law. Indeed, the debate about the proper basis for interpreting legal documents is really just part of a much wider debate about the proper basis for interpreting something as law. For example, the discussion about the existence of separate Scottish and English systems has, so far, proceeded on the basis of a particular assumption. That assumption is that laws can only be identified as belonging to the same system if they can be traced to the same source - discussed so far in the form of a specific constitution (or some norm underlying it).

In consequence, the first possible interpretation of the effect of the Treaty and Acts of Union was said to cast doubt on the existence of a Scottish legal system but to allow for the continuation of the English one. The second two interpretations led to the view that there is a

---

[34] See cases cit ch III nn. 55, 57 and this ch n. 28.

British legal system but no separate Scottish or English ones. The fourth suggested the possibility of three legal systems being in place - the Scottish, the English and the British. The fifth interpretation implied the existence of Scottish and English legal systems but allowed no place for a British one. Yet all of these assessments fly in the face of at least some facts. While the assumption on which they are based is itself open to serious challenge.

It is to a questioning of this assumption and to wider problems with the notion of legal system that the next chapter turns.

VIII

LAW IN WHOSE TERMS?

The assumption questioned at the end of the last chapter was that we must begin with a notion of what it is for something to be a legal system and then proceed to identify things as laws because they fit within that notion. It would be equally possible, however, to start by identifying things as laws and then look for some criterion that will allow us to determine whether or not they belong to the one system. That different conclusions can be reached, depending on which approach is used, can be shown by considering the European Convention on Human Rights in the context of the United Kingdom.

As mentioned at the beginning of chapter VI, international treaties and conventions only take effect within the domestic laws of the United Kingdom to the extent that they are expressly incorporated by Act of Parliament. The European Convention has not been so incorporated. In consequence the courts regard its provisions as having a very limited effect on their decisions. In England they have been willing to use them as an aid to construction where the terms of a United Kingdom statute have been ambiguous. In Scotland, however, a much more restrictive approach has been taken. Indeed, in *Kaur* v *Lord Advocate*, Lord Ross stated:

> So far as Scotland is concerned, I am of the opinion that the court is not entitled to have regard to the Convention either as an aid to construction or otherwise. I respectfully share the view. . . that a convention is irrelevant to legal proceedings unless and until its provisions have been incorporated or given effect to in legislation. To suggest otherwise is to confer upon a convention concluded by the executive an effect which only an Act of the legislature can achieve.[1]

Lord Ross's view was endorsed in *Moore* v *Secretary of State for Scotland*.[2] Although the Convention did receive consideration in the case of *Budh Singh*,[3] this related only to its relevance as a test for

---

[1] 1981 SLT 322, at p 330.

[2] 1985 SLT 38. See also *Leech* v *Secretary of State for Scotland* 1993 SLT 365 (Ex Div); 1992 SC 89.

[3] *Singh, Petitioner* 1988 SC 349.

unreasonableness in relation to executive action. Neither it nor a couple of other cases in which some mention was made of the Convention[4] have really eroded the *Kaur* approach. It has been argued that: 'Consequently, within the 23 member states of the Council of Europe, it is the legal system of Scotland which accords the Convention the least recognition.'[5]

Accordingly, if, as in the last chapter, one regards a legal system as a body of laws created in accordance with a particular Constitution or some norm underlying it,[6] it seems to follow that the European Convention on Human Rights cannot be counted as law where citizens in the United Kingdom are concerned. The same applies if one takes any other kind of source based approach to a legal system, such as explaining it as a series of commands, backed by threat of sanction, issued by some sovereign who is habitually obeyed,[7] or as a set of rules applied by the one group of courts and officials.[8] For it is clear that the Convention does not fit into any of these categories.

As has already been mentioned, though, the fact that significant numbers of U.K. citizens have sought redress through the Strasbourg machinery does suggest that there is something odd in ruling out even the possibility of counting the Convention as law where they are concerned. Yet, on the other hand, if it is so counted, a different problem arises. The basis for identifying things as law appears to have become undesirably vague. It has also, perhaps, become undesirable in other ways. Do we want to admit that, contrary to our ordinary constitutional understandings (whereby only Parliament and the courts

---

[4] *Martin* v *City of Edinburgh District Council* 1988 SLT (OH) 329 and *Ralston* v *H.M. Advocate* 1989 S.L.T. 474.

[5] J L Murdoch, 'The European Convention on Human Rights in Scots Law' (cit. ch VI, n. 2) at p 40. Since the article was written the number of member states has been enlarged to 39.

[6] As Kelsen does in *The Pure Theory of Law* (cit. ch I, n. 2).

[7] John Austin, *The Province of Jurisprudence Determined* (cit. ch I, n. 12).

[8] As H L A Hart, *The Concept of Law* (cit. ch V, n. 40), Alf Ross, from the logical point of view at least, in *Directives and Norms* (London: Routledge & Kegan Paul, 1968), John Bell in 'Legal Revolutions and the Continuity of Public Law' in *Shaping Revolution* (cit. ch IV, n. 53) p 125.

can make law),[9] the executive's granting of the right of individual petition was sufficient where the Convention was concerned? The notion that executive action is capable of making law is the very point that Lord Ross was concerned to deny in *Kaur*. It seems, too, to run contrary to Dworkin's view that 'the most abstract and fundamental point of legal practice is to guide and constrain the power of government'. Yet Dworkin also insists that 'force not be used or withheld . . .except as licensed or required by individual rights and responsibilities flowing from past political decisions about when collective force is justified'. The question then becomes one of just whose political decisions are to be counted. Does the fact that so many individual citizens have taken advantage of the right of petition suggest that, given such popular endorsement of the executive action concerned, the Convention should be counted as law, irrespective of what the courts may say?

The problem is, of course, far from limited to issues relating to the European Convention on Human Rights. Previous chapters have identified a range of matters - sometimes classified as "soft law" - from codes of practice to principles that do not readily fit into a specific source based approach to the identification of law. How, then, are these to be explained? In Chapter II it was suggested that a society could be understood as a grouping of people orienting their behaviour toward one another in terms of shared understandings and expectations. These understandings may or may not extend to a distinction between "law" and "non law". How should the legal theorist approach such understandings? Any predetermined notion of what law is may lead her or him to deny that something is law, even though distinguished as such by members of that society - because, for example, it is lacking, as was much of Nazi law, in acceptable moral content or, as in many tribal societies, certain institutional structures.

Even if he or she avoids this and concentrates on the actual understandings of the members of the society, there is still a problem. It is that of determining just whose understandings should be looked to, whether some understandings should be given greater weight than

9 Note the contrast here with France and the distinction between *lois* enacted by Parliament and *decrets* and *arrêtés* emerging from the executive, both employing powers afforded by the 1958 Constitution, Arts 34 & 37 particularly.

others and on what basis. Those who view law, from very different perspectives, as a tool of civilisation or an instrument of repression tend to look primarily to the understandings of some kind of elite. In the case of modern Western legal systems this is likely to be those of the legislature or the legislature and the higher judiciary.[10] By contrast, Eugen Ehrlich, though acknowledging the role of "norms for decision" (or official law), drew attention to the importance of the living law that influenced them. He argued that:

> the scientific significance of the living law is not confined to its influence upon the norms for decision which the courts apply or upon the content of statutes. The knowledge of the living law has an independent value, and this consists of the fact that it constitutes the foundation of the legal order of human society. In order to acquire a knowledge of this order we must know the usages, relations of domination, legal relations, contracts, articles of association, declarations by last will and testament, quite independently of the question whether they have already found expression in a judicial decision or in a statute or whether they will ever find it.[11]

If Ehrlich's line is followed, we need to accept that there are two forms of law operative in society - the law as understood and operated by officials and the law as understood and operated by members of society as a whole. In this context a distinction is sometimes drawn between the internal legal culture (that of those professionally engaged in the law) and the lay legal culture (that of the rest of the population). For those who see law as solely the province of officials, the lay legal culture is confined to the attitudes toward the official law held by that population or groupings within it. For example, is, as in the United States, the lay legal culture litigious or, as - until recently at least - in Japan, one which is averse to involvement in formal dispute resolution processes? For those, however, who count the "living law" as law, the lay legal culture embraces both such attitudes to the official law and all the understandings involved in the living law itself.

---

[10] What Jerome Frank called "The Upper Court Myth" - see *Courts on Trial* (Princeton; Princeton University Press, 1950) esp pp 24, 74, 222. See also William Twining, *Karl Llewellyn and the Realist Movement* (London: Weidenfeld and Nicolson, 1974) and the reference at p 379 to "appellate-courtitis".

[11] Eugen Ehrlich, *Fundamental Principles of the Sociology of Law* trans W Moll (Cambridge, Mass: Harvard University Press, 1936) p 502.

Should law, then, be regarded solely as the province of officials? In particular, should it be regarded as the province of some single and united elite? On the second point, much of what has been written in earlier chapters has served to cast doubt on the need for some single elite. The existence side by side of canon law and feudal law in Scotland of the Middle Ages, each with its own body of officials, is one contrary example. In modern times, the parallel existence of domestic law and European Community Law, each with its own institutions, provides another. Of course, some means has to be found for avoiding contradictory behaviour between such elites, whether as with canon law and feudal law, in terms of a mutually agreeable division of labour or, as with domestic law and Community law, the acceptance of some principle of superiority.

Even within the context of one body of law, however, it is difficult to find some elite that can justifiably be called either single or united. The doctrine of "the separation of powers" is deeply embedded in our constitutional thinking. Legislature, executive and judiciary alike attempt to maintain and, sometimes to extend, their own spheres of influence and to guard against encroachment from elsewhere. Admittedly, within the U.K., statute law has priority over judicial decisions - but the courts are reluctant to accept that any change has been made to the previous common law if a statute does not expressly override it. The *Burmah Oil* case[12] and *Anisminic*[13], in their different ways, also illustrate the tenacity with which the courts resist attempts to tamper with their powers. In *Anisminic* the House of Lords was concerned with the interpretation of the Foreign Compensation Act 1950. Parliament had decided that, where applications were made to the Foreign Compensation Commission, determinations of them by the Commission were not to be 'called into question in any Court of Law'.[14] Nonetheless, the House of Lords considered that, in denying compensation in the circumstances it did, the Commission had exceeded its jurisdiction. Since Parliament could not have intended to allow this, it was open to the House to declare the determination null and void.

---

[12] See ch V.

[13] *Anisminic* v *Foreign Compensation Commission* [1969] 2 AC 197.

[14] s. 4 (4).

Further, while the validity of statute law as such cannot be challenged in the courts, that of delegated legislation can. At one level, this can be seen as the courts acting on behalf of Parliament to ensure that some government minister has not gone beyond the powers granted him or her. At another level, however, taken together with a much wider power of judicial review of administrative action, it can be looked on as a means of controlling executive discretion. Notable examples of references to the courts have related to cold climate heating allowance,[15] to immigration matters [16] and to the criminal injuries compensation scheme.[17] Such challenges come, notably, not from some other part of the establishment but from the individual or group adversely affected. Even where not entirely successful in legal terms their political effect has been considerable.

All this serves to suggest that Austin may have been guilty of a degree of oversimplification when he argued that judicial decisions should be understood as 'tacit commands of the sovereign' (understood as Crown, Lords and Commons) and as themselves a form of legislation.[18] The notion that the different branches of government may pull in different directions is reinforced by a consideration of the executive and legislature. Traditionally, the Westminster Parliament was regarded, at least from the mid 17th century on, as the place where the laws of the land were primarily determined. When many of the Crown's powers and prerogatives passed from the Monarch to government ministers it became understood that these ministers were responsible to Parliament, both individually and collectively, for the ways in which they exercised them. Members of Parliament in their turn were accountable to their electorates.

David Marquand argues that 'the net effect was to create a chain of representation and accountability, binding the decision makers in the

---

[15] *Scottish Old People's Welfare Council Petitioners* 1987 SLT 179.

[16] For example, the deportation order relating to Professor Al-Mas'ari and the denial of social security benefits to asylum seekers.

[17] *R* v *Secretary of State for Home Department, ex parte Firebrigades Union* [1995] 2 All E R 244.

[18] *Lectures on Jurisprudence* R Campbell ed (London: John Murray, 1873) Lectures XXXVII - XXXVIII.

Cabinet to the electors in the constituencies'.[19] This, however, he maintains has changed:

> In the first place, the expansion of the electorate and the growth of the modern mass party had transformed the relationship between ministers and members of parliament, on the one hand, and between members of parliament and their constituents on the other. . . A general election was no longer a series of constituency elections in which the constituency's voters decided who should represent them in the Commons. It was a kind of plebiscite in which the national electorate decided which team of party leaders should govern the country. As a result, the power relationships within the House of Commons were quite different from the days when the Westminster model took shape. Formally, Members of Parliament still held ministers to account. But members of the governing party in Parliament - by definition in the majority - had been elected to sustain the government in office and to put its legislation on to the statute book. Ministers had rarely much to fear from them. As for the Opposition, it was by definition in a minority; no matter how successful it might be in debate, it could not hope for significant victories in the division lobbies.[20]

In consequence, he concludes that 'Whatever constitutional textbooks might say, governments were now accountable to the electorate, rather than to Parliament, and checked much more effectively by the prospect of the next general election than by anything that might happen to them in the House of Commons'.[21] At the same time the effect of the growth of government had both 'made it impossible for ministers to take all the decisions that mattered' and the policy making process itself 'enormously more complicated'. The doctrine of ministerial responsibility no longer served as a lever by which Parliament could control the executive but rather as a cloak around which the executive could shelter from parliamentary scrutiny.[22] The consequence of policy being formulated mainly by bureaucrats, together with increasing consultation of organised interested groups, was that 'Parliament still played an indispensable part in the legislative process, but for the most part it was a ritualistic one. Its function was not so much to make law

---

[19] *The Unprincipled Society* (London: Jonathan Cape, 1988) p 179.

[20] Ibid p 180.

[21] Ibid p 181.

[22] Id per J P Macintosh, *The Government and Politics of Britain* (London: Hutchinson, 1977) pp 160-5 and 174-5.

as to legitimise the laws which emerged from this informal process of consultation and bargaining.'[23]

If this analysis is accepted, it not only bears out the view that no single elite is involved in the process of creating law but also the view that whatever elites there are cannot adequately be identified by reference to the legislature and the higher judiciary alone. Contemporary jurisprudence is sometimes said to be biased toward the western world in the way that it tends to ignore the role played by the bureaucracy in other legal cultures. This may well be fair comment. But it seems appropriate to suggest that western jurisprudence also pays insufficient attention to bureaucrats where its own kind of cultural context is concerned. Yet their significance in the UK, at least, has become even more obvious given the operation of the regulatory agencies, including those introduced with privatisation of the utilities,[24] and the "decentralisation" of the civil service through the "Next Steps Agencies".[25]

Further, when a particular elite can be identified, it is clear that its membership will not necessarily have identical or even generally similar views. This is obvious in the case of Parliament, where there is considerable demarcation along party lines. There is dissension within the political parties, too, and this sometimes becomes apparent even within the ranks of government.[26] This applies not just between ministers but also between ministers and their civil servants. Many of the plaudits directed towards the TV series 'Yes, Minister', related to the way it brought out, though by means of a degree of caricature, the

---

[23] Ibid p 182.

[24] Known as Ofgas, Oftel etc. See for discussion, C Graham and T Prosser, *Privatising Public Enterprise: Constitutions, the State and Regulation in a Comparative Perspective* (Oxford: Clarendon Press, 1991) and Anthony I Ogus, *Regulation* (Oxford: Clarendon Press, 1994) esp pp 287ff.

[25] For a brief account, see H W R Wade and F Forsyth, *Administrative Law* 7th edn (Oxford: Clarendon Press, 1994) p 56f. For more detail see, 'The Role of the Civil Service' Report of the Treasury and Civil Service Select Committee HC 27 1993-4.

[26] Consider, for example, the role played by disagreements about the European Community in general and monetary union in particular in the deposing of Mrs Thatcher.

genuine irony underlying the title. Nor do civil servants themselves necessarily have an identical view of their roles, as testified to by the *Ponting* case.[27] Various instances of disagreement within the judiciary, in terms both of the proper approach to and the proper outcome of decision-making, have been considered in the course of this text.[28] Further, if juries can be counted as officials, they can hold very different views of what the law demands from judges, as testified to not just by the Ponting case but also by the acquittals of those who had admitted to assisting in the escape of the spy George Blake[29] and of a man who had shot and wounded two people, one of whom had killed his son by driving a tipper truck over him.[30]

Charles Sampford, in *The Disorder of Law* identifies similar examples of conflict 'between and within the institutions of law' which he argues is caused partly by 'the constant struggle by officials within each institution to reduce the limits placed on them by officials in other institutions, and increase the opportunities for affecting officials in other institutions' and partly by conflicts within society itself, 'the different members being influenced by, or holding values supportive of, competing groups'.[31] Indeed, for Sampford, law should be seen as a mêlée, and as a microcosm of a wider social mêlée.[32]

There seem, then, to be strong grounds for arguing that law is not the province of some single united elite but rather, at most, a matter of equilibrium between competing elites. The problem still remains, though, as to what are to be counted as elites in this context. Should it just be the legislature and the higher judiciary? If so, how do we account for the legislature's often cursory involvement in delegated legislation, particularly statutory codes of practice, and for non

[27] *R* v *Ponting* [1975] Crim L R 318. Equally, too, in that case, the jury took a significantly different view of the world from the judge, although whether this was about the state of the law or their own function was not entirely clear.

[28] See particularly chs VI and VII.

[29] See also *R* v *Central Criminal Court, ex parte Randle* [1992] 1 All E R 370.

[30] *R* v *Owen*, Maidstone Crown Court, May 1992.

[31] *The Disorder of Law* (Oxford: Blackwell, 1989) p 246.

[32] Ibid p 223.

statutory codes and other forms of self regulation? How, too, do we account for those decisions of the lower courts that remain unchallenged? What, also, should we make of the many alternative dispute resolving bodies that have some kind of formal standing? What, again, of the higher echelons of the civil service and of the directions and guidelines issued by them? What, even, of the way that these are interpreted by the people who implement the rules and regulations on a day to day basis?

We may want to bring into account, too, the understandings of a much wider range of those professionally engaged in the law than just those belonging to the people who decide the outcome of disputes. In this case the internal legal culture is seen as belonging to a particular type of legal community. As John Bell puts it:

> The notion of a 'legal community' is somewhat nebulous and requires clarification. Broadly, the legal audience consists of those skilled and knowledgeable in the law, be they judges, practitioners, academics or whatever. Within each legal tradition, there are some specific people who have an important influence within the legal community and from whom a lead is taken as to what is a good legal argument. In the English common law, the twelve judges of Westminster Hall provided the touchstone of what was legally right, while the Lord Chancellor performed the same function in equity. In modern times, Professor Paterson has suggested that the ten members of the House of Lords have that role.[33] In Roman law, a similar role was occupied by the jurists, those with a *ius respondendi.* In identifying the rules, or even in acknowledging the existence of a 'legal revolution', it may suffice that the influential group within the legal community accept it, and the rest will take the lead from them, but that depends on the structure of the legal community within a specific legal system.[34]

Within the United Kingdom, at least, it is difficult to deny that practising lawyers, whether by the way that they advise clients as to how to arrange their affairs or by the way that they use (or avoid) dispute resolution processes, do make a significant contribution both to the actual operation of the law and to the way that doubtful issues are raised before and resolved by the courts and other tribunals. One straightforward example of this is that, in terms of the operation of the

[33] *The Law Lords* (London: Macmillan, 1982) ch 5.

[34] 'Legal Revolutions and the Continuity of Public Law' (cit. n. 8) at p 125.

doctrine of precedent, it is rare for a judge to bring into consideration a case not cited by the lawyers for the parties in court.[35]

A more complicated example can be found with "deeds of family arrangement". Under Scots law it has long been possible for beneficiaries under a Will (or those inheriting on intestacy) to refuse bequests or to redirect them to others. This may be done on a collaborative basis so as to vary the terms of the original Will.[36] When Capital Transfer Tax was introduced in 1975[37] such variations began to become much more common. The advantage lies in the fact that they do not count as a transfer of value, now in terms of the Inheritance Taxes Act 1984,[38] nor as a disposal for the purposes of Capital Gains Tax.[39] In consequence, they may be of considerable financial benefit, particularly where the transfer is between exempt and non exempt beneficiaries. The IHTA requires only an "Instrument in writing" and the Inland Revenue has - intimated by way of a Press Release[40] - a relatively relaxed attitude to the form that it takes. What it also intimated in the Press Release, however, was that the instrument or deed had to be irrevocable and not open to amendment by subsequent deeds. That view was contested, although unsuccessfully, in *Russell* v *IRC*.[41] Yet, had it not been contested, this particular point of "soft" law would never have become hard.

Numerous other examples might be cited - for instance the extent to which solicitors will attempt to negotiate "Minutes of Agreement" between divorcing couples, because of a perception that Sheriffs are reluctant to undertake the division of matrimonial property for themselves, as would then be required of them by the Family Law (Scotland) Act 1985. Indeed, the whole area of out of court settlements generally is of relevance here. Given the extent, then, to which practising lawyers may exert an influence on the development of the

[35] As did Lord Fraser of Tullybelton with the case of *Hyslops* v *Gordon* in his opinion in *Miliangos* (cit. ch VI, n. 27).

[36] *Gray* v *Gray's Trustees* (1877) 4 R 378.

[37] Finance Act 1975 s 47.

[38] ss 17(1) and 142(1).

[39] CGTA 1979 s 49(6).

[40] May, 1985.

[41] (1988) STC.

law, it may be necessary to count them as yet another of the "elites" whose understandings and activities should be brought into consideration. Yet whether they can be said to be an elite in the normal understanding of the term is a moot point. The same applies to lower levels of officialdom, much though decisions taken there may be as effectively unchallengeable by those affected as they would if taken by the highest in the land.

Is what law is, then, to be regarded as determined by the understandings and activities of "elites" or "officials", more or less broadly defined? For Kelsen, not necessarily so. As already indicated, he takes a legal order to be a normative order that monopolises the legitimate use of force, thus regulating the mutual behaviour of men by prescribing the only conditions under which they may be deprived of life, freedom, economic and other values.[42] No particular institutions need to be in place for a legal order to exist. Instead, he expressly states that the monopoly of force may be decentralised. It is so if:

> the individuals authorised to use force do not have the character of special organs acting according to the principle of the division of labour but if the legal order authorises all individuals to use force who consider their interests violated by the illegal conduct of others; in other words if the principle of self help prevails.[43]

In somewhat different vein, Hart gives an account of a legal system as a union of primary rules of obligation and secondary rules of change, adjudication and recognition, which can be found where the primary rules, as recognised by officials, are generally obeyed and where those officials effectively accept the rules for recognition, for change and for adjudication as common standards for their own behaviour.[44] It is possible, though, that there is no major disagreement involved. Hart does appear to allow that law can exist even where a legal system does not.[45] In consequence it may be that the proper parallel is between Hart's legal system and Kelsen's state, for:

> To be a state, the legal order must have the character of an organisation in the narrower and specific sense of this word, that is, it must establish

[42] *The Pure Theory of Law* (cit. n. 6) ch 1, esp pp 30-36.

[43] Ibid p 37.

[44] *The Concept of Law* (cit. ch V, n. 40) chs V and VI, esp p 116.

[45] Ibid p 86.

> organs who, in the manner of division of labor, create and apply the norms that constitute the legal order; it must display a certain degree of centralisation.[46]

The fact that both of them distinguish their legal system/state from, on the one hand, the law/legal order of a primitive society and, on the other, from the super - (or inter -) state international law/legal order, supports this kind of interpretation.

What we may then wish to question is, first, whether we do wish to identify the notion of legal system with that of the state and, second, whether we wish to accord such a degree of prominence to officials. On the first point, Kelsen himself admitted that very few modern states are unitary ones and that there may be only a limited number of positive norms valid for the whole territory (or, at least, most of it). Indeed, in the extreme case, the only common norm may be the presupposed or fictitiously posited basic norm.[47] More will be said in this respect in the next chapter. On the second point, however, it does seem that, within the state, officials have come to take on the same kind of importance for Kelsen as for Hart. On the understanding that 'law is the primary norm, which stipulates the sanction'[48] it becomes primarily addressed to judges in the form of authorisations to apply such sanctions. Thus, for Kelsen, what we usually take to be law - a set of behavioural standards to be conformed to, inter alia, for the purpose of avoiding being on the receiving end of sanctions - is merely a batch of secondary norms that are parasitic on the primary ones.[49]

Alf Ross argues on similar lines, in that for him legal rules: are not rules maintained by the exercise of coercion but rules about its exercise; they are rules which are in general not enforced but followed voluntarily, that is in virtue of the feeling of validity which endows the rules with binding force. Legal rules are directed at those in authority - the organs of the state - and their source of effectiveness is the allegiance of officials towards the constitution and the institutions

---

[46] *The Pure Theory of Law* p 286.

[47] Ibid pp 314-5.

[48] *General Theory of Law and State* trans A Wedberg (New York: Russell and Russell, 1961) p 61.

[49] *Introduction to the Problems of Legal Theory* trans B L Paulson and S L Paulson (Oxford: Clarendon Press, 1992) p 29f.

derived from it, together with the non violent sanctions of disapproval and criticism that are implied in this attitude.[50]

By contrast with Kelsen, and in common with Hart, Ross dubs such rules - those prescribing how cases are to be decided - secondary rules. Such secondary rules, he argues, are all that are needed from the logical point of view. For primary rules, demanding a certain type of behaviour from citizens, contain nothing not already implied by the secondary ones. Nonetheless, from the psychological point of view, two sets of rules do exist:

> Rules addressed to citizens are felt psychologically to be independent entities which are grounds for the reaction of the authorities. If we apply our definition of the existence of a norm, primary rules must be recognised as actually existing norms, in so far as they are followed with regularity and experienced as being binding.[51]

Ross, then, appears to be accepting a Kelsenian monism[52] for the purposes of structural analysis but to be opting for dualism where the identification of law as it actually exists is concerned. For officials there is a set of rules setting out the conditions for the exercise of coercion, these conditions being followed out of a mixture of allegiance and a desire to avoid disapproval. For citizens there is a set of rules both directive of their behaviour and justificative of official reaction to it, followed because of an experience of such behaviour as binding. This "experience of bindingness" is explained as a special type of psychological impulse toward the behaviour. Ross argues that for the individual 'the compelling impulse has a stamp of unintelligibility and mystery, as if it did not arise from his own nature but was a dictate coming to him from outside'.[53]

The question is whether one can separate law from the "logical" and "psychological" points of view in this way. Setting aside any difficulties there may be with the notion of an "experience of bindingness", Ross's analysis suggests problems about the status of a

---

[50] *Directives and Norms* (cit. n. 8) p 90ff.

[51] Ibid p 92.

[52] Philosophically, the view that there is only one kind of substance or ultimate reality, eg. there is only mind or there is only matter, or that such reality forms a unitary whole. In this context, the view that law is to be quantified on one level - that of authorisations to officials.

[53] Ibid p 85.

law where it is either not followed with regularity or experienced in such a way or both. For example, the Community Charge or poll tax proved to be a largely unpopular measure. A considerable proportion of the population clearly felt no "compelling impulse" to pay. Some of these did pay for reasons unconnected with there being a legal requirement to do so. Many did not. In the April 1992 General Election Tommy Sheridan, of the Anti Poll Tax Federation, stood as a candidate in the Glasgow Pollok Constituency. He obtained 6287 votes (19.26%), coming second to the returned Labour member. At the time he was in Saughton Prison in Edinburgh, serving a six month sentence for contempt of court. This resulted from his presence at a demonstration attempting to prevent Sheriff Officers from seizing goods belonging to non payers of the poll tax and from his tearing up of a court order forbidding him to attend such demonstrations. In the local elections in May 1992, along with another Scottish Militant Labour candidate, and while still in prison, he was returned as a member of the Greater Glasgow District Council.[54] While, of course, one cannot know the actual motives of all the individuals who voted for him, it does seem reasonable to assume that, whether or not they had actually paid the tax themselves, most, at least, had not experienced the requirement to do so as binding.

More certainly, where they were concerned, Hart's conditions for the existence of a social rule cannot have been met. Like Ross's norm, this calls for regularity of behaviour. Instead of an experience of bindingness, however, a "critical reflective attitude" toward deviations is the second feature required to convert a mere habit into a rule.[55] Since Hart's use of the term "critical" here implies an adverse reaction to the deviation concerned, one can readily question the existence amongst the relevant voters in Pollok of the existence of any social rule to the effect that one ought to pay one's poll tax.

Hart himself, however, appears to consider that the existence of such social rules about obedience to legal rules is not necessary. All he specifies is that his primary rules of obligation must be generally

---

[54] He was returned again in the 1995 local elections, following the change to the unitary authorities, to the new City of Glasgow Council.

[55] *The Concept of Law* (cit. n. 44) p 57.

obeyed.[56] It is not made clear whether this anything more than a matter of habit or, indeed, whether the primary rules even need to be recognised as legal rules by the public at large. Perhaps, though, he would argue that, while the primary rules of obligation do not each need to be supported by specific social rules about their individual observance, there must be some general social rule requiring obedience to the law. Alternatively, it may only be the officials that require to hold a critical reflective attitude toward deviations. If the second interpretation is correct, how close does this bring him to Kelsen's view?

Kelsen, on the other hand, seems to be unconcerned with questions about the occurrence of "experiences of bindingness" and the existence of "critical reflective attitudes". In the *General Theory of Law and State,* he argued only that for a legal order to exist it had, as a whole, to be "by and large effective". What distinguishes a legal order from any other normative order is the kind of monopoly it has over the use of force.[57] This does not involve total control over the actual use of force - clearly people may be deprived of 'life, freedom, economic and other values' by non legal means. Rather, the legal order must have at least enough of a monopoly over the actual use of force for this to outweigh, overall, any other use. Revolutionary situations apart, it is a matter of simple observation to tell if this condition is fulfilled and by whom. Besides this effective monopoly over the actual use of force, however, Kelsen requires the legal order to have a complete monopoly over the valid or legitimate use of force. Whether the use of force is valid or legitimate in any given case is determined ultimately by whether it is 'carried out only under the conditions and in the ways determined by the "fathers" of the constitution or the organs delegated by them'.[58]

It is very difficult to see just what Kelsen is claiming here. His legal scientist, in describing a given legal order, simply works on the basis that the conditions laid down by the fathers of the constitution for the

---

[56] Ibid p 116.

[57] Indeed, all the norms within the order can be formulated as the various sets of conditions under which some human being or group of human beings becomes authorised to impose a sanction.

[58] *The General Theory of Law and State* (cit. n. 48) p 116.

valid or legitimate use of force are themselves valid or legitimate ones - that they ought to be adhered to. This does not mean that the legal scientist need have any kind of moral or political commitment to the conditions.[59] Rather, that coercive acts ought only to be carried out under them (the basic norm) is just an assumption that is made for the purposes of the investigation in hand.[60] Can, however, the legal scientist really afford to proceed on this particular assumption? Why should he or she make it anyway?

Does Kelsen regard it as an analytical truth, like two plus two equalling four, that force is legitimate if constitutionally exercised? If so, just how does the constitution confer such legitimacy? Presumably, it does so through its own legitimacy. What then renders the constitution itself legitimate? Is it so by definition, rather as a metre is what the metre bar in Paris says it is? In which case, just how is the constitution grounded in social reality? After all, the metre bar in Paris only defines what a metre is because it is accepted as doing so. Does the constitution require similar acceptance? If it does, by whom - those exercising the force or those subject to it or both? Or is Kelsen slipping in here some kind of substantive claim, to the effect that what makes the use of force legitimate is its compatibility with past political decisions? In which case Dworkin's arguments offer a striking parallel with his.

Alternatively, perhaps Kelsen believes that officials do actually make their decisions in ways constrained by a constitutionally constituted normative framework, so that in making the assumption the

---

[59] On this point see J W Harris, 'Revolutions and Normativity' in Attwooll ed, *Shaping Revolution* (cit. n. 8) p 1.

[60] Confusion sometimes arises because of the fact that Kelsen, at a late stage explains the basic norm as fictitiously posited. The resolution would seem to be as follows. The legal scientist is concerned with identifying the legal norms and stating them as legal rules. In the context of such acts of understanding the basic norm need only be assumed. Actual norms, however, can only come into existence as the result of human decision (of acts of will). The basic norm that 'coercive acts ought only to be carried out under the conditions. . .' must, as the foundation of the legal order, be understood as resulting from an act of will. Since no actual such act can be traced, it has to be regarded as a fictitious one. (See K Olivecrona, *Law as Fact* 2nd edn (London: Stevens & Sons, 1971) p 114.

legal scientist is reflecting what is happening in practice. What, though, if he is wrong about this? And, even if he is right, is enough being said? The days are gone when natural science was regarded as simply concerned with reporting the state of natural facts. It is now acknowledged to be about producing theoretical explanations that account for the information that we have about the physical world, such explanations also indicating what other information we might expect to acquire if the theory is a good one. A theory will be maintained only for so long as it is accepted - for whatever reasons - as giving a better account than any other. If this view of science is extended to legal science, then we may argue that the task of the legal scientist is to give the best possible explanation of the information that is available about the law.

So far, on this alternative account, it seems that we can say that a legal order exists when officials, though applying force only 'under the conditions and in the ways determined by the "fathers" of the constitution and the organs delegated by them', succeed in making it predominant. It remains unclear, however, in what sense their activity is to be regarded as legitimate. The questions asked earlier recur. Nor are matters made clearer by the claim, to be found in the second edition of *The Pure Theory of Law*, that individual norms within the order also need to be "by and large effective". In this context Kelsen argues:

> a norm is not regarded as valid if it is never obeyed or applied. In fact a legal norm may lose its validity by never being obeyed or applied - by so called *desuetude*. *Desuetudo* may be described as negative custom, and its essential function is to abolish the validity of an existing norm. If custom is a law-creating fact at all, then even the validity of statute law can be abolished by customary law.[61]

Such a rule of "desuetude" was understood to apply to Acts of the Scots Parliament prior to 1707, as it still does in certain civilian systems today.

In addition to others already mentioned,[62] a contemporary example can be found in road traffic law. It is the practice of intentionally law abiding (or perhaps just honest) motorists, who do minor damage to a parked car in circumstances where the other driver is not present, to

---

[61] *The Pure Theory of Law* (cit. n. 6) p 213.

[62] Such e.g. as the non-prosecution of homosexual activity.

leave a note with name and address tucked under the windscreen wipers. What section 170 of the Road Traffic Act 1988 actually specifies, however, is the following:

(1) This section applies in a case where, owing to the presence of a motor vehicle on a road, an accident occurs by which-
(a). . .
(b) damage is caused-
(i) to a vehicle other than that motor vehicle or a trailer drawn by that motor vehicle,. . .
(2) The driver of the motor vehicle must stop and, if required to do so by any person having reasonable grounds for so requiring, give his name and address and also the name and address of the owner and the identification marks of the vehicle.
(3) If for any reason the driver of the motor vehicle does not give his name and address under subsection (2) above, he must report the accident.
(4). . .
(5). . .
(6) To comply with a duty under this section to report an accident. . . the driver-
(a) must do so at a police station or to a constable, and
(b) must do so as soon as is reasonably practicable and, in any case, within twenty four hours of the occurrence of the accident.

Obviously it is open to Procurators Fiscal to prosecute in circumstances where the letter of the statute has not been observed, in the sense that the particulars have not been handed directly to a some appropriate person. It is suggested, though, that the likelihood of their doing so is slim. Even if there was "a clamp down", it is guessed that this would do more to alter motorists' perception of what "the system" requires than to change their actual practice. For it expects them either to engage in an indefinite wait for the right person or to seek out a policeman or a police station. They may well consider, as did Mr Bumble, squeezing his hat emphatically in both hands, 'If the law supposes that, the law is a ass - a idiot'.[63]

Kelsen appears to accommodate situations of this kind almost as readily as Ehrlich. For he accepts that his primary norms, parallelling Ehrlich's norms for decision, may go out of existence as a result of law created by contrary custom. What is not entirely clear is whether it is sufficient that the primary norm is never obeyed or whether it is also

---

[63] Charles Dickens, *Oliver Twist* ch 51.

necessary that it is never applied. Further, customary norms may be created on a more general basis 'by the behavior of individuals who are subject to the legal order'[64] Such norms exist prior to any law applying act. Of course, their actual application depends on the courts, but then this is also true of legislation. Customary norms can be of considerable significance for they may have a 'canceling effect in relation to formal constitutional law; and even in relation to formal constitutional law that expressly excludes the application of customary law'.[65] Where Kelsen, then, appears to differ from Hart is in the latter's view that, while non compliance generally may affect the existence of the legal system, it does not affect the validity of individual laws. This results entirely from their recognition by the officials. For:

> In our own system, custom and precedent are subordinate to legislation since customary and common law rules may be deprived of their status by statute. Yet they owe their status of law, precarious as this may be, not to a 'tacit' exercise of legislative power but to the acceptance of a rule of recognition which accords them this independent though subordinate place.[66]

With Kelsen, however, these norms are already there to be recognised.

Whatever the correct interpretation of Kelsen and Hart in these respects, both are clearly acknowledging that law has to be seen as part of the world of social fact. It "lives" in that it conditions and is conditioned by the interactions of actual human beings. In neither case is it just as clear as it might be how the law is founded in the world of social fact. What seems to be puzzling about both thinkers, too, is that, whilst they tie the existence of a legal order or legal system to actual human behaviour, the grounds on which they distinguish them from other features of the social world seem, on the face of it, to involve nothing more than competing personal choices as to how the notions "legal" and "order" or "system" should be defined. The next chapter considers some of the issues involved.

---

[64] *The Pure Theory of Law* (cit. n. 6) p 228.

[65] Ibid p 227.

[66] *The Concept of Law* (cit. n. 44) p 98.

IX

AND WHAT KIND OF SYSTEM?

If, then, there are difficulties in the way of identifying law as the province or creation of officials (and particularly of some united elite within officialdom), is there some alternative way in which laws and legal systems can be distinguished from other aspects of the social world? The trouble with any attempt to find one by beginning with the notion of a legal system is that the term "system" is used in so many different, and often imprecise, ways. The most common feature of such usage, however, seems to be the understanding of a system as having something to do with parts in the context of wholes. This introduces an immediate complication because, as mentioned in chapter II, there are at least three different views about the relationship between parts and wholes. Attempts to understand the notion of system are complicated still further by the fact that the term can be understood both statically and dynamically. The static understanding has to do with ordered presentation, the dynamic one to do with procedures and processes.

Where ordered presentation is concerned, system may be identified with *method*, as when we speak of "the Dewey system" for classifying books in libraries. Equally, system may be identified with *layout* - the place taken by the parts vis a vis one another, together with the form of the connections between them. Thus we might speak of the electrical system of a modern house as involving a number of lighting and power circuits connected via the circuit box and the meter to the mains supply. Similarly we might spell out the hierarchy of the courts within the Scottish criminal legal system, specifying the levels at which appeals may be heard. Sometimes, too, system may be identified with *diagram*, with a map or plan that depicts the kind of layout just described.

Most important for jurisprudence within the static understanding, however, is the identification of system with *combination*. This involves explaining some particular whole as a set of parts united by a common characteristic or characteristics. With Kelsen's legal order such characteristics can be found on two levels. First, the norms have in common that they regulate the mutual behaviour of men by prescribing the only conditions under which they may be deprived of life, freedom, economic and other values. This much they share with law generally. Second, they are given unity by the fact that they all have the same basic norm as the reason for their validity.[1] It is this feature that makes them part of the same legal order. Hart approaches the matter differently, placing emphasis on the variety of functions that laws can fulfil.[2] In consequence, a legal system is explained as a union of different types of rules - specifically, of primary ones of obligation and secondary ones of change, adjudication and recognition. What unites them is that a rule or rules of recognition, specifying the criteria for identifying the primary rules, and the rules of change and adjudication are 'effectively accepted as common public standards of official behaviour' by the officials.[3]

Within the dynamic understanding and a concern with procedures and processes, system may be identified with *mode of operation*, with the way in which something works. This may just involve an analysis of the ways in which parts combine and to what effect. So we might explain the electoral system in the United Kingdom as determining the membership of Parliament by means of constituency based nomination, voting and counting procedures according to which the candidate in each constituency who is identified as the sole choice of more voters than any other candidate in the same constituency is deemed elected.

Often, however, when system is identified with mode of operation, it is being looked at as part of a wider context and in terms of the role it plays in relation to other things. It is this notion of system we might have in mind when suggesting that family disputes would be better settled by a system of conciliation than of adjudication. In this kind of context the system may be seen as a *tool*, as something which is designed to produce a particular type of result. Thus Lon Fuller and Roscoe Pound regard law respectively as 'the enterprise of subjecting human conduct to the governance of rules'[4] and as there to achieve 'the

---

1 *The Pure Theory of Law* (cit. ch I, n. 2) ch 1, esp pp. 30-36.

2 *The Concept of Law* (cit. ch V, n. 40) ch III passim.

3 Ibid p 116.

4 Lon L Fuller, *The Morality of Law* (cit. ch I, n. 18) p 91.

maximum satisfaction of wants with the minimum of friction and waste'.[5] Such understandings of system are usually termed "instrumental".

Alternatively, the system may be seen as a particular type of *linkage* in the chain of cause and effect. This may involve a consideration of how the system has come to operate as it does or of how that operation serves to produce its own effects or both of these. Such understandings of system are usually termed functionalist. They frequently involve certain claims about the extent to which the operation of the system is determined by outside factors, as also, about the extent to which its operation can, or even must, be productive of some particular effect. Thus, within Marxist theory, there is a divergence of opinion about how far the economic system (or base) determines the legal system (part of the superstructure) and, similarly, how far, if at all, the legal superstructure can produce changes in the economic base.

Finally, within the dynamic approach, system may be identified with *interaction.* Here the concern is with how the parts of the whole adjust to one another and with how the whole adjusts to factors outside itself. The main disagreement between theorists in this area is as to whether such interaction and, thus, any change produced by it is itself systematic. To some, change - if not immediately, certainly ultimately - follows an ordered path and laws of development can be found. Others, by contrast, regard change as something that occurs variously by accident or by deliberate design and, whichever, as having no necessary pattern to it.

Even if the first view is correct, recent research in the natural sciences, with major implications for the social sciences, suggests that any laws of this kind are still a long way from being understood and that there are almost overwhelming difficulties in gathering sufficient, and sufficiently precise, data to allow us to reach such an understanding - at least for the purposes of making really accurate predictions.[6] Putting such difficulties to one side for the moment, though, the identification of system with interaction does seem to

---

[5] Roscoe Pound, *Social Control Through Law* (New Haven: Yale University Press, 1942).

[6] The development of "chaos theory" in mathematices. See e.g. Ian Stewart, *Does God Play Dice?* (Oxford: Blackwell, 1989).

suggest an important insight. The dynamic approach, in its concern with procedures and processes, lays stress on the way in which the parts affect and are affected by one another, the whole and factors outside the whole. Even with a whole in which there is no change, the parts must still stand in some kind of relationship with one another. Our experience tells us that everything in the world does change, though some things at a very much slower rate than others. The ordered presentation offered by the static approach, therefore, only captures the whole at a given moment in time. It is rather like using the "hold" button on the remote control to freeze one frame of a video. It follows, then, that, even within the static approach, a properly developed account of any whole cannot afford to ignore its layout - the placings of the various parts and the form(s) of the connections between them. Explaining the whole in terms of other sorts of characteristics shared by the parts may be important but it is not enough.

What consequences, then, does this have for a discussion of legal system? First, most courses entitled 'the X Legal System', like most attempts by analytical jurisprudence to explain the concept, are within the static mode. They are concerned with offering an ordered or systematic presentation of a whole body of law or, in the case of analytical jurisprudence, with the criteria that should be used in doing so.[7] Courses entitled 'the X legal system' proceed accordingly on the basis of certain presuppositions about the common characteristics of the parts (the laws), the relationships between them and the way in which they are connected together. Analytical jurisprudence asks whether these presuppositions are correct.

Back in chapter II it was argued that, if wholes are purely fictitious, we can draw the boundary around them wherever we wish - at least we can do so if we can come up with some plausible principle by reference to which we can justify treating the parts as having a common characteristic or characteristics and as connected in a way that places them in some kind of meaningful relationship with one another. On such a view, then, we can treat various laws as belonging

---

[7] See, particularly, Joseph Raz, *The Concept of a Legal System* (Oxford: Clarendon Press, 1980) and J W Harris, *Law and Legal Science* (Oxford: Clarendon Press, 1979).

to the one body of law (the X legal system) if we can establish a plausible connecting principle of this kind.

If, on the other hand, the whole is taken to exist "over and above" its parts, its boundaries are already drawn for us and the parts are already ordered together in accordance with some principle or principles governing the whole. We are limited to trying to discover where the boundaries are situated and what the governing principles are. In consequence, in seeking to offer an ordered presentation of a whole body of law, plausibility is not enough. We have to identify a set of parts that are truly connected together, classifying both them and the whole that they form as legal by reference to an understanding of what law really is. Our whole has to exclude anything that does not fall into this category.

Even if this understanding is rejected, it raises a point of major significance for the "plausible principle" approach. This is that, when drawing the boundaries of a whole, it is not enough to explain it in terms of parts having a common characteristic or characteristics and as connected in a way that places them in some kind of meaningful relationship with one another. It is also necessary to bring out the basis on which we are separating the whole from other wholes and from the parts that belong to them. With Kelsen and Hart we find that what unites the norms or rules into a system is also what marks the system off from everything else - respectively, the basic norm and recognition by the same set of officials.

This raises the central question of the type of separation that is appropriate. Undoubtedly the strongest case for arguing that things belong to a single whole is where they can be isolated from everything else. Where a system is being looked at, it can then be termed a closed one. This does not mean that it is immune to outside influences. It only means that what is part of it at any given time can be decisively determined by reference to some definitive dividing line. An analogy might be that of a cell wall. Whilst that wall may be permeable, foreign substances do not become part of the cell until they have permeated it.

Kelsen, with his device of traceability to a presupposed or fictitiously posited basic norm, is clearly attempting to isolate the legal order in this kind of way. It seems appropriate to ask, though, whether a legal order can be isolated along such lines, either from other legal orders or from other aspects of the social world. On the first point even Kelsen himself raises a certain doubt, since the basic norm of a municipal (i.e. domestic) legal order is held to survive as such only courtesy of the basic norm of international law.[8] On a more practical level, too, those involved in the law do regularly take notice of rules found in other legal systems. This is markedly so with private international law, even though, as seen earlier, such rules are sometimes regarded as matters of fact rather than matters of law.[9]

Further, it may just be enough for the legal scientist to presuppose the existence of the basic norm of the municipal legal order when engaged in describing the content of that order. Yet some mere hypothesis about the legitimacy of the coercion involved seems insufficient to explain the way in which law actually conditions the behaviour of participants. If law can indeed be distinguished from naked force, then the difference must be somewhere in the perceptions of such participants. Rather than explain this difference in terms of the fictitious occurrence of some ancestral act of will, it seems more plausible to locate it in contemporary attitudes. This is not, of course, to deny that such attitudes may be influenced by a belief, conscious or otherwise, in the legitimacy of some historically first constitution, of which the United States Constitution would be a prime example. It is only to argue that what counts as law for some given set of interacting individuals can best be determined by reference to the ideas they hold and the actions they engage in at that moment in time.

Clearly, though, if one were convinced that what differentiates a particular legal order from law in general is the possibility of isolating it, there would be major difficulties in arguing for the existence of a separate Scots legal order (or system). For, if any coherent single unifying basic norm can be found anywhere at all, it must somehow be related to the Treaty and Acts of Union.[10] Whatever the precise interpretation put on them, they clearly do not offer any basis for regarding the law applicable to Scotland as existing in isolation.

---

[8] *The Pure Theory of Law* (cit. n. 1) pp 331-339.

[9] See ch VII, n. 57. For more detail A E Anton and P R Beaumont, *Private International Law,* 2nd edn (Edinburgh: W Green, 1990) p 775ff.

[10] See G Maher, 'The Identity of the Scottish Legal System' 1977 *Juridical Review* 21.

Perhaps, though, being able to isolate it from everything else is too stringent a test for calling something a whole. It may just be sufficient for it to be self-contained. This condition would be satisfied where none of its parts were shared with any other whole. Clearly, the law of Scotland is not a whole in this sense, since the Westminster Parliament passes numerous statutes that are common to various parts of the United Kingdom. It has to be said, though, that if bodies of law require to be self-contained it is doubtful whether - given its membership of the European Community - we can find a single body of law for the United Kingdom as such. One may also enquire about the self-containedness of any system that incorporates rules of international law. In the Netherlands, for example, although no Treaty can be ratified until it has received the approval of the States-General, once ratified and published its provisions take precedence over domestic law.[11] In certain circumstances, too, law making and applying powers may be conferred directly on international organisations.[12]

It would seem, then, that at best a limited number of bodies of law are separate in the sense of being self contained. Yet, self-contained or not, we have no difficulty in recognising distinct bodies of law - such as Dutch law, French law, German law - and in thinking of these in terms of legal systems. It may be, of course, that we are mistaken in thinking this way and that these are not (or are not any longer) appropriate shapes into which to carve the world of law. Alternatively, we may just need to find a more suitable way of viewing a whole.

One such possibility might be that of a whole as something which is independent of anything else. This does not necessarily mean complete self-sufficiency. Rather, it means that the whole has adequate mechanisms for adapting itself to its environment, converting selected aspects of that environment into parts of itself and adjusting its parts to one another. This understanding of a whole is reflected in Hart's view that primary rules of obligation alone are too uncertain, static and inefficient to constitute a legal system. Only when such defects are remedied, respectively, by secondary rules of recognition, change and adjudication do we have anything more than 'a set of separate

[11] Articles 65 and 66 of the Netherlands Constitution.

[12] Ibid Article 66.

standards, without any identifying or common mark, except of course that they are rules which a particular group of human beings accepts'.[13]

In this light, one might argue that a legal system exists only when all the institutions required for making and applying law were present. The search would be on for a set of laws, created and applied in particular ways, involving distinct organisations with distinct procedures, staffed by distinct personnel with distinct qualifications, and capable of performing all the necessary tasks. This approach still does not really allow us to claim that Scotland has a separate legal system, again for the reason that Scotland does not have her own legislature.

One might try to get round the difficulty by arguing for the (quasi) federal interpretation of the Constitution and saying that the Westminster Parliament, in legislating for Scotland, is a distinct body or by drawing attention to the different procedures, involving the Scottish Grand Committee, adopted for non controversial Scottish legislation. One might even bring in the fact that Scottish Bills are drafted within the Lord Advocate's Department and not within the Office of Parliamentary Counsel. This is not a very strong case, though, and it is weakened still further by the point, made earlier, that many of the laws coming from Westminster apply to other parts of the United Kingdom as well.

On the other hand, there are undoubtedly still some areas in which the law of Scotland remains untouched by the Westminster legislative hand or by that of the House of Lords. Provided one accepts the idea that courts count as law making institutions, then some law in Scotland, at least, can be separated out as independently maintained. The difficulties in deciding the extent of the laws falling into this category and of presenting them as connected into a single whole, however, look to be considerable. Nonetheless, the notion of independence, in the sense of self-maintenance, does seem to be relatively helpful in identifying separate bodies of law. It would enable us, for example, to account for the situation in the United States, where Federal/State legislative/adjudicative bodies keep within their own spheres. Even so, the distinction becomes blurred by the fact that it is the Federal Supreme Court that has the ultimate authority to avoid

---

[13] *The Concept of Law* (cit. n. 2) p 92.

state legislation as unconstitutional. In Canada things are even less clear cut, since the same local courts adjudicate on both Federal and Provincial law.

The obvious disadvantage of this approach, then, is that it does not fully allow us to separate out bodies of law in the context of groups of people whose membership does not coincide with the whole population of what are, in effect, sovereign states. We cannot accord the dignity of having a legal system to the inhabitants, for example, of Scotland or Quebec or Oklahoma. We appear, in effect, to have been driven back to the idea of some overarching basic norm. Yet, even if this is taken to imply self-containment rather than isolation, it has already been found inadequate to account for all the situations that may arise.

Another difficulty, too, with the independence approach is that it appears to prejudge the issue of whether, contrary to Hart, we can find such a thing as a legal system in the absence of distinct law creating and applying institutions, as, for example, with the customs of certain tribes. All that seems to be left, then, is a very watered down version of the notion, in which a whole is allowed to consist in any appropriate combination of parts that is not identical with any other combination.

In order for something to be regarded as not identical with something else it must fulfil one or more of three conditions. Either it must have at least some different characteristics or, though sharing the same characteristics, have at least some of them in different amounts or, else, at least some of them in differing combinations. It is clearly not necessary, however, for the two things to have nothing in common. On this account, then, the fact that Scotland shares a considerable amount of law with the rest of Britain and, indeed, with the rest of the European Community, does not stand in the way of the assertion that she has her own legal system. For we can undoubtedly find a unique mix of Scottish, British, United Kingdom and European Community law. Depending on our viewpoint, we may even want to put international law into the melting pot as well.

Unfortunately, looking at wholes in this way may take us further than we want to go. For even a brief glance at its actual operation will show that just what the law is can be subject to widely different interpretations - as for example between one Sheriff Court area and another. This is not just a matter of geography. What satisfies one

Environmental Health Officer as satisfying the law may not satisfy another, even though both work for the same local authority. Divergences are even greater when a considerable amount of discretion is built into the law. Anyone familiar with the workings of the Licensing (Scotland) Act 1976 will be only too well aware of this point. In consequence, using the non identical criterion could result in us finding almost countless "legal systems" in operation within any group whose membership is at all broadly defined. We may, of course, try to avoid this degree of untidiness by finding some means of showing that these are not actually separate legal systems, even by the non identical criterion, since their contents do not really count as law. This, however, seems to push us back into the kind of elitism that was questioned earlier.

An alternative approach might be to try to reach some new understanding of legal system that allows us to treat them as sub-systems of it. Here the advantages of a Durkheimian approach become apparent. Since its starting point is that wholes are simply systems involving parts, we are taken directly into questions about the location and operation of those parts. Because such relationships between the parts are seen as belonging to the real world, as matters of fact, our drawing of the boundary around any whole is limited by the actual extent of these relationships. Looked at in this way, the question to be asked, in the course of identifying a legal system, becomes 'what is the law as a whole for some set of interacting individuals?' As indicated earlier, this involves specifying the common characteristic or characteristics of the things being counted as laws, indicating the nature of the relationship between them and bringing out the basis on which we are separating out the law as a whole from other parts of the social system. Put a different way, we need to distinguish the legal system from the non legal environment(s) in which it operates.

In chapter II, a society was explained as a grouping of people orienting their behaviour toward one another in terms of shared understandings and expectations and as amounting to a stable system of interaction. At this stage it seems preferable to revise the account slightly and to distinguish between the notions of society and social system, equating the former with the groupings that are constituted through people becoming engaged in stable interaction and the latter with the ways in which relationships between members of the group are structured by those forms of interaction. The social system thus becomes understood both as something generated by the culture, or at those least aspects of it that are stable in kind, and as part of that culture. As also suggested in chapter II, there can also be societies within society, each with their own forms of interaction and intra-systemic relationships. Such forms of interactions, it was suggested, might be merely habitual or might take place in terms of some kind of normative standard, it being possible to characterise societies according to the relative dominance of these. What was not canvassed, however, was the possibility that the interactions themselves might take place on almost entirely different premises, according to the area of social life involved . This idea is developed in the systems theory of writers such as Niklas Luhmann and Gunther Teubner.[14]

For both, all social interactions take the form of communications. The social system is thus to be understood as a communication system. It is not, however, one uniform system but, rather, extends to a multiplicity of specialised sub-systems. Whilst every communication conveys information, the character of the information conveyed will be different from one sub-system to another. That character will depend on the function the sub-system has and the code according to which the communications are produced. With the legal system the function is that of maintaining normative expectations in the face of disappointment and the code is a binary one distinguishing between what is legal and what is illegal.[15] By contrast, it might be said that the function of the economic system is the handling of scarcity and that its code distinguishes between what is efficient and what is inefficient.

What is significant about these systems is that they are self-referential. That is to say, the communications all result from other communications within the system, so that the process is a circular one. Put in simple terms, the ultimate answer to the question

[14] See G Teubner, *Law as an Autopoietic System,* trans A Bankowska and R Adler, ed Z Bankowski (Oxford: Blackwell, 1993) which has an extensive bibliography.

[15] The German *recht/unrecht* does not seem to entirely adequately translated by "legal" and "illegal". To use "legal" and "non-legal" would, however, probably open the distinction up too much to reflect the kind of binary coding that Luhmann considers to be characteristic of autopoietic systems.

'Why is it illegal?' will be 'Because the law says it is illegal'. Teubner puts it as follows:

> As soon as legal communications on the fundamental distinction between legal and illegal begin to be differentiated from general social communication, they inevitably become self referential and are forced to consider themselves in terms of legal categories. This leads to 'vicious' and 'virtuous' circles, tautologies, contradictions, paradoxes and infinite regress. The law is forced to describe its components using its own categories. It begins to establish norms for its own operations, structures, processes, boundaries, environments - indeed for its own identity. When it actually uses these self descriptions, it has begun to constitute its own components. This leads to the emergence of self referential circles in relation to legal acts, legal norms, legal process and legal dogmatics, with the result that the law becomes increasingly 'autonomous'. The law determines which presuppositions must be present before one can speak of a legally-relevant event, a valid norm and so forth.[16]

For both Luhmann and Teubner, however, law is not just self-referential - it is autopoietic. This involves more than just all the components of the system being produced and maintained by the system itself. The system has to be able to describe the distinction between itself and its environment and to regulate its own reproduction exclusively in terms of what it considers to be part of itself. Thus, for Teubner:

> Law becomes autopoietic when its self descriptions develop and practice a theory of legal sources in which norms can be generated by precedents or other processes of law creation internal to the law itself.[17]

One issue on which Luhmann and Teubner appear to disagree is as to the extent to which a system can be autopoietic. For Luhmann, it must be either so or not. There is no equivalent of being "a little bit pregnant". For Teubner, on the other hand, autopoiesis can be a matter of degree.

A great deal can be built upon this kind of model. As all the social sub-systems, such as politics, economics and law, involve radically different constructions of reality, they all operate independently of one another. For each sub-system all the other sub-systems simply form part of its environment, constituted for itself according to its own lights. Thus, if, for example, the law attempts to introduce a price

---

[16] *Law as an Autopoietic System* (cit. n. 14) p 33.

[17] Ibid p 41.

freeze in the economy we find that 'Through the device of a price control norm the law is merely observing its own operations, imagining all the while the economy functions in such and such a way'.[18] It follows that no sub-system can intervene directly in the operations of any other sub-system. The best it can do is to produce a sort of noise or interference to which the other sub-system may react in its own terms. Accordingly, the law can only regulate other areas of social life in a manner that is indirect and uncertain. Appreciating this, and how it is consequential upon the autopoietic character of the sub-systems concerned, will allow both a fuller understanding of the reasons for law failing in its regulatory aims and an exploration of the ways in which it can adapt itself so as to become more successful.

This kind of theory does, however, pose certain problems of its own. First, if both the social system in general and the various specialised sub-systems construct themselves and their own environments, and thus have no real contact with anything from outside themselves, where do they draw their information from? Further, how are they related to one another? Luhmann solves the problem by allowing the social system access to one type of environment - a "materiality continuum", comprising matters such as physical and chemical processes and human sense data - which is capable of informing it directly. It then develops its operations and structures in ways that may make use of this information. The social system itself, including particularly the language it employs, then forms a similar materiality continuum for law and the other sub-systems, providing them with information allowing a common 'participation in the social construction of reality'.[19]

Teubner, however, is critical of at least the second part of this analysis, arguing that, since Luhmann does not think the operation and structures of the social system are the same as those in the materiality continuum, he should not assume that those within the sub-systems will be anything more than superficially like those in the general social system. Nor, for Teubner, will the sub-systems themselves have more

---

[18] Ibid p 77.

[19] Niklas Luhmann, 'Closure and Openness: on reality in the world of law' in G Teubner ed, *Autopoietic Law: a new approach to law and society* (Berlin: de Gruyter, 1987) at p 340.

than a limited amount in common. For they really only resemble one another in four ways. First, they all operate by means of communications, the contents of which have meaning. Second, they employ forms of communication, such as interaction and organisation, that are also forms of general social communication. Third, they may make use of structures found in the social system generally, such as the existence of expectations. Finally, they may share in the same "communicative events". Teubner argues, however, that, in according meaning to these, the sub-systems regard the structures and constructions of reality to be found in wider social communication only as a point of departure. So:

> Social subsystems use the flow of social communication and extract from it special communications as new elements. They use social structures (expectations) for the construction of legal norms and social constructions of reality for the construction of legal reality. They do not need to create these from scratch, merely to imbue them with a new meaning.[20]

Presumably, then, it is because the sub-systems employ forms of communication in common with the social system and because at least some of their structures are revamped versions of social ones, that we should regard them as parts of the social system and not as independent entities. Yet, at the same time, this would seem to deny the fierce autonomy that the theory itself demands. Part of the problem seems to arise because, the further we move away from some kind of materiality continuum, the less the systems appear to have any visible means of support. Yet each one continues to reproduce itself.

One direct - but perhaps naive - line of attack might be to suggest that communications do not occur by some kind of spontaneous combustion but actually take place between human beings. In consequence it is just mystification to talk of the system developing itself when, simply, human beings are developing it. Yet there are problems with this approach. If autopoietic theory is even partially correct in claiming that reality is constructed, then it is at least arguable that humans themselves are simply constructs. The sense in which this might be so can be seen by turning to the legal context and to the concept of a legal person. Kelsen's analysis is as follows:

> What, now, does the statement of traditional theory mean that the legal order invests the human being, or a group of human beings, with the

[20] *Law as an Autopoietic System* (cit. n. 14) p 87.

> quality of legal personality - with the quality of being a "person"? It means that the legal order imposes obligations upon, or confers rights to, human beings, that is, the legal order makes human behaviour the content of obligations and rights. "To be a legal person" or "to have a legal personality" is identical with having legal obligations and subjective rights. The person as a holder of obligations and rights is not something that is different from the obligations and rights, as whose holder the person is presented - just as a tree which is said to have a trunk, branches, and blossoms, is not a substance different from trunk, branches and blossoms, but merely the totality of these elements. . .[21]
>
> The so-called physical person, then, is not a human being, but the personified unity of the legal norms that obligate or authorise one and the same human being. It is not a natural reality but a legal construction. . .[22]

Just as the legal person is constructed by the legal order or legal system, then, it may be that the human being or human person is something constructed by the social order or social system. This does, however, leave a puzzle or two. First, each sub-system will be constructing the human being or the human person for itself. The constructs will thus differ both between each sub-system and between all the sub-systems and the social system in general. Is the human person, then, a somewhat confused amalgam of them all or only that which is constructed by the social system in general or is no single construct possible? Further, if the middle choice is made, what exactly is left to do the constructing once the sub-systems, including the economic, the political and the legal ones, have been taken away?

Second, we may wonder whether the system produces something from which we, as individuals, can detach ourselves, or whether we actually become constructed by it. Teubner's view seems to be that humans are independent psychic autopoietic systems.[23] In which case it would seem that we do have the capacity to detach ourselves. What is not so clear, however, is whether the psychic system operates entirely in its own idiom and solely as a reaction to noise, so that our own autopoiesis is a purely psychodynamic one, or whether it engages in the creation of structures of the same type as those within the social

[21] *Pure Theory of Law* (cit. n. 1) p 172.

[22] Ibid p 174.

[23] Postgraduate Seminar, University of Edinburgh, 1991. See also Teubner, *Law as an Autopoietic System* (cit. n. 14) p 45.

system. Since, to return to the earlier point but at a deeper level, social systems are the outcome of human activity, the theory actually seems to require humans to have this kind of capacity. If so, it is possible that we can, individually, do something to reconstruct ourselves. What is more, we can do so in a way that makes our own self at least partially distinct from the persona society has constituted for us.

The room for manouevre may, however, be limited. For instance, one of the types of interference to which Teubner thinks systems may react is role interference, which occurs when people have an overlapping membership of two or more sub-systems. While he accepts that this may allow communication between them, he is sceptical about the possibilities of this leading to any structural change. In the same way one might expect scepticism about the extent to which changes in individual (or even group) self perception may lead to structural change in society. Equally, however, it is dangerous for any system to use the structures and constructions of reality belonging to another one. For, in doing so, it may begin to disintegrate. If systems are to both to maintain themselves and to operate harmoniously, then, this has to be done by adapting their programmes. This does not mean seeking to achieve certain pre-determined results. Luhmann argues that legal programmes must be conditional, allowing the selection of the appropriate value as the basis of determining what is legal and what is illegal in a given situation.[24] Teubner also points out that this will lead to legal indeterminacy, a reduction in internal consistency and an increasing differentiation in law with, for example, the law of delict being replaced by specialised delicts.[25]

As an approach this is unlikely to commend itself to those lawyers, legal theorists and lay persons who regard consistency and coherence as virtues that the law should strive to achieve, even as ones that are defining characteristics of law. In this context, the English law of provocation provides an interesting example. Following the sentencing of Sara Thornton to life for the murder of her husband, in circumstances where there had been a long history of provocation but where none was being immediately offered, considerable concern was

---

[24] Erasmus Seminar in Legal Theory, Brussels, 1992.

[25] *Law as an Autopoietic System* (cit. n. 14) p 105ff.

expressed as to whether the law as it stood was sufficiently responsive to the experience of women and to the circumstances under which they might lose control. In the subsequent appeal of Kiranjit Ahluwahlia against her own conviction and sentence, the then Lord Chief Justice, Lord Taylor, expressed reluctance to put a new interpretation on provocation. This was because it involved a public policy element to prevent people taking law into their own hands. Defences such as it, self defence and diminished responsibility were used to find a way round the mandatory life sentence for murder. A better approach might therefore be to make a life sentence no longer mandatory.[26]

This attitude gives support to autopoietic theory to the extent that it evidences a legal construction of reality that, as in the cases of *Smith* and *Brennan*,[27] distances itself considerably from more general social constructions. At the same time, it suggests a strong disinclination to introduce anything like the kind of flexibility required by Luhmann's conditional programmes - almost a demand for judging each case on its merits - into the body of the law. If such programmes are to be employed, it is argued then their employment should be restricted to the sentencing process where they properly belong.

The theory also suggests a degree of indeterminacy about what is to count as law. First, it would seem that any communication using the code legal/illegal is a legal one and thus should qualify to be regarded as part of the legal (sub-) system. At the same time, however, the function of such communications is to maintain normative expectations in the face of disappointment. This function can be fulfilled with greater and lesser degrees of success. That may be why both Luhmann and Teubner, while rejecting a top-down model of law,

---

[26] *R* v *Ahluwahlia* [1992] 4 All E R 889. Kirinjit Ahluwahlia was, nonetheless, sent for retrial on the basis that whether she was of diminished responsibility had not been properly considered at the original trial and she was subsequently convicted only of manslaughter. Sarah Thornton failed in her first appeal ([1992] 1 All E R 302) but was retried (after a reference by the Secretary of State to the English Court of Appeal and at its direction) in May 1996 and similarly found guilty only of manslaughter. Having already served more than five years in prison, the judge considered this to have been an adequate sentence and she was released.

[27] See ch II and ch VIII respectively.

do adopt a centre-periphery one. In this context the centre is where paradoxes within the system are resolved. For the legal system, the centre is formed by the courts. A hierarchical organisation will be necessary. Luhmann, however, argues that this does not mean that the centre is any more important than the periphery because it is there - with, for example, legislation and contracts - that variety is imparted to the system. It is just that, with the centre, there is no possibility of saying 'This is not law'.[28]

Teubner, similarly, draws a distinction between state law and various "social quasi legal orders". Yet, at the same time, he seems to want to reject this type of prioritisation, showing sympathy with the kind of pluralism developed by Boaventura de Sousa Santos, where different legal orders are seen not as 'separate entities coexisting in the same political space' but rather as 'different legal spaces superposed [sic], interpenetrated and mixed in our minds as much as in our actions. . .'[29] For, 'We live in a time of porous legality or of legal porosity of multiple networks of legal orders forcing us to constant transitions and trespassings. Our legal life is constituted by an intersection of different legal orders, that is by interlegality'.[30] If, though, we ask in whose minds this interpenetration occurs, the answer would appear to have to be, in major part at least, that of legal professionals. For autopoiesis itself is highly dependent on the use of self descriptions by the system, on its developing and practising 'a theory of legal sources in which norms can be generated by precdents or other processes of law internal to the law itself'. This is primarily a matter for the community of those whose business is the law and the culture to which they are committed.

It would appear, too, that it is only the fact that they still use the code legal/illegal that prevents us from regarding increasingly differentiated areas of law, and the inconsistent constructions of reality found within them, as simply parts of the legal sub-system rather than as further sub-systems of it. Yet the whole logic of autopoiesis seems

---

[28] Erasmus Seminar (cit n. 24).

[29] Boaventura de Sousa Santos, 'Law: a map of misreading' (1987) 14 *Journal of Law and Society* 279.

[30] Id.

to push us in that direction. This raises the question of whether such a simple binary code is actually adequate for the role that it is given in the theory and, indeed, whether the theory does not overstate the extent of the autonomy that sub-systems can achieve, if not from one another, then at least from the more general system of social communication that they are concerned to recast. Similar issues, although in different terms, are explored by semiotic theory, to which the next chapter turns.

X

THE LANGUAGE OF THE LAW

This century, philosophy - with legal theory in its wake - has paid considerable attention to language. Initially philosophers were concerned to eradicate the sort of confusion they thought was brought about by the looseness of everyday communication and the belief that there must be something in the world to which the words used in it referred. This led some of them to try to produce, by way of alternative, a logically exact language that was actually capable of mirroring reality.[1] This enterprise foundered, largely because of increasing doubt as to what, if anything, there was in reality that could be mirrored in this way.

Attention then moved to the slightly less perplexing question of what uses of language might legitimately be regarded as making assertions about reality.[2] The view was taken that such use was restricted to the making of statements that could, in principle at least, be tested for their truth or falsity by experimental means.[3] In consequence, a number of thinkers came to view words that could not form part of such statements with considerable suspicion. Sometimes they wanted to eliminate them from discourse altogether. Thus, in the legal context, A V Lundstedt argued:

---

1 The "father" of this approach, known as logical atomism, is usually taken to be Bertrand Russell, see e.g. *Principia Mathematica* 1903, 'On Denoting' *Mind* 1905, 'Knowledge by Acquaintance and Knowledge by Description' *Proceedings of the Aristotelian Society* 1910-11. Many of these ideas were developed further by Russell's pupil, Ludwig Wittgenstein, who was, however, later to become himself the "father" of ordinary language philosophy.

2 This approach, known as logical positivism, originated in the 'Vienna circle' of the 1920s. Its first comprehensive expression in the English language came in 1936 with the publication of A J Ayer's *Language, Truth and Logic* (London: Gollancz, 1936).

3 This "verification principle" was first formulated by Ayer in the 1936 version of *Language, Truth and Logic* and offered in slightly revised form in the introduction to the 1946 one.

> The chimera, against which we have above all to fight, consists in interposing this imaginary something, a right, between the facts and the possible legal consequences. Nobody has ever been able to give real grounds for the existence of this something. [4]

Sometimes, instead, they wanted to identify the function such words and the sentences in which they were found really performed. This might, perhaps, be one of allowing us to express certain feelings. It is in this light that Alf Ross regards a demand for justice. He claims that 'to invoke justice is the same thing as banging on the table: an emotional expression which turns one's demand into an absolute postulate'.[5] Alternatively the function might be that of attempting, successfully or otherwise, to motivate people to behave in certain ways. To tell people that something is their legal duty may, for example, even be rather like casting a spell over them - inducing a belief in them that here is some force that they are powerless to resist.[6] Less colourfully, Karl Olivecrona argues that words like right and duty actually designate nothing, not even imaginary entities, but that they do still have a function in legal language, namely that of helping to provide guides to action.[7]

Whilst views like these were typical of the Scandinavian Legal Realists, a parallel to them developed even earlier in the United States, based on a different philosophical approach. According to this the meaning of whatever we might say or write had to be found in what followed from it in practical terms and its truth gauged by reference to

---

[4] As reproduced in Karl Olivecrona, *Law as Fact* (cit ch VIII, n. 60), A V Lundstedt, (1932) 1 *Die Unwissenschaftlichkeit der Rechtswissenschaft* p 268. The influence of logical positivism on Kelsen's treatment of rights and even duties is also worthy of note.

[5] *On Law and Justice* trans M Dutton (London: Stevens & Sons, 1958) p 274.

[6] See the ideas of Axel Hägerström, *Inquiries into the Nature of Law and Morals* ed K. Olivecrona, trans and intro C D Broad (Uppsala: Almqvist & Wiksell, 1953) esp xvi.

[7] See *Law as Fact,* esp chs 6 and 9.

whether or not it proved useful when it came to action.[8] So, the statement 'diamonds are very hard' conveys to us that, for instance, diamonds are likely to scratch but are unlikely to be scratched by various other substances. We find it to be true when, for instance, we find that a diamond tipped tool can successfully be employed in the engraving of glass.

This kind of understanding is reflected in what is sometimes called "the bad man" view of law. The full quotation from Oliver Wendell Holmes, briefly mentioned in Chapter I, runs:

> Take the fundamental question, What constitutes the law? You will find some text writers telling you it is something different from what is decided by the courts of Massachusetts or England, that it is a system of reason, that it is a deduction from principles of ethics or admitted axioms or what not, which may or may not coincide with the decisions. But if we take the view of our friend the bad man we shall find that he does not care two straws for the axioms or deductions, but that he does want to know what the Massachusetts or English courts are likely to do in fact. I am much of his mind. The prophecies of what the courts will do in fact, and nothing more pretentious, are what I mean by the law.[9]

An allied approach is that concepts can best be understood in terms of the operations by which we would determine whether something would fit into the category that the concept embraces.[10] Thus, we understand the concept of a mile in terms of the steps we would take (perhaps literally) to establish whether or not the distance between A and B was one. Again, for the American Legal Realists, this leads to an emphasis on the role of the courts, as providing the forum in which such operations are conducted where the law is concerned. These two

---

[8] The version of pragmatism offered by William James in e.g. *Pragmatism* (New York/London: Longmans, Green, 1907) rather than that in the initial account by Charles Sanders Peirce in an article entitled 'How to Make Our Ideas Clear' in *Popular Science Monthly* 1878. A later version is to be found in John Dewey, *Reconstruction in Philosophy* (London: London University Press, 1921) and *Human Nature and Conduct* (New York: H Holt & Co, 1922) with attention turned from the individual to the social usefulness of the theory.

[9] 'The Path of the Law' (cit ch I, n. 25) at p. 460.

[10] This is in line with the theory of operationalism enunciated by Percy W Bridgman in *The Logic of Modern Physics* (New York: Macmillan, 1927).

approaches - the pragmatic and the operationalist - come together in another quotation from Holmes:

> a legal duty so called is nothing but a prediction that if a man does or omits certain things he will be made to suffer in this way or that by a judgment of the court.[11]

A contract is similarly seen as a contingent liability to pay damages. Not all philosophers, though, felt the same kind of need to eradicate such concepts from our language or to redefine them in factual terms. Their concentration was on language as an activity and on the functions that it performed. Besides conveying information, sentences could be used to question, to command, to prescribe, to evaluate, to authorise and so on. Just as sentences should be understood in terms of their function, so too should the words that they contained.

Like the Legal Realists they took the view that the fact that we use words such as 'good', 'tenacity', 'causality', 'choice' and 'contract' does not mean that there needs to be something somewhere to which the words must refer. This was, they agreed, to indulge in mystification, to treat features of language, designed solely to assist communication, as indicating the existence of strange entities. They came to a different conclusion, however, about the consequences of this for philosophy. It should not, they argued, concern itself with attempts to demonstrate whether or not reality does contain such things. It should, rather, concentrate on how what is asserted in the course of the ordinary use of language resembles a common sense view, how it reflects the way human beings actually find the world.[12] All philosophy can, and should, do is to make explicit the various conditions under which it is appropriate to use the various words that form part of our language and to help eliminate the errors that may arise from misunderstandings of the role they fulfil.

The idea of specifying the conditions under which it is appropriate to use a word or phrase points to the fact that language is not merely an activity, it is a rule-governed activity. Thus, in *Philosophical Investigations*,[13] Ludwig Wittgenstein developed the notion of

---

[11] 'The Path of the Law' (cit. n. 9) p 458.

[12] This aspect of their ideas was largely as a result of the influence of the philosopher G E Moore.

[13] Trans G E M Anscombe (Oxford: Blackwell, 1953).

"language games". Just as in chess or cricket playing by the rules which govern the moves can be said to **be** the game, so it is with language. The practice by its 'players' of the rules governing the way that words in it are used **is** the language game. Whilst these rules are sometimes difficult to state with any precision, they can be explained by reference to settled cases of usage. To attempt to use words in a way that is not compatible with the settled or "paradigm" case is not to play the game - just as the boy at Rugby School who picked up the ball and ran with it was no longer playing what we now know as soccer.

For Wittgenstein, however, the use of any language involves the playing of a considerable variety of language games. These can be classified in two different ways. First, there are those games that can be identified by reference to the context of the general type of human activity to which they relate. The legal language game and the medical language game are examples falling within this classification.[14] Secondly, language games can be identified by reference to the particular functions that are performed in playing them - by reference to what the various moves within them are designed to achieve. Language games may, for instance, be concerned with asserting or authorising or questioning or justifying or pleading and so on.

Language games tend to have their own specialised rules for the use of words. Confusion, sometimes even sheer nonsense, may result if a word that appears to be common to two or more language games is used according to the rules of a different language game from the one that is being played at the time. Compare, for example, the conditions under which it is appropriate to use the term "lesion" in medicine and in the law. Some theorists would also argue that serious logical errors can be made when moving from one language game of the second type to another - for instance from that of stating the facts in a given case to that of justifying a decision upon it - if one believes that one is playing by the same rules in both. Indeed, the whole question about the possibility of judges coming to their decisions by deductive means turns on whether such an error is being made by those who claim that they can do so.

[14] Linguists usually refer to these as different "registers" of language.

The most obvious example of an ordinary language philosopher in the context of legal theory is that of Hart. True to the project of looking to see how language is actually used, he designated *The Concept of Law* 'an essay in descriptive sociology'.[15] Similarly, he brings out his allegiance to the idea of settled cases of usage as early as page four of the text:

> it is not a peculiarity of complex terms like 'law' and 'legal system' that we are forced to recognise both clear standard cases and challengeable borderline cases. It is now a familiar fact (though once too little stressed) that this distinction must be made in the case of almost every general term we use in classifying features of human life and of the world in which we live.

Again, the way in which he divides up rules - initially into primary rules of obligation and into secondary, or parasitic, ones that confer powers; later into primary rules of obligation and into secondary ones of change, adjudication and recognition[16] - shows the importance that he attaches to the function that uses of language have.

There are, however, times when Hart appears to move beyond the kind of remit that ordinary language philosophy allows. At one stage in *The Concept of Law* he argues that 'There are therefore two minimum conditions necessary and sufficient for the existence of a legal system'.[17] Equally, in his inaugural lecture 'Definition and Theory in Jurisprudence' he sets out to specify the conditions under which the statement 'X has a legal right' may be said to be true.[18] These conditions, he says, are fulfilled when there is in existence a legal system containing a rule or rules of a certain type, namely one(s) placing an obligation on Y to act in a certain way if X so chooses. These accounts appear to involve more than just specifying the functions performed by the words 'legal system' and 'legal right' in our language and more, even, than stating the conditions under which it is

---

[15] See the Preface to *The Concept of Law* (cit. ch V, n. 40). Arguably, however, this is not something he sustains throughout the text.

[16] Compare chapters II and V of *The Concept of Law*. A particular puzzle is provided by the status of the rule of recognition, since it is not clear whether it is a power conferring rule or a rule of obligation operating at the secondary level and even whether it is a legal rule at all.

[17] p 116.

[18] (1954) 70 LQR 37.

regarded as appropriate to use the words 'This is a legal system' and 'X has a legal right' within our legal language game. They seem to embrace an attempt to make the truth of such statements depend on their correspondence with a set of social facts that hold good irrespective of the particular language game being played.

Olivecrona, for instance, claims that all that Hart can properly argue is that he is stating the conditions under which, within a particularly legal system, the statement 'X has a legal right' would be correct.[19] This point is of importance for Olivecrona because of the extent to which the influences of ordinary language philosophy are evident by the second, 1971, edition of *Law as Fact*. There he suggests that the idea that pivotal words of our legal vocabulary signify supersensible entities covers up the real function of our legal language. In reality there is only the regularised use of language in connection with uniform ideas about correct behaviour, fixed attitudes and relatively common scales of value. The nature of the social machinery, including language itself, is such, however, that it actually directs our behaviour - causes us to act on certain assumptions. This gives the supposed entities counterparts in real life. In consequence 'information ostensibly referring to them becomes a basis for making inferences concerning actual conditions in society'.[20]

Ordinary language philosophy has been criticised on a number of grounds.[21] The two main ones are that, first, it makes the mistake of assuming that ordinary usage is legitimate usage - that, for example, there is nothing wrong with discussing miracles when we cannot know that these really do happen. In others words, the way we actually talk cannot be regarded as settling issues about how we ought to think. Second, if there is a variety of language games, all equally valid, then we can never give a definitive account of any concept. The most we can do is list the various permutations of meanings given to it in

---

[19] *Law as Fact* (cit. n. 7) p 273.

[20] Ibid p 258.

[21] Those that follow are along the lines of those offered by Ernest Gellner in *Words and Things* (Harmondsworth: Penguin Books, 1968) pp32-62 but others can be found e.g. in Bertrand Russell 'The Cult of "Common Usage"' in *Portraits from Memory and Other Essays* (London: Allen & Unwin , 1956).

different contexts - as, for example, we seem to be required to do for the law where a concept like "possession" is concerned.[22] Surely, it is argued, we should look beyond the mere efficiency with which a concept is employed in any language game to some overall criterion by which its value can be assessed. In the legal context this would require us to seek some specific form of a relationship between a person and a thing according to which we could (? justly) say they were in possession of it, no matter our reason for enquiring whether such a relationship existed. In sum, however, these criticisms amount to a re-assertion of the view that there must be something, somewhere "out there" to which the words we use refer.

A similar philosophical debate has arisen out of the development of structuralism in linguistics. There, though, it takes the form of a dispute, not as to whether words refer to something "out there", but rather as to whether the structures we find within language itself and the forms in which we employ it are in any way rooted in human nature.

The origins of structuralism in linguistics are usually found in the *Cours de Linguistique Generale* compiled mainly from lecture notes taken by students from the Swiss scholar, Ferdinand de Saussure, and published in 1916, three years after his death.[23] Saussure himself placed great emphasis on living language, on how it manifested itself in speech and on how it related to its social context. For the purpose mainly of this type of study he drew a distinction between "*langage*", "*langue*" and"*parole*". *Langage* was to be understood as the capacity almost all human beings have for speaking, which requires the right kind of stimuli in order for it to develop properly.

For various thinkers the most interesting aspect of Saussure's thought was his emphasis on *parole*, on language as a set of events occurring in the world. This led some of them to equate language with

[22] Thus "possession" may take on markedly different meanings in criminal law and property law. This is what Gellner calls "polymorphism" and what structuralist writers call "polysemicity". For a discussion of the concept of possession in English law and further references, see R W M Dias, *Jurisprudence,* 5th edn (London: Butterworth, 1985) esp p 277ff.

[23] From the notebooks of E Constantin/F de Saussure, French text ed E Komatsu, 3rd English edn, trans R Harris (Oxford: Pergamon Press, 1993).

behaviour, both being seen as sets of stimuli and responses.[24] Others, however, thought that *parole* could only be understood in terms of the rules by which it was governed, such rules being found within *langue*. This approach fitted more closely with that of Saussure himself, who treated *langue* as a system of mutually defining signs. Signs were to be understood as consisting of two elements - the "signifier": the patterns of sound made in the act of speaking or the patterns of ink on paper made in the act of writing and the "signified": the idea that it conveyed. Signs could be found in two different types of relationship with one another - the "syntagmatic", with other parts of speech (from the notion of syntax or grammar), and the "paradigmatic", with the same parts of speech.

The sign itself was taken to be arbitrary. That is to say the pattern c-h-e-e-s-e just happens to be used for a foodstuff made from processed milk and the pattern c-h-a-l-k for soft limestone. It could well be the other way round. The notion of the sovereignty of Parliament is sometimes illustrated by saying that, while it could not actually turn chalk into cheese in the sense of altering its composition, it could legislate that henceforth chalk shall be called cheese and vice versa and, even, that the chemical components be renamed accordingly. There are problems with this notion of the arbitrariness of the sign since, of course, we use the words we do for the things we do as the result of what is usually a long historical tradition. The structuralist would respond that this is irrelevant to the analysis of language as it is operating at a particular moment in time.[25]

Where students of linguistics began to disagree was about the extent to which the sign was arbitrary. To some this was only entirely true of the signifier, the particular pattern of noise or ink. To others the arbitrariness extended to the whole sign, signifier and signified, the idea it conveyed, alike. For this second group language had to be seen as reflecting the fact that 'human societies somehow "construct" the

[24] For example, Otto Jespersen, *Language: Its Nature, Development and Origin* (London: Allen & Unwin, 1922) and Leonard Bloomfield, *Language* (London: Allen & Unwin, 1935).

[25] Saussure himself drew a distinction between "synchronic" linguistics (the study of a language as it lives at a given moment) and "diachronic" linguistics (concerned with detecting changes in the form and content of language through time).

world of social experience out of a relatively undifferentiated and unstructured continuum'.[26] Benjamin Whorf represents this view when he writes:

> In English we divide most of our words into two classes, which have different grammatical and logical properties. Class 1 we call nouns, e.g. 'house, man'; class 2, verbs, e.g. 'hit, run.' Many words of one class can act secondarily as of the other class, e.g., 'a hit, a run,' or 'to man (the boat),' but, on the primary level, the division between the classes is absolute. Our language thus gives us a bi-polar division of nature. But nature herself is not thus polarised. If it be said that 'strike, turn, run,' are verbs because they denote temporary or short-lasting events, i.e., actions, why then is 'fist' a noun? It also is a temporary event. Why are 'lightning, spark, wave, eddy, pulsation, flame, storm, phase, cycle, spasm, noise, emotion' nouns? They are temporary events. If 'man' and 'house' are nouns because they are long-lasting and stable events, i.e. things, what then are 'keep, adhere, extend, project, continue, persist, grow, dwell,' and so on doing among the verbs? If it be objected that 'possess, adhere' are verbs because they are stable relationships rather than stable precepts, why then should 'equilibrium, pressure, current, peace, group, nation, society, tribe, sister,' or any kinship terms be among the nouns?[27]

The consequence of all this is that we find that we cannot define things and events and objects and relationships from nature but only through the grammatical categories that our language employs. Indeed, the ways in which we use language actually determine the ways in which we perceive the world. We are, in effect, prisoners of our language. And, since language is a social phenomenon, this makes us prisoners of the society in which we live.

By contrast, other students of linguistics argue that what is signified, if not by individual signs, at least by the ways in which these are combined together, cannot be explained away as entirely socially conditioned. Part of the impetus toward this approach came from the ideas of Noam Chomsky.[28] He argued that the methods of classification used in linguistics to date - largely dividing language up into word parts, words, classes of words, sentences and types of sentences - could not properly explain the almost infinite number of

---

[26] Max Black, *The Labyrinth of Language* (Harmondsworth: Penguin Books, 1972) p 95.

[27] Benjamin Whorf, 'Science and Linguistics' (cit. ch I, n. 35) para 15.

[28] *Syntactic Structures* (The Hague: Mouton, 1957).

sentences that a language could generate. Nor could it explain either how sentences composed of the same sequences of grammatical parts might actually have an entirely different grammatical structure. Nor, again, could it cope with the ambiguities involved in sentences such as 'The police were ordered to stop drinking at midnight'.[29]

Chomsky came to the conclusion that similarities of surface grammar disguised the different underlying or "deep" structures of such sentences. Instead of trying to classify languages into elements, linguistics should turn to establishing a set of grammatical rules that could generate any one of the almost infinite number of sentences belonging to a given language but could not generate anything that was not such a sentence. For this purpose what required study was not different sets of sentences but how it was that someone could both produce and understand sentences she or he had never heard before.

His investigations in this respect Chomsky to the view that we must have from the beginning a tacit or unconscious knowledge of grammatical rules. This view was, he argued, supported by studies of children learning to speak. And, he concluded, such innate grammatical rules must somehow be connected with the structure of the human brain. If he is correct, then, the question, asked in Chapter I, as to whether reality as it is for human beings has to take the shape it does, must be answered in the affirmative, at least where language is concerned. For we clearly cannot be seen as constructing this part of our social reality in some fashion that seems convenient to us. Its structures - if only of a grammatical kind - are derived from the way we ourselves are structured and that is not something over which we have any real measure of control.

Various of Chomsky's followers, however, came to view his analysis as too restricted. In their view the idea of a well formed sentences did not just depend on grammar but on matters of semantics (or word meaning) as well. For instance, as Chomsky himself pointed out, a sentence such as:

Curiously deep, the slumber of crimson thought:
While breathless, in stodgy viridian,
Colorless green ideas sleep furiously.[30]

[29] D Crystal, *Linguistics* (Harmondsworth: Penguin Books, 1971) p 211.

[30] From John Hollander, 'Coiled Alizarine' in *The Night Mirror* (New York: Atheneum, 1971).

while acceptable enough as a sequence of grammatical parts is not a well formed one in the context of the English language. In consequence, understanding the grammar of a sentence has to start with a description of its meaning and any rules about the sequence that the parts of sentences may follow have to be seen simply as rules for expressing meaning. This view goes to the very root of Chomsky's theory for, if issues of structure and word meaning cannot be separated, it seems unlikely that the existence of the same deep structures underlying all languages can be maintained - unless, of course, it is the meanings that are generated first, on some common basis, and the grammatical forms adopted to reflect them. This returns us to the whole question of the basis on which we construct reality, with the additional problem of how there can be so many apparent variations at the surface level.

One way of approaching this issue that has had considerable influence upon legal theory is to be found in the works of A J Greimas. Just as the anthropologist Claude Levi-Strauss had claimed to find a unified human nature underlying cultural variety and governing social structures, so Greimas detects certain deep-down universal conditions that must be met in order for human discourse to have any meaning at all. For instance, much of such discourse consists in the telling of stories or "narratives". Even where the discourse does not itself involve the telling of a story, a story can still be told about the discourse. When - as is mostly the case - the story is concerned with human action, it depends on such action being understood as goal directed. Since the achievement of goals can be helped or hindered in various ways, there will be roles of a helping and of a hindering kind to be filled. Further, such roles need to be filled at different stages of the action - that at which the goal of the actor and her or his competence to achieve it is set, that at which the actor does something directed toward achieving the goal, and that at which this is seen to be successful or not.[31] The requirement for certain roles to be filled at certain stages will hold good no matter the story being told and will

[31] These stages are called respectively those of "contract", "performance" and "recognition".

provide its deep structure.[32] What particular actor or actors fill which roles and at what stages will, however, vary from one story to the next, just as they do in the human actions that the story relates.

This kind of analysis of action can be illustrated, in the legal context, with the example of contract. At stage one we are concerned with the nature of the obligation the party is undertaking - what the French call the object of the contract - and its appropriateness in legal terms and with her or his capacity to make that kind of commitment; at stage two with, first, the formalities, if any, that have been gone through and then, second, with what, if anything, is actually given or not given or done or not done subsequent to them; at stage three with the extent to which the other party is satisfied. If he or she is not sufficiently so, we may also become concerned with what a court (or some other "referee") makes of the whole sequence.

Not only will the roles the actors fill and the stages at which they do so vary from story to story but so too will the sorts of words and phrases that are used. This is partly because both the story concerned and any discourse it describes will be conditioned by the goal to which the action is directed and by the types of actors filling the roles that affect the achievement of that goal. In addition, the telling of the story itself can also be seen as an action about which a further story can be told.[33] Thus, in the legal context, we can distinguish between the stories told in the course of the trial (by different witnesses, by counsel

---

[32] For Greimas, there is only one deep narrative structure of the kind just described. see e.g his *Semantique structurale*, 1966, trans D McDowell and others as *Structural Semantics* (Lincoln and London: University of Nebraska Press, 1983); *Du sens* (Paris: Seuil, 1970), trans P J Perron and F H Collins as *On Meaning* (London: Pinter, 1987); and (with E Landowski) 'Analyse sémiotique d'un discours juridique' in A J Greimas ed, *Sémiotique et sciences sociales* (Paris: Seuil, 1976). Contrast the view of Vladimir Propp *The Morphology of the Folktale* Russian edn 1928, trans L Scott, 2nd edn rev and ed A Wagner, intro A Dundes (Austin: University of Texas Press, 1968) and the view that there are thirty-one different narrative functions (or types of deep structure).

[33] On this point see Bernard Jackson, *Law, Fact and Narrative Coherence* (cit. ch IV, n. 56) ch 3, referring to W L Bennett and M S Feldman, *Reconstructing Reality in the Courtroom* (New Brunswick: Rutgers University Press, 1981).

for the prosecution and the defence and - in English law - by the judge in his or her summing up), stories of the trial (the trial as its conduct is reported in various different newspapers and on radio and television) and, even, stories of the stories of the trial (reflections on the different versions of the story of the trial that have been offered by the media).

Another reason that the words and phrases used will differ from one story to the next also results from the nature of human action. At one level our physical behaviour can be seen simply as a set of muscular movements. For that behaviour to be regarded as action, certain interpretations need to be made of the events concerned. At one level my hand is just moving in a certain pattern, at another it is being used in conjunction with a pencil to put a cross on a piece of paper, at yet another I am voting in an election. Interpreting something as human action may, however, relate only incidentally to physical behaviour. Speaking, for example, is a form of human action and its significance comes not so much from the patterns of noise emerging from the larynx as from the meanings accorded to these. Further, as well as being a form of human action, speaking is a method by which certain other actions can be performed. Thus, in certain circumstances, use of the single word "done" may be enough to perform the action of accepting an offer and so complete the complex of actions by which a contract is concluded.

If, then, human action is to be understood as directed toward goals, it is not unreasonable to suppose that patterns of usage will develop that are peculiar to particular goals. These patterns may include not just the adoption of a specialised vocabulary or the attaching of specialised meanings to certain more generally used words and phrases but the development of a whole style of communication or discourse.[34] The discourse may include a characterisation of itself as being of a particular kind, as "legal" or "political" or whatever. Nonetheless there may be considerable variations within the different kinds of discourse, depending on the actors and the goals that are involved. As Bernard Jackson argues:

---

[34] Jackson identifies within legal discourse a high degree of restriction of words to one meaning only and a heavy use both of nominalisation and of double expressions. See his *Semiotics and Legal Theory* (London: Routledge & Kegan Paul, 1985) p 35ff.

> We may, for example, find that the lawyer-client discourse has more in common with that between doctor and patient than with other types of "legal" discourse. We may find that the means used for conveying that a particular discourse is "legal" is entirely different when the discourse is between layman and layman, lawyer and lawyer, client and lawyer, lawyer and judge etc.[35]

Despite the common deep structure that gives rise to discourse, then, Jackson sees Greimasian semiotics allowing both for considerable variation in its actual operation at the surface level and for a variety of approaches to understanding that operation. In particular, he claims, it allows legal discourse to be seen, as it is by critical legal studies, as a kind of discourse of power.[36] For other thinkers, however, this kind of approach is still too wedded to the notion that there is anything beyond discourse. To accept, as Jackson does, that where semiotics 'interests itself in universal semiotic phenomena, it thereby suggests the existence of a universal (thus, not socially constructed) subject'[37] is to accept the unacceptable.

Thus Peter Goodrich argues that meaning has, instead, to be understood as entirely socially determined and as constituted solely through "discursive processes".[38] While such discursive processes may be both numerous and ideologically divergent, meanings within them will reflect the structures of the institutions through which the particular "registers" or "codes" governing the different processes are developed. Since the structures of these institutions are themselves the outcome of the way in which power is distributed, such power relationships will reemerge within the register or code concerned. The effect will be to limit - even to determine - what can meaningfully be said within the discourse and, even, the circumstances under which it is sayable. As Goodrich puts it:

> Linguistic structure itself encodes inequalities of power and is also instrumental in enforcing them. The linguistic structure of a text or particular institutional practice is thus a matter for critical interpretation.[39]

---

[35] Ibid p 32.

[36] Ibid ch 7.

[37] Ibid p 190.

[38] *Legal Discourse* (London: Macmillan, 1987) ch 4.

[39] Ibid p 79.

For Goodrich, a failure to appreciate how law and legality operate as a modality of power will, amongst other things, perpetuate the idea that there is only a limited class of people competent to read legal language, this idea itself being geared to the reproduction of an economic elite and the discriminatory values that such an elite serves. Instead, legal language should be understood as a form of rhetoric and jurisprudence should concern itself with identifying 'the persuasive and argumentative mechanisms that permit the law to postulate that it is based upon and adequately reflects a consensus as to values and as to social justice'.[40]

This approach, he acknowledges, will not produce a concept of law. Indeed it would be a mistake to believe that everything we encounter as legal, whether it is legislation, institution or juridical practice, could be fully explained through discourse analysis. It does, however, act as a corrective to those approaches that have attempted to find some unified concept of law based in its essential relationship to some external factor, such as reason, nature or economics. For it presents law as '. . . a social practice formally tied to particular institutions and apparatuses and primarily, though by no means exclusively, defined by its use of particular types of discourse'.[41]

Legal discourse needs to be looked at from two perspectives. One perspective is concerned, first, with the institutions to which the discourse is tied and the way in which these institutions ensure that it is socially authorised. This perspective is concerned, second, with the way in which the language the discourse employs takes a form that presents it as authoritative, as being both rational and universal, and as scientific, as being, for example, both precise and predictable.[42] These are, however, closely related, for:

> It is contradictory. . . to suppose that the dialogic nature of legal discourse is solely a feature of its semantic presuppositions and choices alone, without at the same time showing that legal language in its entirety is embedded in the history of its institutionalisation and in the complex

---

[40] Ibid p 111.

[41] Ibid p 159.

[42] This perspective is what Goodrich calls "intradiscourse".

> interrelations of various languages, multiple audiences and frequently divergent communicative and practical effects.[43]

Similarly, the form the language takes cannot be understood independently of the other perspective - namely, how legal discourse is related to other discourses and to the social whole.[44] Goodrich argues that legal discourse will define out all other discourses that run counter to its basic belief system, using:

> techniques or mechanisms which work precisely to perpetuate the social image or rhetoric of an authorised discourse, a univocal and closed control of meaning, which is persuasive in large measure by virtue of the success with which it systematically denies or excludes its intertextuality, its embeddedness or imbrication within surrounding discourses and socio-political practices.[45]

Legal discourse thus constitutes itself as 'authoritarian, distanced and closed',[46] and yet, at the same time, represents itself as establishing a unified network of true, or objectively valid, meanings that are unproblematic since they reflect 'a consensus as to values and as to social justice'.

A major task for legal theory, then, is to examine the actual nature of legal discourse. In doing so it must avoid both falling into the trap of accepting the claim it makes for itself of unity and objectivity and, at the opposite end, into that of regarding it as 'purely and simply the malleable or transparent instrument of ideological purposes'.[47] To do the former is to ignore the extent to which it is rooted in power and hierarchy, to do the latter is to ignore the extent to which it has become institutionalised and to do either is to ignore the extent to which it is embedded in social practice.

One of the difficulties in this analysis seems to be in determining what amounts to legal discourse. If it is to be identified by reference to particular forms of vocabulary and sentence construction then, in theory at least, anyone can join in. In practice, however, such usage is the province of a professional elite and the dialogue, for those outside that elite, comes over as monologue. This seems to argue a return to

---

43 *Legal Discourse* (cit. n. 38) p 169.

44 What Goodrich calls "interdiscourse".

45 *Legal Discourse*, p 187.

46 Id.

47 Ibid p 169.

a legalist approach, in the sense that it makes law the domain of the few. Further, there appears - short of revolution - to be no way out of this, given the way in which legal discourse is rooted in power and hierarchy, the result of institutionalisation and embedded in social practice.[48]

Another of the difficulties with the analysis concerns the degree to which law can be successful in excluding discourses that run counter to its basic belief system. It must be able to do so to some extent, for it to be capable of arriving at an image of itself - however false it may be - as unified and objective. Yet, insofar as it does exclude other discourses, and develop the univocality of meaning that Goodrich argues is characteristic of it, it necessarily achieves a degree of unity. Further, since on Goodrich's account there are never any univerally valid meanings but only socially determined ones, its claim to objectivity is as good (or as bad) as that in any other discourse. In addition, to the extent that it succeeds as portraying itself as socially authorised it actually becomes so.[49]

These two difficulties, when taken together, give rise to a degree of tension in Goodrich's approach. Despite the avowal that there is a multiplicity of discourses both within and outside law, legal discourse as a whole is seen as the province of the powerful and identified largely at the black letter level. Yet, at the same time, that discourse is to be criticised in terms of what it excludes. Instead of being taken to involve a 'code which. . . forms a series of necessary truths', it should be considered in terms of what, in a self protective manner, 'it systematically endeavours to deny or obscure'.[50]

The method advocated is that of "deconstruction", the approach favoured by United States Critical Legal Studies. This returns to the structuralist view that one level at which parts of speech can be studied

---

[48] Although Goodrich does suggest that a start might be made by a different approach to the education of lawyers. On this point see also David Sugarman, '"A Hatred of Disorder": Legal Science, Liberalism and Imperialism' in Peter Fitzpatrick ed *Dangerous Supplements* (London: Pluto Press, 1991) p 34 and numerous contributions from those involved in American Critical Legal Studies.

[49] A similar point is made by Unger, *Law in Modern Society* (cit. ch II, n. 55) at p 56f in relation to the Rule of Law.

[50] *Legal Discourse* (cit. n. 38) pp 205-6.

is the paradigmatic, which concerns the relationship they have with other parts of the same kind. It is argued that to use one word or phrase is to exclude another that might have been used, in particular its polar or binary opposite. Thus, "male" excludes "female", "white" excludes "black", "public" excludes "private", "employer" excludes "worker" and so on. Legal texts - whether statutes, judgments or, for example, contracts - can be read in this light and, indeed, the law as a whole considered in terms of the poles that are systematically disfavoured or excluded.[51]

The problem faced by adherents of this approach arises out of their commitment, like Goodrich, to the view that meanings have no universal validity but are merely socially constructed. While this allows them to criticise judicial decisionmaking, pointing out the political nature of what is presented as an a-political process, it affords them little room to propose an alternative. A programme of replacing the existing poles or values with the hitherto excluded ones - however desirable from the emotional point of view - cannot be supported on any objective grounds. On their own understanding of the world, it would simply involve substituting one form of favouritism for another.[52]

One person who has tried to break free of this constraint is Roberto Unger, with the development of what he calls "superliberalism". Part of the object is to break down existing structures and to introduce a new fluidity into social and legal relationships. Social life would come to:

> resemble more closely what politics (narrowly and traditionally defined) are already largely like in liberal democracies: a series of conflicts or deals among more or less transitory and fragmentary groups. . . All this stands in contrast to a mode of social organisation that to a significant extent pegs people at fixed stations in a more or less pacified division of labor.[53]

---

[51] The case of *Duke* v *GEC Reliance* (see ch VI) provides a useful illustration.

[52] A point strongly made by David Jabbari, 'Critical Legal Studies: A Revolution in Legal Thought?' in Z Bankowski ed, *Revolutions in Law and Legal Thought* (Aberdeen: Aberdeen University Press, 1991) 155.

[53] 'The Critical Legal Studies Movement' (1983) 96 *Harvard Law Review* 563, at p 602.

In order to achieve and maintain this form of social life, new kinds of rights would be needed: immunity rights, supporting individuals in their 'near absolute' claim to security against the state, organisations and other individuals; destabilisation rights, providing individuals with claims directed to the disruption of the established institutions and forms of social practice that have achieved the very sort of insulation and have contributed to the very kind of crystallised plan of social hierarchy and division that the entire constitution wants to avoid;[54] market rights, giving a 'conditional and provisional claim to divisible portions of social capital';[55] and, finally, solidarity rights, entitlements arising out of communal life.

On this basis, it would appear that Unger has only broken free at the cost of implying that his vision of social life, and the values it promotes, has merit independent of these values being entertained within any actual society. If so, he seems to be conceding that there is something beyond that which is contingent and socially determined.

Similar problems relating to issues of contingency and social determination faced by both feminism and post modernism are considered in the next chapter.

[54] Ibid p 600.

[55] Id.

XI

SOME DIFFERENT CRITIQUES

Some feminists claim that the law is male. This claim is not simply to the effect that the legal process is dominated by males - though this may be true for most or all systems, as it clearly is for Scotland.[1] It is not even just one alleging that, since males hold the power by means of which the world is defined or constructed, their perspective on the world is what will emerge in social structures and discourses and become dominant in social life. It involves asserting that their perspective will be made to appear as if it were objectively valid, as if it offered the only possible account of reality. Thus, not only will all areas of life, including legal rules and practices, reflect this male perspective but they will do so in a way that suggests it is beyond question. This, it is argued, can be amply demonstrated by an investigation of the operation of the law relating to rape or domestic violence or, as mentioned in the previous chapter, provocation.

The feminist claim, however, can be widened from individual legal rules and practices to cover the idea of law as such. Law as such, it is argued, is male in that it embodies male values. One account of this kind suggests that the values with which men are concerned are those of being objective, of being rational and of maintaining emotional distance. This is the Kantian "ethic of justice". Contrasted with this are the female values involved in the "ethic of caring", which emphasises what is context dependent and a matter of feeling, which is concerned with connectedness and the responsibility for sustaining relationships. The ethic of justice, 'is founded on the idea that everyone should be treated the same, while the ethic of caring means that no one should be

[1] In June 1996, 8 out of 104 permanent Sheriffs were women. The first ever woman Senator of the College of Justice was appointed at the beginning of July 1996, having served previously both as a Sheriff and as a temporary judge. (In England, at the same time, out of all ranks of the judiciary, 2804 were men and 312 women, with one woman Court of Appeal Judge and seven on the High Court Bench).

hurt'.[2] Whether or not the distinction is a good one, in the sense that natural dispositions towards the former are exclusively, or even predominantly, the province of those with male sexual characteristics and natural dispositions towards the latter the province of those with female ones,[3] it does seem reasonable to suggest that the law - with its emphasis on formal fairness, on rights and on choosing between opposing claims - favours the ethic of justice.

Indeed, the very notion of the Rule of Law may be said to express such an ethic. As MacCormick argues:

> There is always something to be said for treating people with formal fairness, that is, in a rational and predictable way, setting public standards for citizens' conduct and officials' responses thereto, standards with which one can choose to comply or at least by which one can judge one's compliance or non-compliance, rather than leaving everything to discretionary and potentially arbitrary decision. That indeed is what we mean by the 'Rule of Law'. Where it is observed, people are confronted by a state which treats them as rational agents due some respect as such. It applies fairly whatever standards of conduct and judgment it applies. This has real value, and independent value, even where what is done falls short of any relevant ideal of substantive justice.[4]

Yet, the penalty to be paid for avoiding arbitrariness, by requiring conformity to standards that have been set in advance, is a reduction in the chances of responding according to context and to actual individual needs.[5] It is impartiality, not sympathy, that is prized as a judicial value.[6] Further, the Rule of Law does not only require that

---

[2] Taken from Carol Smart, 'Feminist Jurisprudence' in Peter Fitzpatrick ed, *Dangerous Supplements* (cit. ch X, n. 48) at p 150, commenting on the work of Carol Gilligan, *In a Different Voice* (Harvard University Press, London, 1982). The chapter provides a useful bibliography of feminist jurisprudential writings.

[3] Equally it may be suggested that both types of disposition are to be found, in varying proportion, in all individual human beings, although fostered (and thus made more apparent) or discouraged (and thus kept hidden) as a result of socialisation.

[4] Neil MacCormick, 'The Separation of Law and Morals' in R P George ed, *Natural Law Theory: Contemporary Essays* (Oxford: Clarendon Press, 1992) at p 123.

[5] Except, perhaps, as a matter of coincidence.

[6] Even if, as some would claim, it is a mythical one.

standards be set in advance but also that these standards are general in their terms. Again this means that it cannot cater for the particularity of individual situations. It must, instead, operate at a level above them and, so, at a distance from them. Similarly, insofar as the dispute resolution process operates by means of adjudication - by way of finding for one party at the expense of the other - the extent to which it can function to preserve relationships is a highly limited one.

In sum, from this point of view, law - in its pursuit of objectivity (by the establishing of fixed standards that are taken to be serviceable irrespective of variations in the human condition, whether of capacity, disposition, experience or circumstance); in its rationality (its commitment to the view that set solutions to any problems that may arise can and should be derived from these standards by logical means); and in its detachment (its impassiveness in the face of the destructive effects this kind of approach has where actual human lives and relationships are concerned) - offers only one particular way of organising the world and not a very appealing one at that.

It is not difficult to find instances showing the success of law in developing this kind of character. Where objectivity is concerned, the maxim '*ignorantia juris neminen excusat*' or 'ignorance of the law excuses noone' is just one. More amusingly - although now effectively in disuse - '*solus cum sola in loco suspecto non praesumitur paternoster dicere*' or 'a man and a woman on their own in a secluded place are deemed not to be saying their prayers' is another. One may also cite the imputation of *mens rea* on the basis of external evidence and the use of the McNaghten test for insanity[7] in England or the *Brennan* decision in Scotland in the criminal law and the use of the standard of "the reasonable man" in the law of negligence.

In relation to rationality, almost any case will serve where the judge expresses sympathy for the predicament of one party but claims to be bound by precedent to find against him or her. The decisions of the Inner House of the Court of Session and of the House of Lords in the

---

[7] *McNaghten's Case* (1843) 10 Cl & Fin 200: '. . . the party accused was labouring under such a defect of reason, from disease of the mind, as not to know the nature and quality of the act he was doing, or, if he did know it, that he did not know he was doing what was wrong' - sometimes characterised as posing the question 'Would he still have done it if there had been a policeman at his elbow?'.

Kay case offer an illustration of this, even though policy may have been as influential as precedent there.[8] Where detachment is concerned, the *Kay* case is also relevant in that the small sum of damages eventually agreed as appropriate had already been more than swallowed up in legal costs. At a more general level, one can instance the provision relating to the reduction of benefit levels for mothers who refuse to name the natural fathers of their children.[9] One may even wish to argue that the whole criminal justice system ignores the reality of the fact that, in imprisoning or fining those who are convicted of crimes, it is also "punishing" the innocent to the extent that their families suffer deprivation in consequence.[10]

One problem posed for feminists is as to whether law necessarily operates in this kind of way - as to whether, if claims to objectivity, rationality and detachment are indeed male characteristics, law is intrinsically and irredeemably male. If so, then feminist action must take the form of attempting to reduce (or even eliminate altogether) the role that law plays in social life. Feminists of the kind who regard law as irredeemably male, and so to be discarded, however, face certain special difficulties. This is because, instead of arguing that the male perspective on reality is simply one that is made to appear objectively valid, they appear to be conceding that it is somehow objectively valid, that law cannot be anything other than what men make it to be.

This may suggest that they are, consciously or unconsciously, assuming one of two things. First, that law does have certain essential characteristics, discoverable by a process of reason. This level of reason is shared by men and women alike. (Or else how could women, as well as men, reach the same theoretical understanding of law as involving objectivity, rationality and detachment?) The difference comes in that men do and women do not regard something with these characteristics as a satisfactory basis for the organising of social life.[11]

---

8 See chapter VI.

9 Child Support Act 1991 ss. 6 & 46.

10 See e.g. Ted Honderich, *Punishment: The Supposed Justifications* (London: Hutchinson, 1969).

11 One could argue as to whether this is a matter of emotion or of the operation of a different level of reason, that of practical reason, in terms of divergent male and female interests and purposes.

The alternative assumption is that, while law is merely something constructed, its construction inevitably reflects aspects of the male character and cannot be divorced from them. This approach does not, of course, place what law is like beyond human control. It does, though, seem to go beyond a claim that there is a link between the creation of law and a commitment to 'objectivity, rationality and detachment'. It appears to involve a belief in the existence of a nature that is fundamentally male and of which this kind of commitment is part.

Both these assumptions are problematic in that they embrace the idea that there is some kind of reality outside that which humans have made for themselves. The first of the possible assumptions creates an obvious problem, since the notion that there is something "out there" discoverable by reason is regarded by many feminists, particularly those who regard the law as intrinsically male, as itself a male construction. In consequence, they cannot hold to it without self-contradiction. Yet the second assumption - that law is tied to one form of human nature - is seen by many as the more insidious, since it involves attempting to universalise about the world in a way that is, but is not easily recognised to be, male. If there is some nature that is fundamentally male, the implication is that there is also some nature that is fundamentally female.

Whether or not they accept an account in terms of a disposition to the ethic of caring mentioned earlier, it is clearly the belief of a number of feminists that there is such a separate and different female nature. Indeed, a common feminist cry against men is that they construct "women" in ways that actually belie women's true nature or do injury to it. The feminist task is seen, therefore, as being not just that of identifying this nature but of ensuring that it is accorded its rightful value. Frequently this is taken to involve not just a rejection of the commitment to rationality, objectivity and distance that is attributed to males but an espousal of their opposites. In particular, the tendency is to an anti-rationalism which:

> celebrates the designated and feminised irrational, invoking a strong notion of difference against the gender-neutral pretensions of a rationalised culture that opposes itself to nature, the body, natural contingency and intuition. This project sees itself as a disloyal opposition and envisages a social order that would better accommodate women in

> their feminised difference rather than as imperfect copies of the Everyman.[12]

The practical end point of this kind of argument, when coupled with the claim that law is irredeemably male, would seem to be a social order in which law applies to males, whom it suits, but not to females, whom it does not. Short of this result, though, the argument is liable to backfire on its proponents. For it may reinforce amongst males those very constructions of women according to which they seek to justify excluding them from 'a rationalised culture' and to which they currently admit them only on the basis of pretensions to gender-neutrality.

Regarding law as tied to male nature creates problems at the philosophical level too. For, if subscribing to the view that there is a fundamental human nature is the result - as suspected - of male reasoning about the world, then a claim that there are, instead, two fundamental human natures - male and female - seems to be an insufficient departure from that way of reasoning. To overcome this problem feminists tend either to argue that nature is itself something constructed or else to abandon nature and locate what is feminine in the realities of women's actual experience. This approach is not always consistent, though, in that such experience may still be implicitly attributed to "men being men" in some purely biological or psychological sense. Also, once both of the two assumptions are abandoned and law is seen neither as having certain inherently male characteristics (or ones of value only to males) nor as being tied to some male nature of an unconstructed kind, it becomes difficult to sustain the idea that law is irredeemably male.

Further, if law is not irredeemably male, then a programme of reform directed to introducing law of a new, and more responsive, type may be a viable option. It is not altogether clear what such a law might be like, nor how far it might fit with and how far it would be required to replace existing law. In recent times, however, the call has largely been for law that places women on a genuinely equal footing. This does not mean, as at present, treating them as if they were men. It means, rather, recognising what is different about the way in which

---

[12] Christine Di Stephano, 'Dilemmas of Difference: Feminism, Modernity and Postmodernism' in Linda J Nicholson ed, *Feminism/Postmodernism* (New York & London: Routledge, 1990) p 63.

women actually experience life. As Catharine MacKinnon writes:

> Equality will require change, not reflection - a new jurisprudence, a new relation between life and law. Law that does not dominate life is as difficult to envision as a society in which men do not dominate women, and for the same reasons. To the extent feminist law embodies women's point of view, it will be said that law is not neutral. But existing law is not neutral. It will be said that it undermines the legitimacy of the legal system. But the legitimacy of existing law is based on force at women's expense. Women have never consented to its rule - suggesting that the system's legitimacy needs repair that women are in a position to provide. It will be said that feminist law is special pleading for a particular group and one cannot start that or where will it end. But existing law is already special pleading for a particular group, where it has ended. The question is not where it will stop, but whether it will start for any group but the dominant one. It will be said that feminist law cannot win and will not work. But this is premature. Its possibilities cannot be assessed in the abstract but must engage the world. A feminist theory of the state has barely been imagined; systematically it has never been tried.[13]

As she herself admits, 'not all women agree with the feminist account of women's situation, nor do all feminists agree with any single rendition of feminism'.[14] Many women might, for example, not wish to agree, from their own experience, with a wholesale rejection of the values that the Rule of Law currently seems to espouse. Many feminists do not in fact agree with MacKinnon's own locating of the sole cause of women's oppression in sexuality. Indeed, there are those who think it inappropriate to look for any single cause at all. The reasons for this are to do with the issue of whether women's experience can actually be universalised across cultures or, even, across sub-cultures within the one wider culture.

At one of the hearts of modern philosophical debate lies the issue of what, if any, kind of universalisation is possible, and, indeed, whether there is any way in which one culture can actually "speak" to another. The debate begins with a dispute about what we are like and what sort of knowledge we can have. According to Enlightenment ideas, which are equated with those of modernity, human beings have reason. This reason allows us insight into ourselves. When made use of, it tells the

[13] *Toward a Feminist Theory of the State* (Cambridge, Mass. and London: Harvard University Press, 1989) p 249.

[14] Ibid p 115.

individual that she or he is a unity, has a "self" that is a coherent and relatively unchanging whole. This self is not just something located in the world: it has considerable power to change the world, both natural and social. Such change, however, depends on a proper knowledge of the world and of any limits it imposes. Through philosophical enquiry, reason leads us to an understanding of what such proper knowledge is like and how we can achieve it. First, it will be true knowledge, in the sense that it will reflect the world in an unbiased and uncontrovertible way. Second, it will be universal knowledge, in the sense that it will hold good in relation to every aspect of the world to which it refers. Scientific knowledge thus becomes seen as the pattern of proper knowledge. It is impartial, it tells us global truths and it allows us to change things to good purpose.[15]

Aside from the fact that this appreciation of the character of scientific knowledge is an outdated one, not least in the eyes of scientists themselves,[16] the whole philosophical basis of the Enlightenment is currently under attack. Most radical amongst its opponents are the postmodernists. It would be inconsistent on the part of any postmodernist to attempt to state precisely what postmodernism involves. But the following assessment by two of its opponents, Deryck Beyleveld and Roger Brownsword, provides a useful introduction:

> As we understand 'post-modernism', it refers to a general movement which comprises a number of general theories and positions. Central to all of its variations, however, and most fundamentally, is a degree of scepticism about the employment of reason. . . More conservative proponents of post-modernism might accept that it is uncontroversial that we ought to be rational; but they will insist that 'rationality' is a relative

[15] Although put in my own way and in less detail, I am indebted for the basis of this summary of Enlightenment ideas to Jane Flax, 'Postmodernism and Gender Relations in Social Theory' in Nicholson ed, *Feminism/Postmodernism* (cit. n. 12) at p 41f, although I have omitted her assessment of the relationship between reason, autonomy and freedom (partly because I am not convinced that this approach is attributable to all Enlightenment thinkers and partly because it would complicate the present argument), as also the reference to language, for the second of these reasons.

[16] See for example, Thomas S Kuhn, *The Structure of Scientific Revolutions* 2nd edn (Chicago, London: University of Chicago Press, 1970)

> and variable concept, and they will deny that we ought to be rational in the sense of 'deductive and inductive logic', on the alleged grounds that 'deductive and inductive logic' is merely one discourse of rationality amongst many alternative 'rationality discourses', having no privileged cognitive status. . . More radical proponents of post-modernism might go even further, and claim that all rationality discourses are, when subjected to their own rationality criteria, incoherent or ungrounded in the final analysis.[17]

They conclude that, whichever form postmodernism takes, it denies the possibility of any absolutely certain foundation for human knowledge being found.

The term "postmodernism" was coined by Jean-François Lyotard.[18] For Lyotard, there are two possibilities for those who cling to Enlightenment ideas in the contemporary world. The first is for them to see society as a whole serving some identifiable end or ends. Knowledge, particularly scientific knowledge, is thus regarded as something functional. It is equated with "performativity", that is with the power to achieve the identified ends. What legitimates power is its actual achieving of them. In this way power actually legitimates itself.[19] The second possibility for adherents of Enlightenment ideas is to look on society as internally divided or as an arena of conflict. What is needed is the development of the kind of critical knowledge that will empower human beings to become reconciled to one another. What is sought is agreement about the truth.

For various thinkers, including Lyotard, however, neither of these approaches can be sustained. It is no longer credible to try to give any single account of knowledge; nor is it so to argue in terms of finding any kind of universal truth. The reasons for this are: First, we have

---

[17] 'The Implications of Natural-Law Theory' in Anthony Carty ed, *Post-Modern Law: Enlightenment, Revolution and the Death of Man* (Edinburgh: Edinburgh University Press, 1990) p 145

[18] *The Postmodern Condition: A Report on Human Knowledge,* trans G Bennington and B Massour (Manchester: Manchester University Press, 1984).

[19] It can be argued, however, that this is not so much a modern as a pre-modern view (see later in the chapter) and that theorists such as Luhmann, who wish to rid the world of complexity, are clinging to pre-modern ideas.

learnt that we cannot each, as Enlightenment ideas suggested, stand back from and look in on some coherent and relatively unchanging self. For it is only through our behaviour that we actually become what we are. Thus, it is not because I see myself as ecologically concerned that I buy biodegradable products. Rather, it is the buying of biodegradable products that constitutes me as ecologically concerned. Nor can we regard ourselves as in charge of the world. Instead, in the course of our lives, we both create and are acted upon by social and historical forces that we do not fully comprehend. It is only by gaining some understanding of the play of these upon us that we can come to know ourselves at all. Indeed, on the more radical accounts, there is no self to get to know other than the behaviour that is being produced by a particular constellation of forces at a given moment in time.

Second, we have come to recognise what is wrong with the Enlightenment aspiration to true and universal knowledge. For Enlightenment thinking actually allows to exist only that which we can directly encounter and reduce to order in our thoughts. What is arrived at in consequence is a version of reality constituted in the course of attempts to simplify and control it. This cannot, therefore, be said to mirror the natural and social world in the way that real truth and genuine universality would require. Indeed, the very belief that these are possible reveals itself as part of the "episteme" or way of thinking of a particular age - the modern one. This way of thinking can be contrasted with the pre-modern, which sees the world in constant danger of decay, something only to be avoided by the maintaining of unity and hierarchy, and the postmodern, which recognises the existence of difference, fragmentation and complexity.

Third, knowledge is not something private to us - what we have of it depends on a shared language which, again, does not reflect or represent some inner self or some external reality but, rather, shapes and expresses the understanding of the world that is common to a particular community. As mentioned in the last chapter, Wittgenstein argued that, within such a community, we play a number of different language games, each of which has its own setting and conventions. Two aspects of his argument are of particular importance in the present context. First, with each language game, we both learn the rules and demonstrate what they are as we use them. Second, the language game of describing things as we see them has no greater status than any other of the games that language allows us to play. Of his own illustration of the types of language game that can be played, Wittgenstein writes that they are:

> set up as *objects of comparison* which are meant to throw light on the facts of our language by way not only of similarities, but also of dissimilarities.[20]

One implication that can be taken out of this is, *pace* Wittgenstein himself, that we are as much divided by the language games we cannot play as we are united by the ones that we can.

The problem then becomes that of whether the sets of language games played within different societies or social groups are so divergent that they are unable to communicate with one another. Lyotard has no doubts on the matter. In his view, language games are not merely distinct - they actually have no common basis. This rules out both the possibility of direct translation between them and that of constructing some other language that will allow members of such groups to play one such game or set of games together.[21] One cannot, for example, arrive at a notion of Justice - only explain what justice is taken to mean in a given context.

Indeed, for Lyotard, we should abandon all attempts at 'grand narratives of legitimation'[22] and confine ourselves to the investigation of specific discourses, that is the actual playing of particular language games. If we are to tell any story at all - in relation, for example, to what, for our own group, is regarded as being justifiable or correct - then this can only be by way of describing the practices we actually engage in in the course of the language game concerned.[23] For Lyotard, however, such stories still:

> define what has the right to be said and done in the culture in question, and since they are themselves part of this culture, they are legitimated by the simple fact that they do what they do.[24]

Yet, even though such stories may be legitimate in their own terms, the discourses that they describe have no foundations. Such discourses are

---

[20] *Philosophical Investigations* (cit. ch X, n.13) para 130.

[21] This is the notion of "incommensurability".

[22] *The Post Modern Condition* (cit. n. 18) ch 5.

[23] 'le petit récit'.

[24] *The Post Modern Condition* p 23.

not even a matter of consensus. Rather, they reflect the outcome of a contest.[25] This outcome is not, though, any kind of final one - our discursive practices, the ways in which our language games are played, are continually being modified. In addition, the "self" seems to be constituted simply by the set of discursive practices in which an individual is currently participating.

The problem with this understanding, though, is that it seems to preclude any kind of criticism, either of the story itself, or of the kind of discursive practices it describes or of the sorts of selves that are constituted by them. This leaves open only a highly conservative liberalism or a philosophy devoid of any political content at all.[26] Lyotard himself, however, does seem to think that some measure of criticism is possible by means of the kind of self-reflection engaged in by modern science, which is 'theorising its own evolution as discontinuous, catastrophic, nonrectifiable and paradoxical'.[27]

What might emerge as the result of philosophy theorising its own evolution in the same kind of way is not altogether clear. Most criticism coming from within postmodernist thought remains addressed to Enlightenment style thinking. One aspect of it, particularly commented on in the jurisprudential context, is the way in which such thinking attempts to exclude or redefine anything which does fit not within its categories (what postmodernists call "the other"). This is illustrated in Peter Fitzpatrick's discussion of imperialism:

> unlike the slavery of antiquity or of the Hispanic colonisations, the slave under liberal capitalism was unredeemable-named, recognised as essentially, irrevocably other. In short, racism gave identity to 'the comity of [civilised] nations' as the bearers of universal Enlightenment - an identity constituted in opposition to the savages and barbarians without[28] . . . Anything that resisted re-creation in imperialism's own terms was

[25] Lyotard uses the term "agonistics" - originally to do with Greek sporting activities, such as chariot racing.

[26] The latter is effectively Rorty's position - see e.g. Richard Rorty, *Philosophy and the Mirror of Nature* (Princetown: Princetown University Press, 1979).

[27] *The Post Modern Condition* p 60.

[28] "The Desperate Vacuum": Imperialism and Law in the Experience of Enlightenment' in *Post-Modern Law (*cit. n. 17) p 97f.

denied or suppressed[29]. . . As the repository of present and future truth, Enlightenment could not recognise any efficacy in counter-traditions that was more than evanescent or residual. So, with colonialism, existing social relations were taken, reconstituted in terms of its imperatives and then, as it were, given back to the people as their own. In this, history was denied - the colonised were to be brought into History - and 'custom' created instead.[30]

Yet, on a postmodernist account, such actions did not actually succeed in eradicating the other. Thus Fitzpatrick claims that imperialist law, in constructing and recognising both custom and natives acting in accordance with that custom, stood, at the same time, in constant opposition to them, so emphasising their essential "alterity" or otherness.[31] With the passing of Enlightenment ideas and in the postmodern world, however, boundaries of this kind are in the process of breaking down. The task for postmodern jurisprudence, then, becomes, at least in part, that of examining how the law, in dealing with another discourse, enters into a space between itself and that other discourse and brings in something new which denies the distinct identities of each. This something new is both unsettled and unsettling. It thus allows for questioning and change.

For Costas Douzinas and Ronnie Warrington, with Shaun McVeigh, law - indeed the whole of social life - should be read as if they were texts. In reading these texts, we should aim only to 'tell small-scale, provisional, open stories about our lives and the world'.[32] Telling such stories involves paying 'attention to the repressed and oppressed dialects and idioms that are always in but apparently excluded from complex texts' and having the 'intention to unsettle apparently closed systems and empires of meaning'.[33] In sum:

> Our lives are both texts that we create, and texts created by the laws of others. This interplay opens the space for new reading, writing and speaking, for becoming other than what we are. Postmodern jurisprudence

---

[29] Ibid p 99.

[30] Ibid p 100.

[31] Ibid p 104.

[32] Costas Douzinas and Ronnie Warrington with Shaun McVeigh, *Postmodern Jurisprudence: The Law of Text in the Texts of Law* (London: Routledge, 1991), the Introduction at p x.

[33] Id.

understands the law otherwise and reads the other in the law.[34]

Thus, they write of their own voyage in postmodern jurisprudence that it is not concerned with testing one jurisprudential theory against the other but with letting the texts show how they 'contain both the lofty symbols of a fixed modernity and the lowly marks of an itinerant postmodernity'.[35]

One criticism that may be levelled at postmodernism, however, is that it has a tendency to suffer from an internal contradiction. Rather than just offering a description of the contemporary world and of contemporary ways of thinking, it sometimes seems to set itself up as providing the only possible approach to such description. Thus, Seyla Benhabib criticises Lyotard for privileging one practice of knowledge to serve as a criterion over others. This criterion is provided by the model of a discontinuous, fractured and self-destabilising epistemology, said to characterise modern mathematical and natural science.[36] Similarly, Douzinas, Warrington and McVeigh seem not just to see the law as text but, rather, only as text and only examinable as such. Insofar as it does operate in this way, postmodern theory appears to be demonstrating a belief in the possibility of a single foundation for knowledge of the very kind that it claims to be seeking to destroy.

Yet, even for those it does not entirely convince, postmodernism has the merit of directing attention to the fact that explanations on the grand scale may hide as much, or even more, than they reveal. With feminism, for example, it has had the useful effect of halting a tendency to equate "women's experiences" with those of the white middle class. The problem is, however, that the thrust of postmodernism is such as to cast doubt on the whole feminist enterprise. For, if it is impossible to identify some specifically female way of knowing and experiencing the world, the enterprise seems to have nothing around which it can centre.

The search is thus on for an approach that will allow for the telling of stories on a much larger scale than a strict postmodernism permits but will, at the same time, avoid what is regarded as deficient about

---

[34] Ibid p xiii.

[35] Ibid p x.

[36] 'Epistemologies of Postmodernism' in *Feminism/Postmodernism* (cit. n. 12) at p 120.

Enlightenment beliefs. Such an approach, it is argued, would need to concern itself with particular historical situations and institutions, to engage in comparison rather universalisation, to recognise complexity, to be flexible in the methods and categories it employs and to admit its own fallibility.[37] Allowing that comparisons can be made, though, involves a rejection of Lyotard's belief that there is no possibility of communication between different groups because there is no common basis to the language games that they play. Some ground needs to be found on which such communication can take place.

The main counter to Lyotard comes from those who argue that understanding can be brought about by dialogue. For Hans-Georg Gadamer this understanding is limited to a "fusion of horizons".[38] For Jürgen Habermas, actual consensus is possible. Gadamer's argument focuses on historical rather than transcultural understanding. The problems are, however, similar. For Gadamer, one cannot grasp the events of the past in terms of the understanding that participants had of them. This is because the significance of such events will have changed as a result of other events that have followed them. In consequence, they have to be understood from the perspective of today and according to the assumptions that are embedded in contemporary ways of thinking. For we can only interpret history from a point within history. There is no way of getting outside it.

This holds good for all the ways in which we look at the world. We see it from within a tradition and from the situation in which we find ourselves. With a work of art, for example, the meaning is to be found, not through some attempt to grasp what the artist intended, but in the challenge that the work itself offers to us and our existing prejudices. It makes a claim to truth through which we can each learn something of significance for our own lives. Understanding is thus a matter of participation. It can never be purely subjective because the way in which we apply ourselves to it is always in the context of a tradition. At the same time there can be no one proper understanding because of the way in which our circumstances and concerns differ from one another.

---

[37] See Nancy Fraser and Linda J Nicholson, 'Social Criticism without Philosophy' in *Feminism/Postmodernism* (cit. n. 12) at p 34f.

[38] Hans-Georg Gadamer, *Truth and Method* (cit Intro, n.7) p 273.

Thus, for Gadamer, 'understanding is always interpretation'.[39] Meaning is never determinate. In consequence the fact that we have different histories and that we play different language games does not prevent communication. Rather, these provide the starting point from which such communication becomes possible. If we engage in genuine conversation with others, acknowledging that we are fallible and that their views are potentially true, then a new level of understanding can be achieved:

> Coming to an understanding in conversation presupposes that the partners are ready for this and that they try to allow for the validity of what is alien and contrary to themselves. If this happens on a reciprocal basis and each of the partners, while holding to his own ground simultaneously weighs the counter-arguments, they can ultimately achieve a common language and a common judgment in an imperceptible and non-arbitrary exchanges of viewpoints.[40]

In this fashion, "horizons" become "fused".

What this might mean is illustrated by the following story told by Valerie Kerruish: "Several years ago an aboriginal group living on the outskirts of Perth in Western Australia took objection to the State electricity authority putting a pipe through a brook on land which was 'always sacred, since the beginning of time' to the Aboriginal people. The Aboriginal people's belief is that the Waugal or water-snake 'moved through the area, creating the brook. That is why it is said today, it is the Dreaming Track, wherever it moved across the land'. The Aboriginals wanted the pipe to be constructed over the brook so as not to disturb the Waugul. 'It was to go over the brook and not down into our Mother the Land'. Negotiations with the electricity authority were initially unsuccessful, but the Aborigines succeeded in getting an injunction against the authority from the Supreme Court. Shortly after reading of their success in court, I met the Spokesperson for the Aboriginal people concerned and congratulated him on the victory. He told me, however, that he and his people regarded the court action as a defeat, not a victory. It would have been a victory, he explained to me, if they had been able to negotiate an agreement with the electricity authority. As it was, they had to rely on the goodwill of a liberal

[39] Georgia Warnke, *Gadamer: Hermeneutics, Tradition and Reason* (Stanford: Stanford University Press, 1987) p 82.

[40] *Truth and Method* (cit. n. 38) p 348.

judge".[41]

It is not altogether clear, however, that agreement or consensus is the end to which Gadamer's dialogue is directed. On some readings it is limited to both sides simply expanding their understandings by developing a full appreciation of what the other's point of view actually is. This does not necessarily mean adopting it or some part of it as their own. Indeed, the result could be a position that, though less blinkered, is more entrenched. There is, however, a difficulty with Gadamer's approach. How can we regard the views of others as potentially true or justify accepting or rejecting them, if there is nothing by which we can judge their truth or falsity (or engage in criticism of them) other than the criteria that are accepted in the tradition to which we belong?

It is with accounts, that of Habermas included, of the role of reason in this and other respects that the next chapter is concerned.

---

[41] *Jurisprudence as Ideology* (London and New York: Routledge, 1991) at p 17.

XII

THE ROLE OF REASON

In day to day life we use our reason in two different but related ways. The first of these is directed to relating pieces of information to one another in such a way that we acquire a body of knowledge about the world. For some thinkers the truth of any item of knowledge can be tested by its correspondence with the facts, for others by its coherence with other items of knowledge and for others again by our readiness to agree it with our fellows. Reason employed in this way may be termed theoretical reason. It is concerned with "knowing that". The second use of reason is directed toward guiding our actions, to helping us determine what to do. Reason employed in this way may be termed practical reason. It is concerned with "knowing how".

John Finnis provides one account of what might be involved in such "knowing how" when he argues that worthwhile living requires us to adopt a rational plan of life, in which we pursue various human goods[1] in an efficient way, without any arbitrary preferences between them or between persons, with a commitment to our plan but the capacity to detach ourselves from particular projects within it, while all the time respecting each of the basic goods in all our actions, fostering the common good of our communities and acting according to our consciences.[2] Practical reason will also lead us to the need for human law, for in Finnis's view, 'There are human goods that can be secured only through the institutions of human law, and requirements of practical reasonableness that only those institutions can satisfy'.[3] From this there can be derived a focal meaning for the term law as referring to the:

---

[1] These goods are: life, knowledge, play, aesthetic experience, sociability or friendship, "religion" and practicable reasonableness itself. Although all the goods are equally fundamental, it is open to individuals to choose their own priorities in pursuing them, provided they maintain respect for all of them.

[2] John Finnis, *Natural Law and Natural Rights* (cit. ch I, n. 1) esp chs III, IV and V.

[3] Ibid p 1.

> rules made, in accordance with regulative legal rules, by a determinate and effective authority (itself identified and, standardly, constituted as an institution by legal rules) for a 'complete' community, and buttressed by sanctions in accordance with the rule guided stipulations of adjudicative institutions, this *ensemble of rules and institutions being directed to reasonably resolving any of the community's co-ordination problems* (and to ratifying, tolerating, regulating or overriding co-ordination solutions from any other institutions or sources of norms) *for the common good of that community, according to a manner and form itself adapted to that common good by features of specificity, minimization of arbitrariness, and maintenance of a quality of reciprocity between the subjects of the law both amongst themselves and in their relations with the lawful authorities.*[4][italics added]

So understood, practical reason is clearly very different from the types of reason Lyotard argues are employed by those clinging to Enlightenment beliefs. Its kind of "knowing how" is not about our having the power to achieve certain ends but about our having the "savvy" to do so. One might draw an analogy with the difference between having the physical strength, the appropriate clubs and local knowledge to play a particular hole on a golf course in par and being able to put these together in such a way that par or better is made as smoothly as possible. The first is a matter of capacity, the second one of competence. Nor does Finnis's kind of practical reason seem to stem from a view that society is internally divided and that there is a need for some kind of critical knowledge that will empower human beings to become reconciled to one another.

It may be, then, that Lyotard unduly restricts the roles that reason is capable of playing in modern thinking, even if some, at least, of these might be thought to have more to do with pre-Enlightenment than Enlightenment beliefs.[5] Habermas clearly thinks this is the case. He is concerned in part with establishing a theoretical understanding of the basis upon which both claims about the world and actions are assessed for rationality in actual communities. This involves reconstructing in the form of rules the intuitive "know how" of competent language speakers.

---

4 Ibid p 276.

5 Those of Finnis, for example, are in the pre-Enlightenment tradition of Aristotle and Aquinas.

For Habermas communication between people is oriented toward achieving understanding. We can, of course, say we understand someone when we know the conditions under which we would find ourselves in agreement with them. To Habermas, though, full understanding is only achieved when we do reach actual agreement or consensus. This involves our accepting the rationality of what the other person is saying. When the claim is something about the world, we assess it in terms of its truth; when the claim is about their own intentions, we assess it in terms of its sincerity; when the claim about the forging of relationships, we assess it in terms of its legitimacy.

Corresponding with these types of "validity claims" are various models of rational action. First, there is the kind of action which, given a certain understanding of the world, is directed toward a manipulation of the world. The rationality of the action is judged by reference both to the truth of the claim to understanding the world on which it is based and by the success or otherwise the action itself has in achieving the ends concerned. Such action may be termed instrumental where it is concerned with the physical world and strategic where it is concerned with the social one. Second, there is the kind of action directed toward presenting the actor to the world, with giving effect to feelings and beliefs, motives and intentions. The rationality of such action is judged by consistency between word and deed. Third, there is the kind of action that is directed toward 'creating or maintaining institutions or traditions in which is expressed some conception of right behavior and a good life with others'.[6] Guidance in this respect is provided by accepted norms. The rationality of an action can, therefore, be judged at two levels: as to whether it is in conformity with such norms; and as to whether the norms themselves are valid ones in terms of the criteria by which such validity is to be tested.[7]

---

6 Stephen K. White, *The Recent Work of Jürgen Habermas* (Cambridge: Cambridge University Press, 1988) p 16.

7 White points out that for Habermas these criteria might be expected to involve only the question of the conformity of the norms with other norms that are socially prescribed as being of superior validity but that he actually brings in the 'agent's intuitive sense of what ultimately gives any norm its "ought" quality: whether it incorporates interests which are "generalisable" to all who are affected by that norm.' Ibid p 38.

It can, of course, be argued that these distinctions are not as clear cut as they might at first appear. For example, action in relation to those legal rules that Hart calls power conferring ones, specifying the conditions for making wills and contracts, can be considered both strategic and norm-guided at one and the same time. That said, however, Habermas is concerned to stress that communicative rationality involves competence in testing all the different claims and actions in the course of theoretical and practical discourse with a view to achieving consensus on them.[8]

In particular, Habermas wishes to draw attention to what he regards as the shortcomings of an account of rationality that concentrates entirely on the strategic form. We constitute our knowledge of the world, he argues, in response to certain interests we have as human beings.[9] One of these is in dominating the world, in using objects within it to our advantage. Scientific theory thus constitutes the world as something open to manipulation. Scientific knowledge is judged by its usefulness, by the power it affords us to control the world and by the effectiveness with which such power can be exercised. Scientific knowledge, then, is true knowledge if, in acting on it, we can achieve the ends it serves. Its legitimacy is tested in the same way - it is legitimate because it allows us to achieve these ends.

It may be added that ecological concerns of themselves cast doubt on the question of whether regarding the natural world as there to be manipulated is in the interest - long term, at least - of human beings. More to Habermas's point, however, is that, when transferred to the social sphere, this kind of approach results in human beings being treated as objects, as means to other ends, rather than as agents entitled to dignity and respect. One way of illustrating this is in terms of "rational choice theory" in general and the economic analysis of law in particular.

In most instances, rational choice theory sees the individual as a self-interested being, concerned to gain the maximum satisfaction from life. It can operate at the purely descriptive level, offering an

---

[8] Presumably this must include consensus on which kind of test is the appropriate one in any given instance.

[9] These, it seems are not to be attributed to the existence of some fundamental human nature. Rather, what they are are to be reconstructed out of how we talk and act.

explanation of why people act as they do. It often, however, seeks to say how they ought to act in a given situation. That is, it tries to specify what would be the rational thing to do - this being understood as whatever will bring the greatest satisfaction at the lowest possible cost. Acting rationally is, therefore, a matter of being efficient.

When transferred to the economic sphere, what gives people satisfaction is measured in terms of their willingness to pay for it. Willingness to pay itself turns not just on having the financial resources to do so but also on a calculation of the things that will have to be done without if the payment is made. For example, there may be enough in the bank to take me on holiday to Greece after existing bills are paid but spending the money this way means that the day I can acquire my first ever car recedes even further into the distance. Anything that has to be sacrificed in this way is referred to by economists as an "opportunity cost". Willingness to pay does not necessarily involve actual expenditure. Someone might, for instance, be willing to take the lower waged of two jobs, because of the satisfaction involved in, say, working for a charity, even though this will mean a much more modest life style. Nor can opportunity costs be understood purely in financial terms. The strain of having to worry about making ends meet may well be an opportunity cost of taking the lower paid job.

Given this kind of understanding, together with the facts that resources are limited and that we can acquire ones that give us more satisfaction than those we currently have through processes of exchange, a free market will, it is argued, tend to result in an equilibrium price between those who wish to sell and those who wish to buy, with resources being allocated to those most willing to pay for them. This is "market efficiency". It is said to be efficient not just because it produces a situation in which people are actually gaining the maximum satisfaction at the lowest cost but also because it will allow for the greatest possible production of wealth.

There is, however, one type of cost that will interfere with market efficiency. This is the "transaction cost". One of the simplest examples of a transaction cost can be seen in terms of the ordinary individual buying and selling on the Stock Exchange. What will be paid for a set of shares will be the market buying price plus the broker's charges. Thus the purchase of a small number of shares priced at 45p may, once the broker's charges are taken into account, involve an actual expenditure per share of 48p and so a transaction cost of 3p per share. In real terms, therefore, the individual does not begin to make a profit until the selling price has risen above 48p - for example to 51p once selling costs of say, 2p per share are taken into account.[10]

The basis of the economic analysis of law comes from the Coase Theorem.[11] This argues that whichever legal rule is chosen to regulate a dispute, the outcome will be the economically efficient one, provided there are no transaction costs involved. Mitchell Polinsky gives the following example:

> Consider a factory whose smoke causes damage to the laundry hung outdoors by five nearby residents. In the absence of any corrective action each resident would suffer $75 in damages, a total of $375. The smoke damage can be eliminated in either of two ways: A smokescreen can be installed on the factory's chimney at a cost of $150, or each resident can be provided with an electric dryer, at a cost of $50 dollars per resident. The efficient solution is clearly to install the smokescreen because it eliminates total damages of $375 for an outlay of only $150, and it is cheaper than purchasing five dryers for $250.[12]

He continues that, according to Coase, the same result is reached irrespective of whether the residents are assigned a right of clean air or the factory is given the right to pollute. In the latter case, the residents would also purchase the smokescreen. (For it will cost each only $30 dollars, as opposed to $50 for a dryer or $75 for damaged laundry).

The situation may change, however, once transaction costs are added in. Polinsky asks the reader to suppose that 'it costs each resident $60 to get together with the others (due, say to transportation costs and the

---

[10] A further trap for the unwary is that the price quoted in the financial pages of the newspapers is the median price, with the selling price below and the buying price above it. In consequence, what may at first appear to be a profit situation, even when selling costs are added in, will not necessarily be so.

[11] Ronald H. Coase, 'The Problem of Social Cost' (1960) 3 *Journal of Law and Economics*.

[12] A Mitchell Polinsky, *Introduction to Law and Economics* 2nd edn (Boston: Little, Brown & Co, 1989) p 11.

value attached to time)'.[13] If the residents are assigned the right of clean air, the factory will still purchase the smokescreen. If, on the other hand, the factory is assigned the right to pollute, the cost to the residents of installing the smokescreen will have gone up, as a result of transactions costs, to $450 or $90 a head. This is in excess of the damage actually suffered. The answer, therefore, becomes for each independently to buy a dryer. This is, however, an inefficient outcome.

Once transaction costs are added in, then, there is a basis for preferring one legal rule as against another. The preferred rule is the one most conducive to efficiency because it 'minimizes the effects of transaction costs. These effects include actually occurring transaction costs as well as the inefficient choices induced by a desire to avoid transaction costs'.[14] Various points are of relevance here. First, recourse to the law itself involves transaction costs. Second, legally regulated transactions may be, to a greater or lesser degree, enforced rather than voluntary. It is much more difficult to assess whether these enhance efficiency, although Richard Posner suggests that one might try to guess whether, given zero transaction costs, a voluntary transfer would have occurred in similar circumstances.[15]

Third, the assessment of efficiency is not restricted to the outcome for those directly involved. The smoke screen solution to the smokestack problem, for example, would not be economically efficient if it simply diverted the smoke in a direction that would cause damage of an equivalent or greater kind elsewhere. Actions sometimes do have unforeseen (and, perhaps, effectively unforeseeable) consequences and, even allowing for the predictive force of the notion of human beings as maximisers of their satisfactions, we cannot always be sure just how they will adjust their behaviour in response to legislation or judicial decisions. Law, however, has to limit itself to achieving certain predetermined effects and to proceed on the basis of certain assumptions that may ultimately prove to be unjustified.

---

[13] Ibid p 12.

[14] Ibid p 13.

[15] Richard A Posner, *Economic Analysis of Law* 4th edn (Boston & London: Little, Brown & Co, 1992)) pp 14-15.

Despite such difficulties, proponents of the economic analysis of law argue that it has considerable explanatory power. Posner goes so far as to claim that:

> The economic theory of law is the most promising positive theory of law extant. While anthropologists, sociologists, psychologists, political scientists, and other social scientists beside economists also make positive analyses of the legal system, their work is thus far insufficiently rich in theoretical or empirical content to afford serious competition to the economists. (The reader is challenged to adduce evidence contradicting this presumptuous, sweeping and perhaps uninformed judgment).[16]

Yet, to a lawyer accustomed to judging issues in terms of concepts such as "fault" or according to some kind of principle such as "the polluter pays", this kind of analysis is puzzling. It can be difficult, too, to see a harm as resulting as much from the fact that there are people living close to the factory as from the fact that it is giving off smoke. Nonetheless, legal decisions may well involve viewing matters in this kind of light, as the following newspaper report, dated September 1993, demonstrates:

> A Melbourne brothel has won its fight to have a nearby ballet school closed, arguing that the presence of children was bad for business.[17]

Most proponents of economic analysis argue, though, that they are not claiming that the law ought solely to serve economic efficiency, only that such efficiency is a value that the law does in fact serve and to a major extent. Insofar as economic analysis has any normative or prescriptive force, it is in terms of showing how much efficiency must be sacrificed if other values are to be promoted or with showing what would be the most efficient way of promoting them.[18] Thus Posner admits that 'there is more to justice than economics' but maintains:

> There may well be definite although wide boundaries on both the explanative and reformative power of the economic analysis of law. Always, however, economics can provide value clarification by showing

---

[16] Ibid p 25. In a footnote he cites as evidence Donald J. Black, 'The Mobilization of Law' (1973) 2 *Journal of Legal Studies* 125; Alan Hyde, 'The Concept of Legitimation in the Sociology of Law' 1983 *Wisconsin Law Review* 379; Robert Martinson, 'What Works? - Questions and Answers About Prison Reform' *Public Interest* 22 (Spring 1974).

[17] The Daily Telegraph, 4 September 1993.

[18] *Economic Analysis of Law* (cit n. 15) p 20.

> the society what it must give up to achieve a noneconomic ideal of justice. The demand for justice is not independent of its price.[19]

Yet, at the same time, proponents of economic analysis do seem to want to argue that there is nothing actually unethical in the notion of efficiency, since it requires that the overall benefit equals or, preferably, exceeds any harm done.[20] It can be argued, however, that the approach is much more closely and positively tied to ethics than this admission allows.

First, there is some doubt as to whether a view of human beings as maximisers of their own satisfactions can qualify as purely descriptive. Arguably, in ignoring other ways of characterising human nature, it endorses one particular way of doing so and thus implicitly affords this moral approval. Even if this particular appreciation is contested, the view clearly has certain moral implications. Of course, maximising one's own satisfactions may involve trying to make other people happy - but it does not necessarily involve doing so. The satisfaction maximising model is, therefore, on the face of it at least, compatible with a situation in which each human being regards other human beings solely as potential contributors to or detractors from his or her own satisfactions.

This seems to run counter to what our tradition of morality demands. Taken to the extreme it could make any kind of social cooperation impossible. Stephen White gives the example of Colin Turnbull's study of the Ik tribe in Northern Uganda, where the concern of members for their own individual survival had reached the stage that collective life was disintegrating, with the elderly being left to starve and children over three years of age being driven away by their parents, because both groups were seen 'simply as competitors for scarce food'.[21]

The satisfaction maximising model is, of course, based on the premise that resources, though limited, are actually available for exchange. In such circumstances, the claim is that, if human beings do

---

[19] Ibid pp 25-6.

[20] In the Kaldor-Hicks version. By contrast, Pareto efficiency requires that noone is harmed or is, at least, actually compensated for any harm done.

[21] *The Recent Work of Jürgen Habermas* (cit. n. 6) p.17, referring to Colin Turnbull,*The Mountain People* (New York: Simon and Schuster, 1972).

act in a self interested fashion, then overall happiness will be increased.[22] The problem with this argument is that an increase in overall happiness does not necessarily mean that the happiness of all individuals is maintained or increased.[23] That of some may suffer to a considerable extent. At the economic level the claim is that allowing free transactions between self-interested individuals will increase the available wealth. This will result in an improvement in the position of the worst off. It is possible to argue about how far this claim is supported by the facts. The first part of it does seem to be, given the performance of capitalist as opposed to other economies. The second part is more contestable. On some understandings the effect is an improvement in the actual position of the worst off, even if the gap between them and the best off may increase. On other understandings the effect is to make the worst off even worse off.[24] Perhaps, it is argued, the system might work, given a genuinely "level playing field" to begin with - but that we do not have.

Second, there is an ambiguity in the approach. Its proponents maintain that they are not equating satisfaction with the acquisition of wealth and that other types of satisfaction are just as much grist to the mill:

> Economists are often criticised for assuming that man is wholly materialistic - that man wants "material things". The criticism is unjustified. All we have assumed from the start. . . is that an *individual has desires*. These desires may be embodied in material things such as cocktails and clothes; however, we also fully recognise that men *want* things that are aesthetic, intellectual and spiritual in nature. Some people do want to read Shakespeare and Keats and to contemplate the idea of

[22] On some accounts this actually requires action which does not give any consideration to what one would wish for others, since this will be counter-productive or paternalistic. What one wishes for others are sometimes referred to as "external preferences". See e.g. R M Dworkin, 'Liberalism' in *A Matter of Principle* (cit. ch VII, n. 16) 181.

[23] This occurs only under Pareto superiority, where at least one individual is better off without anyone being worse off, a phenomenon that Posner admits is rare in the course of actual market operations.

[24] For example, the handbook of the UK Child Poverty Action Group, *Poverty: The Facts* (pub Spring, 1996) argues that between 1979 and 1992/3 the poor saw their share of wealth, even after redistribution by taxes and benefits, fall from 9.5% to 6.6%.

beauty. Others want to attend church and worship as they choose. Even a few may want to read this book! We have no quarrel with this (particularly with those who want to read this book). We accept these as values that we must deal with in our analysis. They are part of the data we handle. We emphasise, however, that what we have to say about "material things" is also applicable to those values that are not material. We may talk in terms of "goods," but what we really mean are those things people value.[25]

Willingness to pay can, of course, be quantified in terms of willingness to forego the satisfaction derived from having something one values in favour of the greater satisfaction afforded by something else, as in the case of choosing lower paid work for charity mentioned earlier. Yet, while this may not be true of all economic analysis, there is a tendency, at least, amongst its proponents to move from the view that money is one way of measuring such costs to the view that money is the only way of measuring such costs. Values, so far as possible, are analysed in monetary terms and the efficiency of actions is judged in the same light. In some cases, wealth becomes not just one value amongst others but the overriding one. The notion that behaviour is rational if it conforms to the model of the individual as someone capable of ranking the available options in order of preference by reference to the criterion of what will bring the most satisfaction at the least possible cost becomes the notion that behaviour is irrational unless it is directed to the end of financial reward. Again, at least where this kind of slippage does happen, rational choice theory in general, and economic analysis in particular, cannot be counted as purely descriptive.

Indeed, rather surprisingly, it can be suggested that economic analysis of law is not, as Posner claims it is, a positivistic theory at all but, rather, either a moral theory of law or else a version of natural law thinking. A moral theory of law involves rejecting the positivist claim that a separation of law and morals is possible. On this kind of account, law is seen, for example, as an enterprise that 'can only be conceived in terms of the employment of moral reason'[26] or it is

---

[25] R B McKenzie and G Tullock, *The New World of Economics* (Homewood, Ill: R D Irwin, 1975) p 9.

[26] Deryck Beyleveld and Roger Brownsword, *Law as a Moral Judgment* (London: Sweet & Maxwell, 1986) p 32.

believed that 'Rule judgment is not just legal judgment or chess judgment, but ultimate moral judgment; and nothing less than this is the responsibility of those who make it'.[27] In this context, expressing preference for a legal rule that minimises the effects of transaction costs has to be seen as a matter of moral choice.[28] The second way of seeing economic analysis as non positivistic turns on similarities between its treatment of nature and of rationality and that found in natural law thinking.

Classical natural law theory, as located in the West, may give centrality either to the God-given character of human nature and reason or to human nature and reason as it is actually constituted. In this case, although credit may still be given to God for the forms human nature and reason take, the theory may be detached from theological beliefs. The first approach is found in the works of Thomas Aquinas. To him, God has a plan for the universe, as expressed in his eternal law, which covers all creatures. All of them have a *telos*, an end or ends to which their existence is directed. Divine reason is imprinted on them in the form of a natural inclination toward this end. Human beings, however, are distinguished by a higher level of participation in this reason - 'an imprint on us of the divine light'[29] - that actually allows us access to our part in God's plan. We are thus aware of our *telos* (which might be explained as something like "friendship with God"). We can also 'discern what is good and what is evil, which is the function of the natural law'.[30] Such reason is both of a speculative and a practical kind. Speculative reason allows us to fit our ideas together, as in drawing the conclusion 'one must not kill' from the premise that 'one should do harm to no man'.[31] Practical reason is directed to determining just what such precepts mean in terms of the way we live our lives. Human law is, thus, a dictate of practical reason.

---

[27] M J Detmold, *The Unity of Law and Morality* (London: Routledge & Kegan Paul, 1984) p 22.

[28] This is not to imply that it is the kind of choice that would be endorsed by the authors mentioned above.

[29] Thomas Aquinas, *Summa Theologica*, (cit. ch I, n. 11) Q91, A2.

[30] Id.

[31] Ibid Q95 A2.

On this kind of account, it seems impossible to draw any real distinction between what is natural for human beings and what is rational for them. Nor is there any clear separation between strategic and norm guided rationality. Achieving one's end or *telos* and conforming with what one's *telos* demands come to the same thing. The same connections can be seen in the approach that looks to human nature and reason as they are actually constituted, as represented by the ideas of Grotius. His aim was to:

> refer the proof of all things touching the law of nature to certain fundamental conceptions which are beyond question, so that no man can deny them without doing violence to himself.[32]

These fundamental conceptions are human rationality and sociability. Human beings are impelled to live in society. This is not just a matter of economic advantage, for their sociability means that they want a peaceful, organised life. Further, their rationality is such that, unlike other animals, they can judge the future consequences of their actions and the good or evil that will accrue from them. Human beings need not be carried away by the influence or impulse of the moment. If they were so and were satisfied with what were to their own immediate advantage, ordinary social relations would be impossible. In fact, reason tells human beings that living in society requires a social order. There must be duties to refrain from injuring others, to make good losses caused by fault and so on. Thus:

> the law of nature is a dictate of right reason which points out an act, according as it is or is not in conformity with rational nature, has in it a quality of moral baseness or moral necessity: and consequently that such act is either forbidden or enjoined by God, the author of nature.[33]

Though to considerably different effect, economic analysis of law seems to be making similar connections between nature and rationality. Human beings are naturally inclined to maximise their satisfactions. They are rational in that they are capable of ranking the available options by reference to the criterion of what will bring the most satisfaction at the least possible cost. Behaviour is rational when it actually maximises satisfactions. At the same time such behaviour is rational because it is in conformity with human nature. Equally,

---

[32] *(Three books) On the Law of War and Peace*, trans F W Kelsey (Oxford: Clarendon Press, 1925) vol II, Prolegomena, para 39.

[33] Ibid, I, X, 1.

human beings actually adopt laws that minimise the effects of transaction costs. This behaviour is rational because it is conducive to economic efficency. It is also rational because it is in conformity with the nature of human beings as maximisers of their satisfactions. Once again, strategic rationality and norm guided rationality come to the same thing.

If such arguments are found convincing, then the acceptability of economic analysis of law turns on that of the view it takes of human beings as maximisers of their own satisfactions. The ideas of Adam Smith, as expressed in his *An Inquiry into the Nature and Causes of the Wealth of Nations*[34] and his *The Theory of Moral Sentiments,* [35] provide an interesting contrast in this respect. Under the influence of Newtonian physics, Smith saw human beings as having principles of motion of their own. Such principles of motion are laws in the scientific descriptive sense. But, as they express the will of 'the Author of nature', they are laws in the normative sense too, for, by acting in accordance with them, human beings are achieving the purposes for which they were created. The outcome of their interactions according to these principles will manifest the 'invisible hand' of God.

In the *Wealth of Nations* the principle of motion described is that of selfishness or self interest. Smith considers what happens if every man is left free to pursue his own interest in his own way, and to bring both his industry and capital into competition with those of any other man or order of men.[36]

He argues that this will produce an equilibrium that is conducive to the greatest production of wealth. The role of the state, therefore should be limited to that of maintaining the conditions of peace which allow people to act in this self interested fashion. At least, this is the ideal situation. In practice, economic realities involve the imposition of taxes - to support the administration of justice; to provide basic works, such as roads, bridges, canals and harbours, where these would

---

34 Adam Smith, *The Wealth of Nations*, ed R H Campbell, A S Skinner and W B Todd (Oxford: Clarendon Press, 1976).

35 Adam Smith, *The Theory of Moral Sentiments* (cit. ch III, n. 24). See also the commentary by T D Campbell, *Adam Smith's Science of Morals* (London: Allen & Unwin, 1971).

36 *Wealth of Nations* vol II, IV. ii. 9.

not be profitable for private individuals; and to provide basic education.[37] The state also has a role in law reform - for example, in changing outdated property rules and in breaking monopolies.

In *The Theory of Moral Sentiments*, however, the principle of motion is that of sympathy. Smith argues that:

> How selfish soever man may be supposed, there are evidently some principles in his nature, which interest him in the fortune of others, and render their happiness necessary to him, though he derives nothing from it except the pleasure of seeing it.[38]

We cannot, of course, experience what another person is feeling but we can imagine what we would feel in the same kind of situation. Our reaction is not likely to be as strong as that of the person concerned and we may even feel something that she or he does not. Yet our relationships depend on our having some measure of sympathy, for:

> if you have either no fellow feeling for the misfortunes I have met with, or none that bears any proportion to the grief which distracts me; or if you have either no indignation at the injuries I have suffered, or none that bears any proportion to the resentment which transports me, we can no longer converse upon these subjects. We become intolerable to one another. I can neither support your company, nor you mine. You are confounded at my violence and passion, and I am enraged at your cold insensibility and want of feeling.[39]

The same principle of sympathy by which we may be critical of others provides a basis for us to judge our own motives and conduct. We need to look upon them from a distance and try to view them as an impartial spectator would. This allows us, for example, to measure what would be the appropriate level of retaliation for any injury done to us. It should match the resentment of such an impartial spectator, rather than what we ourselves feel. The reason is that we desire the approval of others. This is not just because we want to be loved. We want to be the natural and proper object of love.[40] Very few of us, though, can be satisfied with our own private consciousness that we

---

[37] Those benefitting, however, should contribute.

[38] *Theory of Moral Sentiments* (cit. n. 35) I. i. 1. 1.

[39] Ibid I. i. 4. 5.

[40] '. . . it is the great precept of nature to love ourselves only as we love our neighbour, or what comes to the same thing, as our neighbour is capable of loving us'. Ibid I. i. 5. 5.

have attained the qualities that make us such a natural and proper object of love. We need to have this acknowledged, at least to the extent of our not being the subject of reproach.

It is not, however, easy for us to be impartial spectators of our own conduct. Nature, fortunately, has afforded us a remedy:

> Our continual observations upon the conduct of others, insensibly lead us to form certain general rules concerning what is fit and proper either to be done or to be avoided. Some of their actions shock all our natural sentiments. We hear every body about us express the like detestation against them. This still further confirms, and even exasperates our natural sense of their deformity. It satisfies us that we view them in the proper light, when we see other people view them in the same light. We resolve never to be guilty of the like, nor ever, upon any account, to render ourselves in this manner the objects of universal disapprobation.[41]

The same process applies in respect of actions that call forth our own approbation and about which we hear others expressing a favourable opinion. In this case, every opportunity of performing such actions is 'carefully to be sought after'.

Smith argues that this is how the general rules of morality are formed, namely 'by finding from experience that all actions of a certain kind, or circumstanced in a certain manner, are approved or disapproved of'.[42] The test for their formation appears to be that they are 'universally acknowledged and established, by the concurring sentiments of mankind'.[43] While it may be too far-fetched to see *The Theory of Moral Sentiments* as containing the seeds of Habermas's notion of communicative rationality, the view that rules come about as the result of a process of interaction and by way of adjustment to the perspectives of others is at least compatible with it. Clearly, too, even if the development of rules were to owe as much to the desire to be loved as to that to be love-worthy or to a natural sympathy for others, and thus stem from a purely self satisfaction maximising strategic rationality, the outcome is the expression of 'some conception of right behavior and a good life with others'. This particular set of Enlightenment beliefs, then, gives further substance to Habermas's

---

[41] Ibid III 4. 7.

[42] Ibid III. 4. 8.

[43] Ibid III. 4. 11.

view that more can be salvaged from modernity than a purely strategic concept of rationality would allow.

What sort of thing, then, does communicative rationality demand? First, communication itself depends on our being able to provide justification for the validity claims we make, whenever others do not find them immediately convincing. This is required because communication is concerned with the forming of human relationships. These become impossible if the truth, sincerity or legitimacy of what is being claimed cannot be sustained. In consequence, someone who denies the need to account for such claims is involved in a "performative contradiction". Further, when the communication concerns issues of legitimacy, there is a performative contradiction involved unless the claim is universalisable. That is to say, it is a presupposition of all argumentation of a normative kind that:

> the consequences and side-effects for the satisfaction of interests of *every* individual, which are expected to result from a *general* conformance to [that] norm, can be accepted *without compulsion* by all.[44]

Only under such circumstances will each member of society be able to regard the norm as legitimate.

Turning to modern society, it is possible to reconstruct, in the form of rules for discourse, further presuppositions about what is involved in normative argumentation. These involve all members of society recognising, first, that other members of society are equal sources of validity claims of their own and, second, that the only kind of force on the basis of which conflict between such claims can be resolved is that of the better argument. The rules for discourse that can be reconstructed in this way set the conditions for rational discussion of questions about the good life. Because such discussions take place within particular "forms of life" the rules cannot determine what the answers should be. What they can do is specify how the answers should be arrived at. It is possible to work out the principles of procedural justice that the presuppositions demand.

Where law is concerned, Habermas argues that:

> Legality can produce legitimacy only to the extent that the legal order reflexively responds to the need for justification that originates from the positivisation of law and responds in such a manner that legal discourses

---

[44] *Moralbewusstsein und kommunikatives Handeln.*(Frankfurt: Suhrkamp 1983) p 103, as reproduced in White (cit n. 6) at p 49.

are institutionalised in ways that are made pervious to moral argumentation.[45]

It is, of course, possible to pursue the implications of this approach for legal theory - for example Robert Alexy's development of a theory of legal argumentation[46] and his thesis that rational discourse would result in a system where individual rights were given *prima facie* preference over collective goods.[47]

Yet, for Habermas, law is a double edged sword. One aspect of modernity is increasing juridification. Law comes to regulate more and more of our life world. It does so in ways adapted to the demands of the economic and administrative systems and of strategic rather than communicative rationality. It becomes "a steering mechanism" that creates conditions of dependency rather than participation. In *The Theory of Communicative Action*, Habermas sees the solution as lying mainly with the development of new and critical social movements that are able to bring pressure to bear on the political and legal systems.

His recent work directly concerned with legal theory - *Faktizitat und Geltung*[48] - appears to have recognised that communicative rationality - as a striving for consensus - cannot on its own provide the degree of knowledge, motivation and organisation that social life requires; further, that the requirement it has for universalisation distances it from the needs and expectations of specific groups. Law, however, is

---

[45] Jürgen Habermas, Lecture I ('How is Legitimacy Possible on the Basis of Legality') of two lectures on 'Law and Morality' (trans Kenneth Baynes) in *The Tanner Lectures in Human Values* Vol VIII (Salt Lake City: University of Utah Press, and Cambridge: Cambridge University Press, 1988) p 243.

[46] Robert Alexy, *A Theory of Legal Argumentation* (Oxford: Clarendon Press, 1989).

[47] 'Eine diskurstheoretische Konzeption der praktischen Vernunft' Plenary lecture to the 15th World Congress on Philosophy of Law and Social Philosophy, Göttingen, 1991.

[48] Jürgen Habermas, *Faktizität und Geltung: Beitrage zur Diskurstheorie des Rechts und des demokratischen Rechtsstaat* (Frankfurt: Suhrkamp, 1992) trans W Rehg as *Between facts and norms: contributions to a discourse theory of law and democracy* (Cambridge, Mass: MIT Press, 1996).

something that is capable of supplementing communicative rationality by producing such knowledge, motivation and organisation as a matter of social fact and in a reflexive form - that is, one which establishes procedures for the conduct of negotiations.

All this, however, increases the possibility of strategic action. In consequence, it becomes even more important that law itself is generated by communicative action. Habermas thus adds to the moral principle of universalisation a new principle of democracy, which allows for equal participation in the formation of public opinion and the public will. This, in turn, generates certain basic rights, such as that to recognition as a member of the community and those to political expression and a share in the political process, which the law is required to guarantee.

Despite his apparently according a more positive value to law than in earlier works, where it is seen primarily as a disturbance to the life world, it still seems that for Habermas its value is a limited one. Important though democratic rights may be in enhancing the individual's emancipation and potential for self-determination, full self-realisation comes only through sharing with one's fellows in a form of life to which all can, without compulsion, agree. Not everyone will agree with the (modified) Kantian basis to Habermas's thought nor accept that the rules for discourse he cites can actually be constructed in the way he claims. In particular there seems to be an uncertainty about whether they arise out of the necessary conditions for communication as such or simply out of the actual presuppositions of competent language users.

That said, the kind of appeal of his arguments have for many is expressed by the earlier words of Lon Fuller, in the concluding paragraphs to the original edition of *The Morality of Law*:

> Hart's search for a "central indisputable element" in human striving raises the question whether in fact this search can be successful. I believe that if we were forced to select the principle that supports and infuses all human aspiration we would find it in the objective of maintaining communication with our fellows.[49]

Fuller continues that it is human beings' capacity for communication that has allowed them to survive in competition with more powerful creatures through a coordination of effort; that if they are to survive

[49] Lon L Fuller, *The Morality of Law* (cit. ch I, n. 18) p 185.

their own powers of self destruction it will be through reaching an understanding with their fellows; and that few would want the kind of vegetable existence in which no meaningful contact could be made with other human beings. Indeed, 'communication is something more than a means of staying alive. It is a means of being alive'.[50] Communication allows us to inherit the achievements of the past, its possibility can reconcile us to the thought of death by assuring us that our own achievements 'will enrich the lives of those to come'. Further, '[h]ow and when we accomplish communication with one another can expand or contract the boundaries of life itself'.[51]

> If I were asked, then, to discern one central indisputable principle of what might be called substantive natural law - Natural Law with capital letters - I would find it in the injunction: Open up, maintain, and preserve the integrity of the channels of communication by which men convey to one another what they perceive, feel and desire. In this matter the morality of aspiration offers more than good counsel and the challenge of excellence. It here speaks with the imperious voice we are accustomed to hear from the morality of duty. And if men will listen, that voice, unlike that of the morality of duty, can be heard across the boundaries and through the barriers that now separate men from one another.[52]

Habermas might disagree with the status Fuller affords to his principle - but it is difficult to see him rejecting the sentiment behind it.

Further, whether or not Habermas is successful in reconstructing rules for discourse out of the practices and presuppositions of competent language speakers, can a similar process of reconstruction bring us any closer to an understanding of law? To this and related questions the next, and final, chapter turns.

---

[50] Ibid p 186.

[51] Fuller quotes the words of Wittgenstein that 'The limits of my language are the limits of my world'.

[52] *The Morality of Law* (cit. n. 49) p 186.

XIII

WEAVING THE THREADS

The notion of reconstruction most immediately suggests the practical exercise of putting back together something which has, by accident or design, been reduced to a set of component parts - for example, an old house that has been dismantled and shipped to a new location. In a philosophical sense, however, reconstruction is concerned with showing how what might appear to be separate and unrelated pieces of data can be seen as fitting together into a larger and more complicated whole. To take the earlier example further, one might liken the task of the reconstructor to that of an architect who has to replicate the design of the dismantled house without any pictures or plans to go by. The principles on which the original building was organised are implicit in the pieces but they have to be uncovered and articulated.

Such reconstruction might, of course, be termed rational simply because it requires considerable thought, insight and imagination on the part of the reconstructor. There is, though, rather more than this to the notion of rational reconstruction. For it takes the principles implicit in the subject matter of investigation themselves to be rational ones. This is particularly so where what is involved is some aspect of human culture. As Zenon Bankowski and Neil MacCormick put it in the context of law:

> Normative order is not a natural datum of human society but a hard-won production of human intelligence.[1]

The rational reconstructor is, therefore, concerned with identifying the principles according to which such intelligence operates and with showing how (or how far) what is being investigated forms a structured and coherent whole.

The aim of rational reconstruction is a descriptive one. Its object is to state what the principles are, not to comment on their merits. For instance, in some jurisdictions slaves or women or foetuses have only a restricted right to life. To give as the reason for this the fact that, within those jurisdictions, they are not (or not fully) regarded as persons is not to condone slavery or patriarchy or abortion.

[1] In R S Summers and N MacCormick eds, *Interpreting Statutes* (cit ch VII, n. 3) Introduction at p 22.

Nonetheless, the rational reconstructor does have certain value commitments of her or his own. First, there must be a belief that objectivity and, thus, neutral description is not merely possible but also worthwhile. Second, there must be a belief not just that humans are rational but also that such rationality is a fundamental human value.

Various challenges to the possibility of objectivity have been discussed in earlier chapters.[2] There is a related problem about the pervasiveness of rationality as a human value, at least as the notion is understood in the contemporary Western world. Even setting these difficulties aside, there is an ambiguity in the claim that rationality is a fundamental human value. This may just mean that rationality is prized in some (or possibly all) societies. Alternatively it may mean that it ought to be so prized - perhaps above everything else.

Thus, although rational reconstructors may argue that a clear distinction can be drawn between description and criticism, there does seem to be an underlying presupposition that what can be reconstructed as principled, structured and coherent is good, acceptable or justifiable. This is probably fair enough, provided that all that is being engaged in is what is known as "immanent critique".[3] That is to say, where it can be established that rationality is being claimed as a value, it can be shown that what is actually being done is inconsistent with it - is unprincipled, unstructured or incoherent. The problem comes when the only test of the "goodness" of a reason for action is that of whether or not it does fit into some structured whole. For other human values may be denied in consequence. The application of too rigid a system of *stare decisis* would be a case in point.

This gives rise to a suspicion that the notion of rational reconstruction places more emphasis on principle, structure and coherence than is warranted by an investigation of the way human intelligence actually operates, even though such theorists themselves admit the unlikelihood of any perfect overall scheme making itself apparent. While rationality may demand that we have good reasons for

---

[2] Principally X and XI.

[3] A method employed by the Frankfurt School, particularly Adorno. For a brief explanation and the raising of some problems, see David Held, *Introduction to Critical Theory: Horkheimer to Habermas* (Berkeley and Los Angeles: University of California Press, 1980) p 382f.

actions, we do not always, or even always want to, make them coherent and consistent ones.

All that said, rational reconstruction is of particular interest in the context of legal theory - not least, although far from entirely, because of the emphasis placed on coherence and consistency within the internal legal culture. More widely, theories of law may involve rational reconstruction at three different levels. First, they do so if they treat law as the product of human intelligence, as opposed to that of forces beyond human control. This applies even where such theories are not concerned with displaying it as some coherent whole. For instance, those who set out to deconstruct law actually presuppose that it can be (re)constructed as text or dialogue to begin with.

Second, rational reconstruction may be directed toward presenting the data of law in a way that reflects the kind of human understanding involved. Rules, for example, are typically reconstructed out of patterns of human behaviour accompanied by some general view of that behaviour - such as a 'critical reflective attitude' or 'an experience of bindingness'.[4] Thirdly, and most strictly, rational reconstruction seeks to fit what has been depicted in this way together into a structured and coherent whole - as with Hart's view of a legal system as 'a union of primary and secondary rules' and as with later criticisms of this for ignoring the integrative role of principles.

In retrospect it can be seen that the earlier chapters of this book - dealing with the law of Scotland in terms of statutes and precedents, principles, codes of practice and so on - took the appropriateness of such reconstructions at the second of the levels largely as a given. There is a sense in which this is unavoidable. It is not just legal theory that makes use of such reconstructions: they are central to the way in which those engaged in or with the law actually understand their own activities. Of course, and as has been seen, this kind of understanding can be explained away as a case of those involved misleading themselves and others, with "what is really going on" described in

[4] Besides H L A Hart and Alf Ross, respectively, see Neil MacCormick and Ota Weinberger *An Institutional Theory of Law* (cit. ch II, n. 7) esp the Introduction and Chapter I.

other ways.[5] Equally, it is possible to see law in both a reconstructive and a functionalist light, as Habermas does in regarding it variously as an output of communicative rationality and a steering mechanism.

If nothing else, such challenges to reconstructive understandings alert those who employ them to the importance of remembering that they are just reconstructions and no more. For there is always the danger of "reifying" the reconstructions, of treating them as fixed and beyond question and of allowing them to dominate us in what we do. And this is to cease to regard them as 'the hard-won production of [a fallible] human intelligence' and to acquiesce in the idea that they are part of some system which has us in its control. This danger is one of which Habermas himself is clearly aware, writing that:

> It is important to see that rational reconstructions, like other types of knowledge, have only a hypothetical status. They may very well start from a false sample of intuitions; they may obscure and distort the right intuitions; and they may, even more often, overgeneralise particular cases.[6]

One might point to the doctrine of the sovereignty of the Westminster Parliament by way of example.

Despite the extent to which the appropriateness of such reconstructions at the second level was taken as a given, rather more caution was expressed in relation to the third level and the basis upon which they might be said to form parts of a structured and coherent whole. One of the things that the later chapters have sought to do is to show that the same data are open to reconstruction in various different ways. Equally, if postmodernism has any credence, they cannot be reconstructed at all because there is no structure, principle or coherence to be found in them. On the contrary, they have to be seen for what they are - 'discontinuous, fractured and self-destabilising'.

As mentioned in chapter XI, however, postmodernism has a paradoxical tendency to self presentation as the only way of viewing

---

5 As with American and early Scandinavian Realism, with Goodrich's view of law as rhetoric and with certain functionalist accounts. For a recent example of the latter in the area of public law, see Martin Loughlin, *Public Law and Political Theory* (Oxford: Oxford University Press, 1992)

6 'Interpretive Social Science vs Hermeneuticism' in N Haan et al eds *Social Science as Moral Inquiry* (Columbia University Press, New York, 1983) p 261.

the world. Similar, although admittedly less paradoxical, tendencies can be found amongst theories in the rational reconstructivist mode. For example, Hart, though resisting the tendency to the extent of reconstructing a legal system as consisting of different types of laws - variously as imposing obligations or conferring powers - still regards law as primarily a matter of rules.[7] It may be argued that this does less than justice to the complexity of the understandings and expectations that are involved. The same may be said even if, as Dworkin would have us do, principles are brought in.

The explanation for such tendencies may, perhaps, lie in reconstruction being an interest driven activity. Just as Habermas argues that there are "knowledge constitutive" interests,[8] so, too, there may be "theory constitutive" ones. By interests here are meant whatever people regard as important, what matters to them.[9] If interests are theory constitutive, this would make it easier to see why both those who regard law as a force for civilisation and those who regard it as an instrument of repression reconstruct it in terms of the understandings and expectations of an elite. One might, as Ehrlich does, find as much (if not more) relevance in the living law as in the official norms for decision.

The idea of theory constitutive interests, too, may allow us to see Kelsen's basic norm as a device for drawing, within a particular society, a clear distinction between the uses of force that are regarded

[7] Although see his admission in the Postscript to *The Concept of Law* (cit ch V, n. 40) p 259 that he had said far too little in the original edition about what his critics call legal principles.

[8] Jürgen Habermas, *Erkenntnis und Interesse* (Frankfurt: Suhrkamp, 1968) trans J J Shapiro as *Knowledge and Human Interests* (Cambridge: Polity Press, 1987).

[9] The influence of interests may be illustrated in the following fashion. Someone is sitting in a moving car and making various movements with the hands and feet. In answer to the question 'what is that person doing?' apart from 'making certain movements' it may be possible to reply 'driving a car', 'changing gear', 'getting ready to turn left', 'going into town', 'fetching the shopping' and so on. All of these may be equally valid as descriptions of the person's behaviour but the appropriate response to the question depends on what aspect of the behaviour mattered to the questioner.

as legitimate and those that are not. Similarly, Dworkin's idea of law as integrity can be understood as presenting a theory of adjudication (rather than of law) designed to minimise judicial discretion. In this kind of light, too, rational reconstruction proper, when seriously engaged in at the third level, can be seen as motivated by a commitment to the kind of ideals involved in the 'Rule of Law'.

Of course, matters are not just as simple as all that. Whether or not there are any fundamental human interests, it is clear that the forms actual interests take - and, particularly, one's preferences for some over others - are constituted by the cultural context in which one finds oneself. It is, for example, difficult for a Scots lawyer, trained in the tradition of Stair, to hold presuppositions of a kind other than those involved in some level of rational reconstruction - even if the notion that contemporary Scots law forms a structured and coherent whole sometimes appears to be more a matter of myth or pious hope than actuality.

For, however else one may characterise the understandings and expectations identified as agreedly or arguably legal in Scotland, they are clearly highly complex in their nature. They arise in a number of different ways. They take various forms and operate to various effects. They are informed by diverse, and sometimes competing, values. The priority to be accorded to these values is disputed within as well as outwith the internal legal culture. One may detect impulses, with MacCormick and Dworkin, toward principle and coherence and, with Luhmann and Teubner, toward indeterminacy and differentiation. Similarly, one may find instances both of the 'ethic of justice' and of the 'ethic of caring'; of the imported and of the indigenous; of the formalist and of the anti-formalist; of the power of the centre and of the pull of the periphery; of the imposed and of the self imposed; and of tensions and accommodations between them.

Finding the law of Scotland to be something of "a mixed bag" is, however, clearly not just a matter of its twentieth century form. The same is true of the middle ages, given the limited survival of Celtic law, the separate operation of canon and feudal law, the granting by the King of rights of judgment to certain Lords and of charters to Burghs, along with the separate development of rules relating to land tenure there and of the law merchant, too, this being largely a matter of self regulation, monitored by the guild courts. It is suspected that similar results would come from an investigation of most, if not all, bodies of law.[10] This would hold for customary law, which contemporary anthropology is coming to recognise as often involving greater internal diversity than originally believed.[11] It would also hold for the greatest direct attempts to engage in rational reconstruction of a practical kind - the major codifications - except, perhaps, at (or, perhaps, even at) "Day One".[12]

If contemporary Western society is to be distinguished from its earlier forms, this would seem to be not just in terms of changed ways of thinking about the world - particularly since it is doubtful that previous modes of thought ever do disappear completely. It is, rather, a matter of the complexity and speed of change of the understandings and expectations involved. This does something to explain current tendencies in the law to maintain unity by tolerating diversity - as evidenced by the introduction of open ended standards,[13] conditional programmes[14] and an increased emphasis on self regulation.[15] A case in point is the way in which the new Dutch Civil Code is framed in terms which allow its ready adaptation to changing circumstances.[16]

---

[10] See e.g. Michael Clanchy, 'A Medieval Realist: Interpreting the Rules at Barnwell Priory, Cambridge' in *Perspectives in Jurisprudence* (cit. ch IV, n. 58) 176.

[11] See e.g. G D MacCormack, 'Anthropology and Legal Theory' 1978 *Juridical Review* 216.

[12] Thus, in France, for example, there is both the role of *doctrine* and the development of the *jurisprudence constante* of the *Cour de Cassation*.

[13] See R M Unger, *Law in Modern Society* (cit. ch II, n. 55) p 192ff.

[14] See the ideas of Luhmann, referred to in ch IX.

[15] Teubner, ibid. See also G Teubner, 'Substantive and Reflexive Elements in Modern Law' (1983) 17 *Law and Society Review* 239; and, for a critical view, Hubert Rottleuthner, 'The Limits of Law - The Myth of a Regulatory Crisis' (1989) 17 *International Journal of the Sociology of Law* 273.

[16] *Nieuw Nederlands Burgerlijk Wetboek*. See the introductory article by Arthur S Hartkampf, 'Civil Code Revision in the Netherlands 1947-1992' at XIII in the translation, respectively, by P P C Haanappel and E Mackaay, into English and French of the Books on Patrimonial Law (Deventer: Kluwer, 1990).

Whether such tendencies will continue is a matter for speculation. Probably the best that can be done for any body of law is to show where the emphasis lies at a particular point in time. All this illustrates the difficulties involved in presenting some set of understandings and expectations as a structured and coherent whole - other, at least, from the perspective of a particular interest or grouping of interests. The particular problems there are in identifying the definitively legal, amongst what is a highly complicated set of understandings and expectations, may account for the heavy emphasis contemporary legal theory places on the judiciary, as the point at which such problems - at least for various practical purposes - can be resolved. Yet this particular approach is as interest driven as any other.

It appears, then, that a decision to adopt some particular theory may well turn both on the questions it seeks to answer and the answers it gives to them. The preferred theory will be that which covers the questions seeming the most important and the answers the most satisfying. If, then, theories, and the choices made between them are interest driven in this way, various things seem to follow. First, the grounds on which other theories may be totally rejected are strictly limited. Thus, one may reject them because of certain beliefs one has about the interests by which they are driven - perhaps to the effect that the pursuit of such interests is untenable either in terms of a set of standards that hold good for humankind (irrespective of their being recognised as such) or of a set of standards that are implicit in human society. Rejecting any theory on this basis, though, requires an admission of a commitment to the existence of such standards - of the interests by which one's own approach is driven. Alternatively, one may simply believe that the pursuit of such interests is pernicious. In which case it is necessary to make clear that one's rejection of the theory is a straightforward matter of political choice.

Second, if theories are interest driven, it has to be accepted that they will seek to exclude or devalue that which cannot be made to fit within them. This only becomes problematic in two cases. One is where the theory ignores or seeks to explain away something for which, in its own terms, it should be able to account. The other is where it fails to acknowledge the interests by which it is driven and holds itself out as being the only possible explanation or reconstruction or the only one of any worth.

The alternative, of course, to espousing one particular theory - or, possibly, a set of compatible theories - is to retain a degree of scepticism about all of them. This approach is reinforced by the fact that the theories themselves are not static - they alter in response both to changes in the world and to challenges from other theories, often in an attempt to accommodate some of the interests by which these theories are driven.[17] This kind of scepticism, though, needs to be consistent. It can neither lend itself to total rejection of any of the theories[18] nor assert its own superiority. For each of these courses implicitly acknowledges the existence of some objective standard by which theories, including this particular theory about how theories should be treated, can be judged. In consequence, the degree of scepticism about all theories, which is the whole basis of the approach, becomes lost.

Yet this kind of thoroughgoing "antifoundationalism" must, on the account just given, be just as interest driven as any of the theories it neither fully accepts nor totally rejects. Quite what these interests are is, however, rather more diffcult to determine. The proponents of antifoundationalism might characterise them as a preference for lack of pretension, for keeping an open mind and for respecting the views of others. Its opponents, with the implication that their own positions reflect arrogance, a closed mind and a contempt for the views of others, might counter that what is presented as lack of pretension is actually an abdication of responsibility, that what is presented as openmindedness is actually a lack of any clear vision and that what is presented as respect for the views of others is actually a readiness to tolerate the intolerable.

This assessment does not seem to be altogether justified. For, insofar as it denies the possibility of "one right understanding", anti-foundationalism is at the cutting edge of critique where such understandings are proclaimed. It is always ready to reassert the other. At the same time, its commitment to pluralism and to doubt prevents it from having any other critical force. Yet, the opposed commitment to universality and certainty is equally limited in the critical scope it

[17] See the arguments of Roger Shiner in *Norm and Nature* (Oxford: Clarendon Press, 1992) esp his concluding remarks at p 326.

[18] Except, perhaps, on the basis that it fails entirely in its own terms.

affords. For while it may allow everything else to be assessed in its light, it provides no basis for questioning of its own merits.

We have not so far discovered any fully satisfactory way of reconciling the two approaches and the human interests - in securing certainty and in achieving flexibility, in maintaining equality and in respecting difference, in developing rational awareness and fulfilling emotional needs - that they represent. The law is just one such attempt. In developing an understanding of it, perhaps we should therefore accept that 'as in spinning a thread we twist fibre on fibre. And the strength of the thread does not reside in the fact that some one fibre runs through its whole length, but in the overlapping of many fibres'.[19] Further, as the Scottish version so amply shows, there may be many different types of thread to the tapestry of the law.

[19] Ludwig Wittgenstein, *Philosophical Investigations* (cit. ch X, n. 13) para 67. He continues 'But if someone wished to say: "There is something common to all these constructions - namely the disjunction of all their common properties" - I should reply: Now you are only playing with words. One might as well say: "Something runs through the whole thread - namely the continuous overlapping of those fibres".

INDEX OF AUTHORS

Law and Philosophy Library

1. E. Bulygin, J.-L. Gardies and I. Niiniluoto (eds.): *Man, Law and Modern Forms of Life.* With an Introduction by M.D. Bayles. 1985 ISBN 90-277-1869-5
2. W. Sadurski: *Giving Desert Its Due.* Social Justice and Legal Theory. 1985 ISBN 90-277-1941-1
3. N. MacCormick and O. Weinberger: *An Institutional Theory of Law.* New Approaches to Legal Positivism. 1986 ISBN 90-277-2079-7
4. A. Aarnio: *The Rational as Reasonable.* A Treatise on Legal Justification. 1987 ISBN 90-277-2276-5
5. M.D. Bayles: *Principles of Law.* A Normative Analysis. 1987 ISBN 90-277-2412-1; Pb: 90-277-2413-X
6. A. Soeteman: *Logic in Law.* Remarks on Logic and Rationality in Normative Reasoning, Especially in Law. 1989 ISBN 0-7923-0042-4
7. C.T. Sistare: *Responsibility and Criminal Liability.* 1989 ISBN 0-7923-0396-2
8. A. Peczenik: *On Law and Reason.* 1989 ISBN 0-7923-0444-6
9. W. Sadurski: *Moral Pluralism and Legal Neutrality.* 1990 ISBN 0-7923-0565-5
10. M.D. Bayles: *Procedural Justice.* Allocating to Individuals. 1990 ISBN 0-7923-0567-1
11. P. Nerhot (ed.): *Law, Interpretation and Reality.* Essays in Epistemology, Hermeneutics and Jurisprudence. 1990 ISBN 0-7923-0593-0
12. A.W. Norrie: *Law, Ideology and Punishment.* Retrieval and Critique of the Liberal Ideal of Criminal Justice. 1991 ISBN 0-7923-1013-6
13. P. Nerhot (ed.): *Legal Knowledge and Analogy.* Fragments of Legal Epistemology, Hermeneutics and Linguistics. 1991 ISBN 0-7923-1065-9
14. O. Weinberger: *Law, Institution and Legal Politics.* Fundamental Problems of Legal Theory and Social Philosophy. 1991 ISBN 0-7923-1143-4
15. J. Wróblewski: *The Judicial Application of Law.* Edited by Z. Bańkowski and N. MacCormick. 1992 ISBN 0-7923-1569-3
16. T. Wilhelmsson: *Critical Studies in Private Law.* A Treatise on Need-Rational Principles in Modern Law. 1992 ISBN 0-7923-1659-2
17. M.D. Bayles: *Hart's Legal Philosophy.* An Examination. 1992 ISBN 0-7923-1981-8
18. D.W.P. Ruiter: *Institutional Legal Facts.* Legal Powers and their Effects. 1993 ISBN 0-7923-2441-2
19. J. Schonsheck: *On Criminalization.* An Essay in the Philosophy of the Criminal Law. 1994 ISBN 0-7923-2663-6
20. R.P. Malloy and J. Evensky (eds.): *Adam Smith and the Philosophy of Law and Economics.* 1994 ISBN 0-7923-2796-9
21. Z. Bankowski, I. White and U. Hahn (eds.): *Informatics and the Foundations of Legal Reasoning.* 1995 ISBN 0-7923-3455-8
22. E. Lagerspetz: *The Opposite Mirrors.* An Essay on the Conventionalist Theory of Institutions. 1995 ISBN 0-7923-3325-X
23. M. van Hees: *Rights and Decisions.* Formal Models of Law and Liberalism. 1995 ISBN 0-7923-3754-9
24. B. Anderson: *"Discovery" in Legal Decision-Making.* 1996 ISBN 0-7923-3981-9

Law and Philosophy Library

25. S. Urbina: *Reason, Democracy, Society.* A Study on the Basis of Legal Thinking. 1996
    ISBN 0-7923-4262-3
26. E. Attwooll: *The Tapestry of the Law.* Scotland, Legal Culture and Legal Theory. 1997
    ISBN 0-7923-4310-7
27. J.C. Hage: *Reasoning with Rules.* An Essay on Legal Reasoning and Its Underlying Logic. 1997
    ISBN 0-7923-4325-5

KLUWER ACADEMIC PUBLISHERS – DORDRECHT / BOSTON / LONDON

MIX
Papier aus verantwortungsvollen Quellen
Paper from responsible sources
FSC® C105338

If you have any concerns about our products,
you can contact us on
ProductSafety@springernature.com

In case Publisher is established outside the EU,
the EU authorized representative is:
Springer Nature Customer Service Center GmbH
Europaplatz 3, 69115 Heidelberg, Germany

Printed by Libri Plureos GmbH
in Hamburg, Germany